M000020938

MY BROTHER THE KING

JUBILEE LIPSEY

Copyright © 2021 by Jubilee Lipsey.

All rights reserved. This book or any portion thereof may not be reproduced or used in any manner whatsoever without the express written permission of the publisher except for the use of brief quotations in a book review.

This is a work of biblical fiction. The characterizations are either from the authors imagination or are presented fictitiously. Any resemblance to similar works is purely coincidental.

Author Photo: Lyndsey Ashmore Photography.

Publishing Services provided by Paper Raven Books
Printed in the United States of America
First Printing, 2021

Paperback ISBN= 978-1-7373447-0-4
Hardback ISBN= 978-1-7373447-1-1

A NOTE FROM THE AUTHOR

The kinship between David and Jonathan has captured the hearts of readers for generations. But I'm convinced their story is not just there for us to gawk at. It's not in the Bible simply to inspire wonder and yearning. As with every Scriptural account, the treasure waiting beneath this story's surface has the potential to transform our lives. Most often, this wealth can be found in the nitty-gritty, not-pretty areas of life that we like to avoid. First and foremost, David and Jonathan's story is about calling. And conflict.

Jonathan was the crown prince of Israel, in line to inherit a throne that God had already stripped from his family because of his father's rebellion. David was a man after God's own heart, chosen to rule in Jonathan's place. It would have been easy for these men to allow this conflict to define and destroy them.

However, instead of fighting to the death over a crown that couldn't belong to both of them, these two men forsook rivalry, and embraced the will of God through a selfless friendship that would withstand the brutal tests of family jealousy and war—a friendship that would change history.

Their rugged commitment to this weighty covenant was not born overnight. It was their diligent pursuit of God that enabled them to stand firm and keep clear vision in the midst of circumstances that could have easily destroyed them.

Few of us may be in situations as life-threatening as theirs. But we're confronted with many of the same heart-challenges, the same questions. How do I pursue what God has put within me? Do I try to work it out in my own strength? Will I allow insecurity to tempt me to downplay or undermine the work of the Lord in someone else's life? Will I try to assert myself in ways that seem humble, but exude the opposite? Or will I reach out to my brothers and sisters, and fight for unity, even if their callings seem to rival mine?

In order to answer these questions, we have to reach even deeper, because we're still not at the root of the matter. The main question calling out to us from the center of Jonathan and David's story is this:

How many of us truly trust God's heart enough to place our futures entirely in His hands?

Even in the Church, we struggle to reconcile the pursuit of our God-given destinies with the contentions that choke relationships. Friendship is often torn asunder by competition and insecurity as gifted dreamers battle for recognition in pursuit of their callings. Lofty promises of loyalty and family love are easily forgotten in the midst of bitter misunderstandings and perceived betrayals that cause us to see one another as rivals instead of brothers and sisters. The flesh is always trying to knock us off balance, get us to stray from the path of an anchored identity in Christ.

But as believers, we've been set free by Jesus, brought from darkness to light, elevated as royal sons and daughters through Christ's finished work (Romans 8:15). We don't have to let the flesh erode our power. We have a daily choice. Are we going to choose to walk in the flesh, which leads to death, or the Spirit, which leads to life?

Insecurity and control are the poisons that break down relationships, and they stem from one thing: fear. Only the pursuit of God and His perfect love will hold us steady in the midst of the storms that will inevitably come against us.

As you explore the friendship of David and Jonathan through this novel, be encouraged to look at your life, your calling, and those around you through God's eyes, and see the greater plan that is unfolding, the plan that you've been invited into. I invite you to face the pain and the hard questions head-on, and realize that yes, there is beauty in it all when you are hidden in Christ.

My desire is for you to read between the battle lines of this classic story and be inspired by the blessings these heroes received by choosing friendship over fear, even in the midst of devastating struggles.

Because world-changing friendship starts with a headlong pursuit of God.

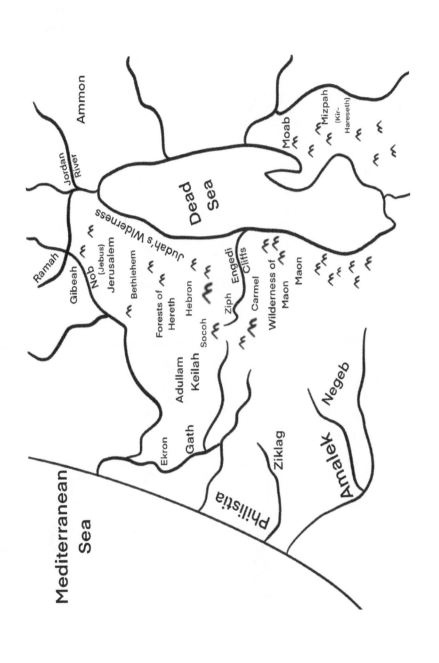

CHARACTER LIST

———◆◆◆◆◆———

Aaron—*David's mentor as a shepherd*

Abiathar—*Ahimelech's son who survives Saul's massacre*

Abigail—*David's childhood friend*

Abinadab—*David's second brother*

Abishai—*Joab's second brother*

Abner—*Saul's general and cousin*

Achish—*Philistine king*

Agag—*Amalekite king, deceased*

Ahijah—*Saul's priest*

Ahimelech—*elderly priest whom Saul kills*

Ahinoam—*Saul's wife*

Ammiel—*Saul's physician*

Asahel (Asa)—*Joab's youngest brother*

Atarah—*Jesse's wife, David's adopted mother*

Ish-Bosheth—*Saul's youngest son*

David—*Jesse's youngest son, anointed second king of Israel*

Eliab—*David's oldest brother*

Ezra—*Jonathan's armorbearer*

Gera—*Saul's armorbearer*

Goliath—*Philistine giant*

Ishvi—*Saul's second son*

Ittai—*Philistine soldier who helps David*

Jehosheva—*Jonathan's betrothed*

Jesse—*David's father*

Joab—*David's oldest nephew*

Jonathan—*the crown prince of Israel, Saul's firstborn*

Joram—*Jonathan's future father-in-law*

Korah—*an outlaw*

Malchishua (Malchi)—*Saul's third son*

Maoch—*Achish's father, Philistine king*

Merab—*Saul's oldest daughter*

Michal—*Saul's youngest daughter*

Naamah—*Jonathan's childhood friend, Michal's servant*

Nahash—*Ammonite king, deceased*

Othniel—*Saul's servant from Judah*

Samuel—*Israel's chief prophet*

Saul—*first king of Israel*

Shammah—*David's third oldest brother*

Shiphrah—*David's birth mother, Jesse's deceased maidservant*

Zeruiah—*Joab's mother, Jesse's daughter*

Ziba—*Naamah's brother, Saul's servant*

GLOSSARY OF HEBREW WORDS

———————◆◆◆◆———————

Abba—*father*

Adonai—*the Lord God*

Adon—*lord (high-ranking official)*

Chesed—*mercy or lovingkindness, favor*

Eema—*mother*

El-Shaddai—*the All-Sufficient One; Yahweh's Name before Moses' time*

El-Jireh—*the God who provides*

El-Roi—*the God who sees*

Ephod—*ancient priest's garment used to inquire of God*

Hakkodesh—*Presence of God*

Hassar—*crown prince, a king's oldest son and heir*

Melek—*king*

Nephilim—*offspring of the giants mentioned in Genesis 6; Goliath was one*

Yahweh—*God's covenant Name given to Israel*

Roeh—*seer or prophet, messenger of God*

Ruach—*Spirit of God*

Saba—*grandfather*

Sar—*prince*

Sarrah—*princess*

Shabbat—*weekly Hebrew service, day of rest*

Shekel—*ancient Hebrew currency*

Sheol—*ancient Hebrew term for the grave*

Torah—*Law of Moses, sacred Jewish writings*

Yeshu-hah—*salvation or deliverer*

PROLOGUE

Jonathan's fourteenth year

———————— ◆ ————————

My heartbeat punches my ribs, and my legs burn from the incline. My bow hugs my shoulders, the bundle of arrows drumming a steady rhythm against my back as I climb. Ezra scrambles up behind me, always keeping within inches of my shoulder, his eyes darting through the trees for any hint that I might need the extra arrows he carries. When I halt in place, he nearly runs into me, his knee thumping against my sword.

"Sorry, my lord."

I bring a finger to my lips, signaling silence, then mouth the words, "almost there," hoping he can see gratitude in my smile.

He's brave to follow me out here. With weapons so scarce in Israel, he's only the bearer of mine, not the owner of any. But when I shook him awake an hour ago, he never asked any questions, just scampered after me with the eagerness of a boy half his age.

"You're not frightened, are you?" I'd teased him a little once we'd cleared the camp. "Because nothing prevents the Lord from saving, by many or by few."

"Do whatever is in your heart, my lord. I'm with you."

His bold answer had scattered any doubts I'd had about bringing him along. Even with the insistent inner witness pulling at me, I'm grateful not to be alone out here. In the chilly breath of dawn, we're just shadows in this forest, the only two of Israel on the trail. And these mountains are crawling with Philistines. To put it simply, we are few, and we will need the Lord.

The hike is intense at this angle. We're pinned in the strip of forest between the mountains Bozez and Seneh, two rocky giants shouldering the towns of Michmash and Geba. And from the fortress in the middle, the Philistine army harasses the people of God. I can see the garrison walls through the clearing trees, hugging the rocks just above us, keeping us from our land. My stomach burns, clenching with a hunger that has nothing to do with food. Everything will change today.

Locking my limbs for a moment of rest, I draw in a long breath and let my senses swim with the forest. The sharp whisper of pine, the sweet, unturned earth, the undercurrent of sweat. Everything fills me, stroking my veins awake like a drink from an ice-cold well, and I tilt my face into the sunlight, awash in it.

I should have left the cave behind weeks ago. This is the freedom my spirit craves. Freed from hiding, released into the hands of Adonai, our Lord. It's so sweet, it obscures the fact that with each step, I'm defying the command of the king.

Since the day the prophet put the crown on his head, it's been my father's mission to drive the Philistines from our land and end their predations against our people, something we could only accomplish with the help of Yahweh. Instead, we've been held back, bound by our refusal to completely follow the God of Israel.

My father's excuses still sting. "I *did* obey the Lord! But my own men were scattering, and the Philistines were amassing, ready to crush us because of my idiot son! So, I felt compelled to offer the sacrifice myself."

I had wanted to sink through the ground to escape the arrow-sharp gaze of the Roeh, Samuel. But there's nowhere to go from the presence that always follows Yahweh's chief messenger.

The prophet had shouted over the awkward silence of my father's councilmen. "You are the people of Adonai! When are you going to start acting like it?"

I shudder, my mind crawling with the chaos of the previous weeks. Only ten days ago, the king had split the army, leaving half with me, and in a flash of confidence, I had led the men in my command against the stronghold in Geba, freeing the city from enemy hands. But I never anticipated the Philistines' reaction.

In a matter of days, they'd unleashed the wrath of their armies on Israel, swarming our border towns like locusts. The turmoil had led to my father's blatant disobedience, then weeks of hiding, blaming God. And the prophet's heavy pronouncement that only my father and I heard—"The Lord has sought out a man after His own heart, and commanded him to be prince over Israel."

In place of King Saul.

My fingers fold into fists, my muscles wound as tight as bowstrings. Barely a year ago, the *hakkodesh,* the very presence of Yahweh, had stirred within my father, uniting our people in our first real military victory in ages. God's anointing had changed everything, turning my father from a sullen isolationist into a bold warrior who rallied armies.

Yet now, we're hiding out with no plans to advance beyond the next season's rains. We're behaving like a country of farmers, and Philistia knows it. After Geba, my father's confidence had dried up.

"You've got to think, Jonathan. You must consider what is best for your people—war or a harvest."

I had considered it, and decided our people needed both. Harvest is rarely attained without conflict.

Frustration tickles my limbs, and I shift onto my knees, tired of crouching.

For centuries, our people have been trying to take hold of the land our God set apart for us, and we're still falling short. Every bit of turmoil in our history has been brought on by our ancestors' unwillingness to trust and obey the God of Israel. How can we fully claim our inheritance when we're so unwilling to fight for it? If we had kept Adonai's commands from the start, we would be prospering in the land as undisputed victors.

But my father has been preaching discouragement for weeks, ever since our armies began disintegrating before our eyes. "God isn't speaking as He used to, Jonathan," he would say. "We have failed Him, and He has abandoned us."

I wince, fighting defeat like a physical pain. We have failed Yahweh, yes. But I refuse to believe that our God will leave us. He is a faithful, merciful God who keeps His covenant of love to a thousand generations.

A screech tears open the silence, and wings beat the air over my head as a hawk sails toward the sun. Time to move. Everything inside me leaps, craving action, but I haul it back, forcing my limbs to unfold one muscle at a time. "No tension. Just zeal. Anxiety makes for poor fighting," my father's cousin Abner likes to say.

I close my eyes briefly as we press farther down the trail. It's not just the yearning for battle that has drawn me out here. The stirring that had shaken me awake this morning was like the pressure of a hand on my shoulder, and I couldn't ignore it. But we still don't have a clear plan.

I have to crouch on these rocky crags like a mountain goat, hugging the hillside to keep from stumbling. Ezra crawls up close, waiting for an order, and I hear the soft pop of twine as he notches an arrow. Folding my fingers around the head of my sword, I exhale, focusing on the silence between every sound.

Adonai, what should we do?

I hold still, locking everything in place except the thumping in my chest. One breath. Two. My eyes locked on the walls of the garrison, I wait for fear to rush in, for misgivings to hold me back. Instead, there's not a doubt in my mind—just energy buzzing inside me.

The feeling intensifies as I think of the presence that follows Samuel. Is this what it's like? Is this what my father felt when he was anointed, and the Spirit of God rushed in on him? Adonai Yahweh must be calling me, activating the faith that has been dormant. To be one with the Lord and His purposes…what more could a man desire?

I pause to breathe, and the plan unfurls in my mind like a banner.

"Let's go up," I say aloud, more to myself than to Ezra. "All the way up to the garrison of these heathens. We'll show ourselves to the archers on the outpost. If they tell us to wait, we will stay where we are. But if they call us to come up, we'll attack. This will be the sign that God is going to fight for us and give them into our hands."

Ezra nods in agreement, zeal flushing his face. We've been waiting weeks to make a move. And this is it. I'm certain.

My pulse leaps in response to my own words, and powerful wings beat in my chest. Something has taken hold of my voice and warbled it, spun it into something heady and shaky, like birdsong. A bold thrust of sunlight winks at me through the scraggly mountain brush like a finger that's pointing, beckoning ahead. Instantly, the sensation is back—the feeling of someone clasping my left shoulder. Sweat pools in my eyebrows, and I swipe it away, along with a tear that I hope no one but the Almighty will see.

I whisper, "Adonai Yahweh, I have not forgotten your power. I am your warrior, and I will fight for you until my last breath." I open my eyes, fixing them on the clearing with the intensity of a lion on the hunt. "And silence the voice of the enemies who come out against us. Let them all know that you are the Lord!"

Glancing back, I nod to Ezra. I'm Hassar Israel, the crown prince. God has chosen me for this.

Excitement shimmers in my veins as we turn and face the stronghold, then walk out into the clearing within perfect range of the archers on the walls. But no one shoots. Pair by pair, enemy eyes lock onto us, and it's clear they're not intimidated.

"I thought Israel was weaponless," one soldier scoffs, the breeze rippling the crown of red feathers adorning his helmet. "Does your king know you have his only sword, Hebrew?"

The distinct lilt of Philistine laughter rides the wind, but it's their words that make my veins hum. "Saul doesn't need it. His army has returned to huddling in the shadows like sheep while their children defend them."

"Come up here, boys," another snickers. "We'll show you how to aim those arrows."

Philistine taunting has never been more welcome, the mockery a clear invitation from God to move forward. Ezra and I spring into action, our movements sharp and precise, our arrows guided to their first marks on the wings of the wind.

The two men left standing gape at us before scrambling for their own weapons, but our arrows take them down as well. The remaining archers flee the battlements, their confidence collapsing. I break into a run after them, the fight building inside me as we approach the lower walls.

"Come on!" I yell to Ezra. "The Lord has given them into our hands!"

What follows feels like seconds and years all at once. The mountain fortress embraces our attack, while the Philistines scramble for order, uncoordinated and unprepared. There's the ring of swords, the clash of iron against bronze, the hiss of a hundred arrows catching wind before slamming into the ground all around us. But they won't take us down. Not today.

I cut left and right, spinning my sword into anyone who comes close, feeling a wall of protection around Ezra and I while we fight. This is what I was made for. I'm an arrow in the hand of God, the great Bowman of Israel.

I count twenty fallen in only the first strike, with Ezra pouncing on the spoil. We race into the camp beneath the garrison, tossing discarded weapons to a dozen Israelite captives who spring into action. With each enemy that falls under my feet, I'm more empowered, more ignited, but the mounting terror assaulting the camp is so much bigger, so much more powerful than us.

A deep, growling rumble mounts on all sides, answering the drumbeat in my chest, and several men glance to the sky, looking for thunderous clouds. But it's no storm. The ground writhes, and the battle heightens as the mountains themselves rejoice, shaking before the God of Israel, who has come down to fight with us. My veins surge with recognition so powerful, it might break me. I know it like I know the sunlight bathing the valley. It's Him.

Yahweh is here. There's no other explanation for the lack of fear, the clear direction, the panic in the enemy camp. He's met me in these mountains, and I know I will never forget the feeling. Unable to hold back, I unleash the battle cry tugging at my lungs even as tears burn my eyes.

This is the air I want to breathe—the deep inner knowing that every move I make is for the Lord of hosts, the Almighty Warrior who has fought for us since the beginning. Victory is out here with Him, not back in the cave. Israel was never meant to hide. And now, we'll have no reason to.

I can't wait to tell my father.

* * * * *

The sharp breath of incense commands my senses, trapping me in the moment I wish I could crawl out of. My father watches me from across the stone altar while our commanders' frightened stares hang heavy on our backs. Tension edges the air like the seething disquiet before a storm. Fresh apprehension has dried up their courage, leaving them as restive and hesitant as shifting shadows.

The battle of Michmash is won, the victory behind us, but now there's no swift rush of boldness—only the restless twisting of my stomach. I chew on parched lips, trying to swallow, but all I can taste is the hint of honey that could end my life. All because of a foolish vow.

My father's men are careful not to look at me. Earlier this morning, I would've sworn they were mistaken. Surely my father wouldn't have vowed to kill anyone who tasted food today. "Until I am completely avenged of my enemies," he'd said, enthused by the disarray in the Philistine camp. But why give an order like that when God had already secured our victory?

On the heels of my assault at Michmash, my father had rallied the army and pounced, chasing the Philistines several miles north to Beth-Aven. By the time we reached Aijalon just beyond, we were exhausted and starving, pushed to our limits by the king's vow of fasting. A vow I wasn't told about until I was dipping some honey to my mouth to keep my strength up. It seems every decision my father makes troubles Israel further. Ever since the unlawful sacrifice he made weeks ago.

But there's no way back. What's done is done.

My father can't hear Yahweh for wisdom on our next move, so he's ordered lots to be cast to find out what has changed, who has gone against him. Heaving air as though he's been running, he hovers over the altar, watching avidly for the results. I watch his face contort, changing with every shadow that pushes across it.

"Are you sure about this, my lord?" Ahijah the priest dares to hesitate, but my father explodes at him, frantic tension straining his brow.

"I don't care if my own son is at fault! I gave an oath. We cannot have rebellion tainting our progress. The guilty one will die."

Dismayed murmurs part the crowd, racing toward me like a troubled tide. As the priest continues, tossing the lots again, everyone steps back apace. The people have been exonerated. It's between me and my father now.

Saul is still bent over the altar, suspicion carved into every line on his face. I stare at him, searching for something merciful and reasonable in his eyes. Some hint of the man Yahweh transformed only a year ago.

"You're my firstborn, Jonathan. The first sign of my strength, and the second strength of the kingdom. The kingdom that will one day be yours."

The pride glowing in him when he'd said those words had been like the sun breaking over a mountain, warming me like nothing else could. Even his innate harshness hadn't stopped the undercurrent of admiration flowing in my veins.

In my fourteen years, I've hardly left his side, first farming Israel's fields, then defending them alongside him. His kingship had strengthened our bond, pulling us closer as Israel's expectations turned into demands, and complaints sharpened into fear. I'd pushed past my youth, and fought my way to a place of honor, completely trusted to be an extension of my father, the king. But now everything is different.

I gave all that up when I defied him, unable to resist the pull of God's presence tugging me out into the open air after victory. The memory still makes my heart race. I'd spent my whole life hoping for a chance to see Yahweh move, to be caught up in Him like that. But now, doubt has dropped a shroud over me. Was I wrong? Was I being led by pride, an attempt to prove myself? Is that why I have to suffer now?

Sweat from the battle still clings to my body, but as the lot is cast toward me, I feel a deep, piercing cold take over, gripping every limb.

"Jonathan," the priest says, and everything stops, even my breathing.

There's utter silence at first, as though the air has been sucked from every lung. And then a collective groan emerges, rippling through the ranks.

Saul's eyes hold mine for a full minute, cold and unblinking, until every bit of recognition drains from them, leaving only the hardened stare of the king. "Jonathan. What have you done?"

It's the first time I've ever hated the sound of my name on his lips. A tremor starts climbing into my chest. Surely, he won't treat an innocent mistake as a rebellious crime.

"Answer me." He steps up closer, letting me feel his height so that I have to look up or bow my head. I do neither, fixing my eyes on the ruby heaving in and out at the center of his breastplate.

"I tasted a little honey, in the forest on the way from Beth-Aven." My own words sound empty and powerless, devoid of all the explanation and pleading that should be there. I'm still in disbelief. How could things change so much in a matter of hours? "It was only a little bit on the end of my staff. Does that deserve death?"

Now I look up at my father. Dare him to reconsider. He doesn't. If anything, my confession seems to fan the flames.

"I gave an oath!" He slaps my chest with both hands, pent-up rage bulging in his neck. "What good are my words if I don't stand by them? What good are your vows of loyalty if you insist on going your own way? Can you not comprehend that *I am king?!*"

His anger breaks off in a sharp puffing breath, and he grinds his fingers in his hair, eyeing me up and down before dropping his arms. "But you don't, apparently. My commands mean nothing to you anymore."

"My lord, I didn't know!" I barely get the words out before he starts railing again.

"How can you continue to put me in this position? You launch into battle, *twice,* recklessly, without my permission. Without any thought to what it might cost me."

His words burn like smoke singeing my skin. What did it cost him? We won! We struck a blow to Philistia that will last for years. Our inaction would have cost us more lives.

But there's no use saying any of it aloud. Not when he's caught in some vortex I can't break him out of. His last words come out in a growl. "May God punish me ever so severely if you do not die for this, Jonathan."

Whispers explode among the men, igniting fear like a flint catching brush. While everyone else reels in place, I feel as though I've been tossed backwards into a net hanging over a cliff, my weight held up only by threads. Out of the corner of my eye, I can see the terror staining the faces of our relatives, and I think briefly of my mother, back in Gibeah, oblivious.

"Take care of him, Saul," she'd said when we left.

When I look back at my father, I wish I hadn't. The calm emptiness I see in his eyes is more terrifying than any flash of Philistine hatred. In that moment, I feel my life's trust shift, hanging in a balance I had no idea existed. Saul is the king, and I'm no longer safe in his hands.

The moment the thought arrives, my heart thumps deeply, and a strange, warm peace breaks through the panic rushing in my ears. It's like the sensation I felt on the mountain, and my fingers creep up toward my left shoulder after it. Yahweh's touched me. I'm not alone. But what am I supposed to do? Escape? Break from my father? Stay and face death?

Adonai, what should I do?

My father's sword pulls free, slicing the silence. "Kneel."

"Abba…" The term of endearment slips from my mouth before I can stop it, before I can rationalize that he's not there. This is not my father. Saul takes one step toward me, and I can clearly read his thoughts. *If your plan is to steal all the glory from me, then you might as well be dead.*

"Saul, no! Stop! You can't do this!" My father's cousin Abner shoves himself between me and the king, and other warriors follow suit. "Jonathan shall not die, Saul! This is madness!"

I can see Saul's anger smoldering, ready to leap out at his general, but Abner talks over it, struggling to rein in his emotions. He's been my father's most loyal supporter, but he's known me since I was a child. He can't watch me die.

"As the Lord lives, not a hair from his head should be harmed." He holds out his hands, imploring. "Why would you kill your son, who fought so valiantly and brought about such a great victory? He worked with the Lord today, Saul! Does that matter less than a little honey?"

Passion digs through the iron shield that typically guards his emotions. Dozens of others voice nervous agreement, holding their ground even when the king turns to look at them.

Abner's words pluck a chord in the center of my chest, setting my heartbeat humming. The resonance fills me until my ears are buzzing with it. Tears slice into my eyes. I fought for Adonai. Not against my father. Why should I have to choose?

I barely hear what Saul says in response, but in a few seconds, he's turning away, sheathing his sword. Without looking back, he stalks toward the trees beyond the tents, his purple robe pulling over the ground.

I take two steps after him, trying to think of a way to apologize. But something else tugs at me, holding me back. He won't ever see me the same way. I'm no longer the warrior he could trust to follow orders without question. And, I remember, in God's eyes, Saul is no longer the king. So, who am I?

The question confronts me as though the Roeh himself is staring me down, waiting for my answer. Whose victory will I fight for? Am I willing to work with Yahweh even if the path doesn't lead to my glory? Even if He has already chosen someone else?

Something breaks inside me, pulling tears down my face. I've been hoping that Yahweh would relent, give my father another chance. That our family could still continue to rule Israel. But what use is a personal empire if God is not with us?

Our ancestor Moses understood this, refusing to go forth into the land of promise without the presence of Yahweh. I think of the stifling cave back in the mountains where our destiny was delayed. And I think of the dizzying height of the cliffs where God displayed His power—through me. Simply because I was willing. And because He's good.

I drop to my knees in the dirt, my palms lifted upward.

"God of Israel, I am yours first. I will work with you. You are my Shield and my Reward. I will fight the battles you lead me to, and defend the ones you choose."

Even if it means I have to face death again.

ONE

Jonathan

———◆———

Twenty-Two Years Later

The Glory of Israel does not change His mind.

Unrest pricks my eyelids, haunting the painful snatches of sleep that I hide in. Resentful, I grip the bedclothes, trying to bury myself further. Even asleep, I can feel myself running, trying to escape the chaotic pull of the surface. I have to rest. But I'm maddeningly alert, fumbling for the sword that still hugs my side. Because I always have to fight. The battle never stops.

The cedar roof over my head groans with thunder, but I barely hear it. Nightmares flicker in and out of focus, twisted revisions of a decades-old conflict. My father huddles on his knees, the Roeh's torn robe in his fist. Samuel's bony hand grips Abba's sword, his eyes flaming. The dreams tug me down dark pathways, demanding I answer the nagging questions they stir up. But in this battle, exhaustion always wins. The troubled haze that imprisons me only breaks for one thing.

The king needs you.

Frantic hammering threatens to break my door from its hinges, but the voice behind it is muffled by the storm tearing through the night. It's still several seconds before actual words find their way through my mental fog, like enemy threats materializing in the distance.

"The king needs you, Jonathan!"

It doesn't take more than a few breaths for my senses to sharpen. My heartbeat is far too wild for this time of night. Ignoring the way sleeplessness stabs the backs of my eyes, I drag my head from the pillow, forcing the rest of my body to comply. I've slept in my clothes, so all I have to do is fumble for the nearest torch.

Staggering to the window, I peer out into torrential darkness, searching for the lights that indicate the night watch. Midnight.

Below my father's fortress, Gibeah still sleeps, barely visible through the tempest launching itself at us in watery fistfuls. Every torch bends sideways in the wind while the customary springtime rains pelt the courtyard. The dark hills beyond seem to wear the prying eyes of the enemy, wondering why they haven't seen me on a battlefield in months.

You can't wait forever, Hassar Israel.

Agitated, I rake my hands through my hair, my fingers catching on the thin, gold band threading through it. I tear it off, tossing it aside, along with the gold armbands that feel too tight. My position weighs heavier every month I'm trapped in this fortress. Raiders still harass our borders, testing our strength. At this time of year, we should be at the training grounds, readying ourselves against outside threats.

I long for earlier days when we understood the attackers, and how to fight them. We've battled countless enemies over the years—Ammon to the east, Geshur to the southwest, Amalek everywhere. I would almost welcome a Philistine.

But tonight, once again, it's the new enemy. The one the king can't fight.

My father's cry of pain shakes the house, and whoever waits at my door throws it open. Abner's expression blooms with warring torchlight and shadows, making him look more spirit than man. Our general has worn that same haunted look since our campaign against Amalek—the last time either of us remember the king being in his right mind.

"He's bad, Jonathan."

Abner is afraid—too afraid to address me as his prince. I'm only Hassar Israel in daylight. At night, we're all just trying to fight our way through to another dawn. And find a way to make the light stay.

The darkness had come over my father gradually, like a mist stealing over a field, until I couldn't look him directly in the eye anymore. Not without feeling like we'd allowed an enemy to take his place. Watching his personality disintegrate by the day, the servants had whispered that he was troubled by an evil spirit, eventually adding, "from God." Their dread is offensive, but also more perceptive than I dare to reveal.

The king has become sullen and reactionary, driving back our allies with mistrust, and fixating on minor skirmishes that might lead to rebellion. At night, he becomes even more unwound, any inhibitions locked away in a place we can't reach. More recently, he rages through nightmares, worked up into a frenzy by unseen threats that taunt him in the dark.

I push my torch into Abner's hand and shove his shoulder.

"Get the singer."

Once he's gone, I edge along the opposite wall, following the moans to my father's chamber.

It's been several grueling weeks since the officials suggested a musician might soothe my father, at least enough to help him deal with the recurrent night terrors. After a few failed attempts to recruit people from Gibeah, a servant from Judah's territory to the south recommended a mere youth, fresh from his father's sheep pastures in Bethlehem. Abner and I disagreed at first, but by then, sleeplessness had burned through our misgivings, and we summoned the boy.

Music has become our only weapon, something to hold the line while I sort through what little I know.

Vague images haunt me when I have the energy to think about them: my father struggling with Samuel, the Amalekite king lying dead at the prophet's feet, and an ominous refrain tolling in my head. *The Glory of Israel is not a man that He should lie.*

But how much of that is a dream? I thought my father had killed Agag years ago. And I'd blocked out what happened shortly afterwards, once Samuel left our camp. I clench my fingers around my sword, trying to choke the writhing. How are these visions supposed to help me? What do they even mean?

Desperate to make sense of it all, I'd sent a message to the Roeh in Ramah, but it's been seven…no, *ten* days since then, and

I fear he won't respond at all. We haven't seen him for years, not since we decimated Amalek. Perhaps if I sent a man…

I stop midstride as Abner's shadow and a smaller one join mine along the stone wall. The young shepherd-singer from Bethlehem arrived earlier today, but I'd barely looked at him. Too tired and distracted to give him any direction beyond, "Sing anything. Play anything. Just do what you can."

But now that we're standing at my father's door, I'm afraid we've made a massive mistake. I hadn't really noticed how young the boy is. His head barely reaches my breastbone, and his frame is light, draped with a loose-fitting, ragged cloak. His eyes are enormous, watching me from behind a tangle of auburn hair.

I wince at Abner. What are we doing? I can't send a boy in there to deal with a volatile warrior who's nearly killed me before.

Pain hums from beneath my rib from being thrown flat on my back a week ago. In the rush of freeing myself without causing Saul harm, the recurrent shock of being attacked by my own father had to be shoved aside, spreading into a deep sting that I haven't had time to grapple with. It has simply joined the rest of the pain I carry, like blurred memories from the battlefield. Except this was a battle I never should have had to fight.

My shoulders jerk involuntarily, trying to shake off the memory like a bad dream. But it's not. The king used to rage once every seven days. Then every four. The mental tally uncovers my fears, dragging them back out into the open. He's getting worse.

"It's all we can do, my lord," Abner pants, his gaze locked on my father's door.

The shepherd boy bows to the ground before me, holding his wooden lyre against his side like a weapon. His eyes meet mine briefly, and I look away, hoping he doesn't see too much. He can't have any idea what he's dealing with.

Abner and I are the closest to Saul, the ones the people see as the approachable extensions of the king. We're trusted to communicate his will, promise stability, address concerns. Yet, with each night of torment, we're losing our grip. Summoning this shepherd boy reveals the truth that I won't speak in front of the people. We're desperate. And it's only a matter of time before they all know.

"Jonathan?" The soft shuffling of voices and footsteps creep toward me along the stone walls and become my mother, Ahinoam, and youngest sister, Michal. Nearly running, my sister elbows her way past her servants, the higher register of her voice dancing on my nerves.

"Eema!" I appeal to our mother. "Why did you let her come down here? I told her not to leave her chambers when he's like this."

Michal tosses her hair over her shoulder. "Don't talk to me like Abba does. You're my brother."

"I'm also your king if anything happens to him."

Michal rolls her eyes, but the second I hear my own words, I regret them.

"Eema, I-I didn't mean that…"

My mother shakes her head, her sad smile brushing it aside. "We all know it's true." She steps around Michal and touches my shoulder. "Are you all right?"

"I'm fine." I pat her hand, wishing I could stop lying to her. It's exhausting. And unnecessary, since she sees through every mask I wear. A thick braid hangs over her shoulder, and she shivers in a thin robe thrown over her night shift. Even in the dim light, I can see the threads of gray running through her hair, matching the silver strands in her robe.

I squeeze her hand again. "Eema, go rest. I can handle this."

"It doesn't sound like you can handle it." Michal shivers also, clasping her elbows to hide it. She shifts from one foot to another, her hair swaying down her back. "I thought you were going to send for the singer."

"He's right behind me. Would you like to go in there and sing to Abba instead, or would you let me take care of this?"

Even as I snap, I can't ignore the grudging affection pushing its way through my annoyance. My eighteen-year-old sister is more similar to me than any of my brothers, and the banter between us comes easily. These days, she's starting to look a bit more like our father. Something in the stubborn slant of her jaw, maybe.

"Where's Merab?" I ask her.

Michal grimaces. "Too frightened."

Our other sister had witnessed our father's torment on the night his dreams started. A few shattered urns later, she was reduced to the frozen, speechless pillar of fear that I refuse to become, no matter how insistently it knocks at my door.

My mother pulls her robe closer, shifting her gaze quickly. Her effort to stay calm is like a dagger in my heart. I take her shoulders and find her eyes. "Eema, I'll fix this. I promise. The music will help him. Now, please, go rest." I kiss her forehead.

"Soon." She smiles, but the pain doesn't leave her eyes. We've been through this before. She moves off to the side. "Michal…"

My youngest sister is leaning on one foot, her fingers tangled in her hair as she watches the kneeling shepherd. Chewing her lip, Michal leans over to me, the ghost of a smile playing on her face. "How old is he?"

The singer? I bend down, looking straight into her eyes. "Go. To. Bed." I give her a shove, and she finally skitters off. A few feet away, my mother crouches against the wall, rocking, with her face covered.

Abner taps the shepherd's shoulder. "Get up."

"Hold it. Follow me." I still don't trust my father to wake up and find a stranger in his chamber. I push past both of them and step over the threshold. But the boy stays right at my side, refusing to cower or drop behind me. For no reason at all, his name finally wakes up among the scattered fragments in my mind.

David. That's it. David, son of Jesse.

I had planned to resent him. An outsider, coming in with all his youthful zeal and being privy to the kingdom's greatest embarrassment—a king driven mad by God's absence. Absence he had chosen with continual disobedience. It felt wrong to uncover this to a shepherd who knows nothing about what has happened to bring us here.

But I can't get over the expression that rests on David's face. Unbroken calm, like the stillness of a quiet morning in the hills. His eyes swim in the torchlight, missing the one thing I searched for and can't find—contempt. He approaches the king like he would a lamb he's about to pull from a thornbush.

I let him stay beside me until we're a few feet from Saul. Then I stop the boy. "Wait there."

He nods, gently lowering himself to the ground. "It's all right, my lord. It will be all right."

I'm not sure whether he's talking to me or my father, but his gentle concern pierces the darkness shrouding the room. Briefly, I wonder if he's crying or if his eyes just glow like that.

Behind a thin veil hanging from the rafters, my father tosses on his bed, his broad shoulders stretching over the side. Sweat pools in the crevice of his throat, matting the dark locks that trail down into a graying beard at his chest. Cords writhe beneath his skin, muscles twitching in his arms and neck. I'm surprised he hasn't torn the bedclothes by now.

Without turning around, I beckon to the boy, and soft notes start floating toward me. My other hand still carefully molded to my sword, I lower myself to one knee. The king can't see anyone standing over him. I've made that mistake before.

"Abba..." I'm steeling myself, but I still have to haul back emotion with a fierce grip. I can't help seeing him as he was on the day of his anointing—his face alive with power and passion, and his hair dripping with oil. The image persists in my mind even though I can't reconcile it with the way he looks at me now. I'll never understand why he turned against me. We're more evenly matched these days, but that doesn't lessen the hurt.

Saul rears up like a disturbed bear, his eyes flashing like lightning from the ceiling to my face. "What do you want?" he mutters. "Is there more I've done wrong?"

I edge away slightly, but exhaustion seizes his rage, dragging it back. Panting, he squeezes his eyes shut as if in terrible pain and drops his head back against the pillow.

"You've been dreaming, Abba. No one is here to hurt you." I string soft words together like I'm speaking to a child. "The musician is here...David."

"David?" he mumbles, frowning without opening his eyes. He groans, covering his face with both hands. "David..."

The boy's playing grows slightly louder, and I watch my father's chest shudder and slowly ebb into a steady rhythm, the trembling in his hands easing away. I release the breath I've been holding and back off, grateful for the shepherd's intuition. Where he learned that at such a young age, I don't know. Hopefully, the king will sleep now and give us all a chance to rest.

I'm halfway to the door when the music stops me. The notes emerging from under David's fingers are purposeful and captivating, strung together into something that causes pain to dance in my chest. Frozen in place, I release a breath and allow myself to listen. The simple peace of the melody pushes through me, touching the tumult inside. David changes the key slightly, drawing everything up a notch, and then begins to sing softly.

"Spirit of God, you bring renewal.

"You renew the face of the ground.

"I will sing to the Lord all my life,

"Each day that I have breath I will sing.

"For by Your breath all life is created,

"And you renew the face of the ground."

My breath catches at the profound sincerity of the words. I had expected the country youth to have relatively simple skill, but this! The music is like a drink offering poured out, like incense changing the air. How long has it been since such pure praises have been lifted to Yahweh from this room? The lamplight swims in my eyes as the words continue flowing.

"You satisfy our yearning,

"You make our faces shine.

"I will sing to the Lord with my life.

"I will sing praises to my God.

"As long as I have breath,

"My voice will bless the Lord God who saves."

A chill creeps over my skin as the room fills. Absently, I reach up to my opposite shoulder, feeling like I should be on my knees instead of my feet.

At Michmash, I could have sworn God was closer than my breath, His hands over mine, guiding each arrow to its mark. His power had shaken the mountains, crumbling the Philistines' defenses into dust. It had been a great victory, my favorite memory, even after two decades. And the king's wrath against me had passed. Do I dare believe Yahweh is here, now?

Will you still have mercy on us, Adonai? Will you renew the ground of my father's heart?

The floor creaks, and Abner's face appears around the door. I edge through it, still looking backwards. "Did he write that? I've never heard these songs."

Abner shakes his head, distracted. "I couldn't say. I need you in the antechamber."

"What for?"

"We need to talk." Already several steps ahead of me, he beckons impatiently. "Where there are no servants."

I glance back. "The shepherd? He's a little preoccupied at the moment. He won't hear us."

Abner shakes his head, frustration straining his neck. "I still can't believe we brought a boy from Bethlehem in here to see this. Of all the tribes, Judah is our harshest critic."

I spread my hands. "We were running out of options. Othniel said he was the most skilled he'd ever heard."

"Yes, yes. I was there." He glances along the wall where my mother is still huddled on the floor, her lips moving in prayer. A maid waits silently beside her.

Abner turns his back to them and finds my eyes. "What do you intend to do if this doesn't work? The land is aflame with rumors, and not just about the king's condition. Every day, we receive reports of Philistine raiders being spotted in another town. One threshing floor burns at Geba, and now everyone is convinced their city will be the next target. We're running out of time, Jonathan."

"To do what?" Weariness pulls at the edges of my eyes. I don't know how much longer I can keep them open.

"To answer the threats coming against us!" Abner's whisper is loud enough to create a short echo. I glance at my mother, but she doesn't lift her head.

Abner's eyes burn into mine, digging deep for my own fears.

"The elders believe these attacks have been purposeful from the beginning. Right now, the Philistines are testing us, but this is not all they will do! Meanwhile, that new king of theirs is said to be more ambitious than his predecessors. He's recruiting the ancient *Nephilim* giants, and every conceivable monster from

Gath and Ekron to be a scourge to us. We don't know the full extent of the army he's amassed."

His words drop onto my chest like a millstone. I'd hoped for more time to decide how to deal with the new Philistine king.

In the past year, I've managed to keep uncertainty at bay outside these walls while my father struggles within them. I've made my brothers generals, appointed judges to mediate local matters, and commissioned spies to the camps of our enemies. Now, my brothers and their thousands wait outside Gibeah for a direct order. An order that should come from the king.

I'm hesitant to seize more power with my father so vulnerable. But I can't wait much longer before the Philistines decide Saul isn't a threat anymore. Their king Achish grows bolder every month that he doesn't see us in battle. And if the *Nephilim* fight with them…

Adonai, give me wisdom.

Abner is a pillar of strength before the army, but here, his anxiety is barely restrained. "My lord prince, we were scheduled to join the others at the training camp weeks ago."

My jaw bunches. If he thinks the king's nightmares are bad here, he should imagine them in the war camp. "I sent Ishvi and Malchishua to join them until Abba was well enough to travel again."

"It's not enough, my lord. The only reports I'm receiving confirm what we've already heard. The threat is spreading like wildfire, and the farther it spreads, the harder it will be to discern and control. This could become very serious very fast."

"I know." The assault after Geba years ago had caused hundreds of Israelites to flee their homes in a matter of weeks. We can't let that happen again. We can't lose all the stability we've fought for. Proactive fighting is easier than trying to win our whole country back.

Abner continues, "Michmash remains their greatest embarrassment to this day. I'm convinced Achish is trying to draw you or the king into battle. Until they see one of you taking charge, the attacks will only grow worse."

Stopping to breathe, he changes his tone, edging into a careful explanation.

"Jonathan, we're family. You know I have every sympathy for the king, but all this uncertainty is bad for the kingdom. The healers leave useless medicines behind and refuse to do more. Instead, they spread rumors about what they've seen here. Every other day, we're approached by elders who wonder how long it will be before one of their cities is burned. Southerners are taking to the hills in increasing numbers, choosing to live outside Saul's jurisdiction. And now, you've trusted the stability of our king to a singer from Bethlehem."

Anger glows in my eyes, but I'm too tired to unleash it. "What is your point?"

"The people need answers. And we want to know what you are willing to do." His last words come out in bites, and his grip tightens around his arms.

"We?"

"The council. But we speak for the army, the people. Everyone." Abner angles closer. When he looks up at me, his face is only inches away. "You know that we cannot go on like this much longer. The Philistine threats must be answered. This was the reason Israel asked for a king in the first place—"

"*Demanded* a king, in spite of God's warnings." Now look where we are.

"—to deal with our enemies," Abner finishes, woodenly. "The position we established years ago must be maintained, or our enemies will be enticed by a weak stance. You are Saul's firstborn and arguably the champion Philistia fears the most."

I clench my teeth. "What exactly are you suggesting I do? Take over the kingdom while Saul is compromised? If I seize power now, there may be no way back. God anointed my father king of Israel. He did not anoint me. And the last time we spoke to the prophet…"

The image of Samuel's torn robe drifts through my mind again. I shake it off and adjust my tone. "I sent a message to the Roeh asking for his counsel."

Begging. Pleading to know what had happened after Amalek to plunge my father into despair. Samuel had returned with us after that battle, but we haven't seen him for years since.

"The Roeh has wisdom from God that we will need in order to move forward," I continue. "I would prefer to wait and see what he says before…what's the matter with you?"

Abner's pinning the ground with his stare, the heavy cloud back on his brow. It's the same sickened look he's shared with me in countless frozen moments over the years. Instead of fumbling for words, he simply reaches into his cloak and pulls out a wrinkled parchment. With the seal broken. "Samuel is no longer our ally."

"You read it?"

I rear over him, but he holds the paper between us like a shield. It's from the prophet. And it can't be good news. Or he would have told me before.

"How long have you had this?" I demand.

"It arrived the day we sent for the shepherd boy."

"Who else has seen it?"

"Just me, my lord."

Unconvinced, I snatch the paper, and Abner steps back. The first words of the Lord we've heard in years, and he was hiding them from me? I turn away, angling the parchment toward the nearest torch.

Just the sight of Samuel's unsteady handwriting sends a spearpoint of hope through my stomach. My eyes devour the contents like a hungry man pouncing on food. But before I'm even finished reading, the words dig into me, clawing deep into the place that I keep hidden. The place I don't touch.

"These are the words of the Lord to Saul ben Kish—

"Does the Almighty take more delight in burnt offerings and sacrifices than in those who obey His voice when He speaks?

"Behold, to obey is better than sacrifice. To listen is better than the fat of rams. For rebellion is like the sin of witchcraft, and presumption leads to iniquity and idolatry.

"As you tore my garment from me years ago, so your kingdom has been torn from you.

"Because you have rejected the Word of the Lord, he has also rejected you from being king."

An instant ache blooms in my throat, spreading down my chest and through my arms. The parchment disappears, the words smearing together, but I continue to stare at them, crushing the paper in my hand. I have my answer from the Lord, and yet it's merely deepened the canyon inside me. What am I supposed to tell everyone? Who will stand with Saul if he's been rejected by God?

Abner clears his throat. "Samuel has chosen to set himself against us. But you are right. We cannot desert the king now." He breathes deeply. "No matter what it takes, we must think of another way to help him if the music doesn't. We have to band together to keep the tribes united, or everyone will talk of how we failed."

His words bend and echo, bouncing off my ears without meaning. It won't be long before I'll have to do something to release what's building up inside me. What hope do we have if we've been forsaken by the God of Israel's armies? Any plans we try to make without Him will unravel, cursed before they even take shape.

Abner drones on, trying to make up for my silence. "Saul was anointed by God, and we have to defend his throne. Will we just stand around until the kingdom falls to another?"

I bend over slightly, feeling as though I've been punched. Without speaking, I turn and stumble toward my chamber, leaning into the wall so Abner doesn't see the answer carved into my face.

It already has.

TWO

David

───◆◆◆◆◆───

A month ago

"I don't understand." I'm shaking my head, feeling cold despite the sunlight.

Abinadab isn't making any sense. It's already strange enough to see my brother here in the pastures, but I can't think of one reason my father would pull me away from the sheep in the middle of the day.

I glance at Aaron. The confusion on the old shepherd's face matches mine. Abinadab is so out of breath, he can't even manage any insults. I can't remember the last time he's had to run all the way to the pastures from town. Watching him bent over, struggling to breathe would be entertaining if it wasn't for the agitation straining his face.

"Why does Abba want me now?" I press him.

"He doesn't." Abinadab shakes his head, rubbing his brow. "It's the Roeh."

"What?" Aaron and I say it at the same time.

"The Roeh—Samuel," I repeat it, making sure my brother isn't teasing. It wouldn't be the first time. But there's not a hint of mirth in his eyes.

"Yes, Samuel. What other Roeh is there?" Abinadab snaps, impatiently. "He's back at our compound. Abba said you are to come at once."

"But why? What is Samuel doing here?" I've never known Israel's chief prophet to come this far south, and it's not even a feast day.

Aaron's face is more serious than I've ever seen it. He takes the staff from me, concern darkening the sunburn on his brow. "I'll stay with the flock. Go on."

Abinadab is already halfway down the hill, and I sprint after him. I've felt uneasy since daybreak, distracted by an undefined anticipation, but this is one step short of impossible. "Samuel—the Roeh from Ramah is here in Bethlehem."

My brother keeps running. "Yes! Samuel! How many times are you going to say that?"

"But what is he doing here? Why do I have to come?" I'm willing to bet anything that my father wasn't expecting this.

Abinadab scoffs, jogging backwards. "Please. David, you've been dying to meet Samuel your whole life. Along with Saul and Jonathan."

And Samuel was probably the least likely of the three.

Abinadab sighs, slowing his pace a little. "He's a strange old man, that's certain. He said he came for a sacrifice, but he only invited our family. And not the whole clan either—just us." He shrugs, keeping his eyes on the path ahead. "He told Abba he wanted his sons to stand before him, so we did. Myself, Eliab, Shammah, all of us. He just kept saying that the Lord hadn't chosen yet. Then he asked if our father had any other sons." His tone tightens. "At that point, Abba had to mention you."

Heat mounts in my face. I'm sure my father avoided it as long as possible, but it would be pointless to lie to the man who speaks for Yahweh. The God of Israel knows that I'm Jesse's son, even if Abba hates admitting it. "So...Samuel wanted me to come?"

Abinadab still won't look at me. "Why else would I have come to get you?"

I swallow, my bubbling excitement shaking into uneasiness. What business would bring Yahweh's prophet all the way out here into the territory of Ephrath? All the important cities are to the north. And what kind of sacrifice would require all my father's sons to be present for it?

Most importantly, what difference do I make? I'm the son of a maidservant, and I've never been required to present myself with the others at any feast.

When we reach the gate of my father's compound, Jesse's wife, Atarah, comes out a side door to meet us. "Hold on. You've come from the pastures." She smiles wryly into my eyes and lifts a waterskin, pouring over my blackened knuckles.

Gratefully, I wash up and down my arms and splash my face. I'm home so rarely that I barely take note of my appearance. My sandals are shredded by brambles, and my shepherd's tunic is torn, exposing half my torso, where the lion wounded me last year. But there's nothing I can do about that.

"Did he say why he wants the boy, Eema?" Abinadab asks her.

The anxiety in Atarah's face is carefully controlled, hidden with her usual stubborn smile. "Because he's a son of Jesse," she says coolly. "That should be enough for you."

I lower my head to hide my own smile. I'm only Jesse's son, not hers. But no one ever tries to tell her that. She's the reason my father finally claimed me, after years of hiding me in the pastures.

We walk through the gate and across the courtyard in absolute silence. It's so quiet, we can hear everything—the hiss of incense, the twitter of birds overhead, the slight push of the wind. A spotless heifer shuffles beside an altar that's been constructed off to the side.

Jesse and his other sons are gathered at the far end of the compound. Atarah pulls her veil across her face and slips in behind them. My father's gaze cuts nervously to the left when he sees me. "Roeh, this is…my youngest."

When Samuel turns around, sudden panic jumps inside me. I've never prepared for this. Should I say something? Bow?

He's not an imposing presence. To an untrained eye, he's just an ancient prophet. Long woolen sleeves cover his bony wrists, and white hair curls into a thinning beard over his chest. But this is the man who has given Yahweh's words to our people since he was a boy, serving in the temple at Shiloh. And in all those decades, Yahweh has not let one of his words fall to the ground.

Heaviness pulls at Samuel's wrinkled face. His eyes are full of what he has seen—both the triumph of Israel's trust and the pain of her failures to believe. His own sons don't follow in his footsteps, and he had grieved when Israel first demanded a human king to lead in place of Yahweh.

The weight of it all makes me want to tremble. I can only imagine how uncomfortable my father is. But Samuel doesn't seem to notice anyone or anything but me. He takes a step forward, both hands resting on the top of his staff. "What is your name, my son?"

Something sharp dances in my chest when he calls me that. "David, sir."

Then his expression opens up, like dawn breaking over a hillside, and I can see the color of his eyes. He holds out his hand, an endearing smile lighting up his face as though he's known about me forever. "Come. Don't be afraid." When I get closer, he leans on my shoulder a little, breathing into my ear, "I have brought the Word of the Lord today."

After that, the familiar motions of the sacrifice go by me in a blur. The Roeh and his attendant kill the heifer, and in a few moments, it's burning on the altar, incense-laden smoke pluming up to join the clouds. I take it all in, refusing to look at anyone or say anything. Whether or not Samuel explains himself, it should be enough that for some reason he wanted me beside him for all this.

Then Samuel turns to me, his eyes finding mine. "Kneel, my son."

Without waiting, he takes my shoulders and eases me down. Startled, I keep my eyes on his, even though the longer I look, the faster my heart races. A few whispers creep toward us, but Samuel cups my face with one hand, keeping my attention on him. With his other hand, he's holding a small golden vial shaped like a horn. The sunlight flashes off the tip as he tilts it against my forehead and releases the contents.

It's oil. So much of it. The heavily scented liquid runs down my face in every direction, dripping from my chin and the ends of my hair, but Samuel keeps pouring until the vial is empty. In awe of whatever blessing he's bestowing, I hold out my hands to catch the excess.

Samuel cups my face, and my heart jumps in my chest when he lifts his voice.

"David ben Jesse, in the Name of Yahweh, I anoint you king of Israel."

Now the whispers explode behind us, but Samuel acts as though he doesn't hear. Bending, he kisses both my cheeks, a satisfied smile on his face. But I'm shaking, inside and out, wishing I had the courage to say what I'm thinking.

It's humiliating, but I have to correct him. He has to be wrong. My neck and face start to burn as I wonder if this whole thing has been a mistake. He can't know what he's doing. I'm no king. I'm barely accepted in my own father's house.

Melek Israel. The title burns in my chest, and tears flood my eyes. Now he's making me want it. But I can't have it. Something like that can't be mine.

I've pulled away slightly, trying to shake my head, but the Roeh takes my shoulders and makes me stand. His hands grip my face, and he presses his forehead against mine, speaking directly into me.

"David, the Lord does not see as man sees. Man sees only the outward appearance, but the Lord looks at the heart. Yahweh sees everything. And He chose you for your heart."

My head can't comprehend it, but I already believe it. Inexplicably, I'm feeling Yahweh's smile—touching every beat of my heart, covering over any uncertainty. I've always trusted He was with me, but this is what it feels like to know, and the joy is taking me over, filling me up as though I've been anointed on the inside. How will I possibly contain this?

Just like that, I don't need to understand. I can only respond. Because it's not just the crown of Israel that's being offered. It's

Him. The God who took me in since I was born, who saw me when no one else did.

Utterly captivated, I stare right into this impossible gift and let my heart embrace it, for better or worse. "I'm all yours, Adonai," I gasp. "I will do whatever you command. You are worthy of every praise. I will fight for you until the day I die."

Then I blink and see Samuel again, a thousand emotions struggling on his face. Holding back tears, he grips my shoulders. "Yahweh is your rock and your strength, your fortress and your deliverer. He has chosen you, and He sees everything you cannot. Only time will tell if you believe Him."

I feel the strength of his hands even after he lets go of me. I do believe. I believe that Yahweh is with me.

And all I want to do is sing.

* * * * *

"They're coming."

Shouldering around my brother, I press my face against the crack in the wall in time to see my oldest nephew barrel through the compound like a wild man. Joab clutches a knife at his side, his hair ragged, his eyes full of fight.

My father lags several steps behind, casting uneasy glances back toward the gate where he'd left the messengers from Gibeah.

Even from a distance, their anxiety seethes toward me, tugging my heartbeat into an unsteady rhythm. Even ordinarily, the arrival of King Saul's men in Bethlehem would be unusual. But seeing them here now cannot be a good sign. I can easily imagine the concern stirring the village elders when the messengers had arrived and mentioned the name of Jesse. Much like they'd reacted a week ago when the Roeh had arrived unannounced.

By the time the king's messengers had reached our gate, Joab had already run ahead to warn us and I had been herded into a back storeroom while my father went to meet them. Shammah waits with me, barely breaking composure, but I can tell he's wound tighter than the sling around my wrist. Two of our other brothers are stationed at the edge of the compound, ready to order me to the hills if necessary.

Joab slams his full weight into the storeroom door, cursing when it won't open. Shammah unlatches it, and our nephew elbows his way through, panting as though he's run all the way from Gibeah. "Jesse spoke to them, and it's true. They've come for David."

Shammah looks at me, heaviness crowding his face. It's what we feared—the end of our hopes that things might return to normal. The suddenness reaches into me and twists my stomach, but Joab grabs my arm before I can speak.

"We have to get out of here." He shoves me toward the door, tossing orders over his shoulder. "Shammah, tell the others."

"Don't be crazy. Wait for Abba…" My brother tries to separate us, but he knows it's pointless. Our sister's son is eleven years older, and one of the most aggressive men in Judah. He tends to act first and think later, and he's been watching for trouble ever since the Roeh came. Even though he still doesn't know why he came.

I plant my fists in his chest. "Stop it, Joab. Just tell me what they said! What do they want?"

"Joab ben Zeruiah!" The full name barely makes it past my father's lips.

He struggles toward us, beads of sweat coating his brow. These days, you can see the strain of his heart in his eyes. His beard trembles as he bends over to breathe, leaning hard into his staff. "Do you think we're going to talk about this in the middle of the compound? All of you, inside. Now."

He shoves his staff in the direction of the house, and Shammah takes his arm, supporting him so he can move faster.

I move to his other side, keeping my voice low. "What happened? What did they say?"

Ahead of us, Joab jogs backwards so that he can face me. "Well, Saul is finally going mad, like we all knew he would. They want someone to come play the lyre for him so that he can sleep. Some imbecile mentioned you."

I glance behind us, then press closer to my father. "So…do they know?"

My father watches the ground, laboring over every step, and his headshake is more of a question than an answer. "Inside."

Shammah leans over him. "Do we have a choice? Was it a command?"

Jesse looks up, and the fear in his eyes makes my stomach drop. "What else would it be?"

The rest of the family is huddled in the main room of the house, waiting to wrestle information from us as soon as we come through the doors. My seven brothers are scattered throughout the room. Joab's mother has a quelling hand on the shoulders of her other two sons. Abishai and Asahel had insisted on wearing weapons. Atarah is planted in front of the door, her wild eyes jumping from face to face. As soon as we get through the door, she shoves it closed, and turns to her husband.

"What's going on, Jesse?" she demands. "What did they want?"

Abba plants his staff, bent over for several breaths. "They are looking for David, to bring him to the king."

Atarah throws her hands up. "We're leaving."

I almost smile. Out of everyone in this room, she's probably the one who cares the most about me.

"Atarah—" My father's shoulders drop as his wife starts shoving items into the nearest basket, calling for servants to come help her.

"I told you, didn't I?" Joab crows, and his brothers spring to his side.

"Should we go too, Eema?" Zeruiah asks Atarah, anxiety building in her face. "At least for a little while?"

Abishai fiddles with his sword. "We could stay with our relatives in Beth-Aven. We could even go to Moab if…"

"Enough! No one is going anywhere!" Abba slams his staff into the ground, but his wife keeps moving.

"What are we supposed to make of this, Jesse? The king's men show up commanding David to the court only days after the prophet—"

"Atarah!" With his voice so shaky with age, Abba rarely uses that tone anymore, but it silences everything in the room, except Joab's ragged breathing. "The Roeh came here for a *sacrifice*. Nothing more. The man is older and more forgetful than I am. He likely doesn't even remember the trip. And nor should we."

He turns on his heel, reminding everyone with his eyes. I'm the one person he doesn't look at. But that's nothing new.

My father has ignored the Roeh's surprise visit ever since it happened, refusing to speak of it or hear it mentioned. Not that there's much to talk about. The experience left all of us with more questions than answers. Still, it's my life that was altered by it. He could at least act like he cared.

Spent, Abba shields his eyes with one hand, easing himself back onto a bench. "What the Roeh does is beyond our control or understanding. That's all behind us. We must decide on the matter at hand."

My mother is as rigid as a stone pillar, her fingers clenched around the rim of her basket. "Do Saul's men know Samuel was here?"

Abba's jaw bunches. "They said nothing about it."

Eema sucks in a wobbly breath, but Joab fills the silence with a dramatic groan. "They didn't say anything, but that doesn't mean they don't know. Saul has his foxes all over the countryside. He doesn't even pay all of them, but everyone knows they watch Samuel."

"Joab, enough!" My father and Zeruiah say it together. Abba holds his hands out, aiming his petulance at the ceiling. "God above, I'm too old for this."

"As far as we know, all they want is a harp player," Shammah placates. Always the peacekeeper.

"A harp player?" Eema lifts her face from her hands.

Shammah nods. "The messenger said Saul has been ill. Troubled by dreams or something. Can't sleep. They've been through healers, and nothing is helping. Someone suggested he bring in a harp player to soothe him."

Now everyone looks at me—except my oldest brother, Eliab, who just rolls his eyes. Everyone who knows my name knows that I play. All my life, I've heard notes everywhere, the way prophets claim to hear God's voice on the wind. The lyre has been in my hands since childhood, and constant practice has honed my skills as sharply as my aim with my sling.

Music fills my days in the pastures, stringing the hours together. I've become well known in Bethlehem, but I had no expectations that my music would reach the notice of anyone in Saul's capital.

Eema folds her arms. "No. Absolutely not."

"How did they even know about him?" Eliab finally weighs in. He's still leaning up against the opposite wall with his arms folded and his face pinched with disgust. He's done his best to avoid me since the Roeh's visit.

Joab smirks, vindicated. "I told you, Saul has servants from every corner of Israel, and they tell him everything they know. Some guard from Bethlehem mentioned David, and he didn't leave anything out. The messenger couldn't say enough."

My father's sigh fills the room, and I recognize the look on his face. It's the same baffled frustration that had twisted his expression when I'd walked in from the pastures at Samuel's invitation. Disbelief that despite all his efforts to shove me aside, other eyes had found me. He hadn't even given the Roeh my name. Why call an afterthought David? Beloved.

"Can't we just refuse?" Eema protests again. "Tell Saul that David is needed here?"

My father lifts a helpless hand in her direction. "Saul is the king, Atarah. I would think we have very little choice."

"But Jesse, is this wise? Sending David to placate a volatile king when not even his healers have made progress with him?"

Joab starts to answer, and then suddenly everyone's talking at once, like a bunch of nervous sheep set off by a single noise. I don't try to speak. I wouldn't be heard anyway. Folding my arms, I lean against the wall and exhale, letting the noises fade into the background while I focus on the charged stillness that follows me now.

Ever since Samuel's visit, the prophet's words have led me like a torch in the darkness, illuminating a path I've been traveling for years, thinking no one noticed. But Someone had.

I close my eyes, gripped by the memory. I had gone back to the pastures that day utterly overwhelmed, ignoring everyone else's confusion. It was as though a deep well had been unlocked inside me, and every empty place was being filled. I wanted to weep, and I wanted to sing for joy, so I did both—in the pastures, where I did everything. Before the One who saw me when no one else did.

The awesome reality had torn my heart wide open. The songs that had poured out of me since then were the best I'd ever written. Declarations of God's greatness that I fling toward the sky during my hours with the sheep. I've always believed that He was with me. Now when I sing, I can feel Him in my own voice.

If I've truly been set apart by Yahweh, chosen out of thousands to be a leader of men and not just sheep, then He will protect me. His hand won't depart from me as long as I remain faithful to Him. No doubt that's what the coming days will prove. He's already shown me what His thoughts are toward me. Now perhaps He's inviting me to make a move.

I'm barely fourteen, too young for the army, even though Saul's sons were fighting at that age. But for now, I have something else that is needed by the king. And it can't be a coincidence that this is happening only seven days after the prophet came.

"I'll go." Somehow, my voice breaks through the frantic chatter, and everyone stumbles to a stop, looking at me. I push off the wall and stand straight, making use of every inch I have. "I'll go and serve the king."

Eliab is the first to protest. "David, this isn't the time to be showing off." Agitated, he appeals to our father. "I told you this would happen. He has something to prove now."

"I don't." I almost laugh. Does he really think that I'm planning to march into Saul's court and tell him to his face what Samuel said? What *God* said?

Just a cursory glance around the room tells me that almost everyone's thinking like Eliab. They're just not saying it. Most of them heard Samuel's pronouncement. But they don't believe that it's real or that I can be trusted with it. The rest of them, like Joab, don't know a thing. And it's better that way.

I lift my chin and look directly at my father, straight into the inattention that I've avoided my whole life. "There's no reason we should refuse King Saul. That would only raise suspicion. I promise, he won't see anything other than a shepherd from Bethlehem."

I'm willing to keep the rest hidden until God Himself uncovers it. He did it before, and He can do it again without my help.

"More than likely, they'll send me home in a few weeks," I continue. "As soon as the king gets a good night's sleep." I try to jest, but everyone's too nervous to laugh.

My father strokes his beard, nodding. I can see the relief dawning in his eyes at the hint of security I've offered him. "Yes, that's true. Most likely, this will all be temporary."

I almost flinch. No doubt he's happy for the chance to continue seeing me the way he always has. I stare at him for another couple breaths, wondering if he'll ever see what God showed Samuel.

He clears his throat. "Well, we shouldn't keep the king's men waiting. I suppose they will want to stay here tonight."

Joab snorts. "No, Saba, don't you remember? They said their orders were to stop for nothing. I should go with him."

"No. You will stay."

I almost chuckle at my father's adamance. My entire life, Joab has frightened everyone with his thirst for battle and his belief in Judah's tribal superiority. He's fiercely loyal but extremely volatile. He is the last one Jesse should send with me.

Eema tries to protest. "Jesse, perhaps Joab should go."

"Joab will stay here! There's no sense in looking for trouble. If we don't hear anything from David in a few days, I may send one of the others. But Saul's messengers are protection enough for now. He'll leave as soon as they are ready to go."

Eema moves up closer to him, but he waves her away, insisting, "He'll be fine. Have your maid pack some bread and a wineskin for him to bring to Saul. David, go choose a goat from the flock. Go on." His glance barely takes me in before he shoves to his feet and leaves the room.

Eema follows me outside, her expression heavy with unrest. "This is unwise. I don't like it at all. If anything happened to you…"

"Nothing will." It's what I always say to her, for whatever it's worth.

She grabs my sleeve. "We wouldn't even know! We wouldn't be told. You know how men disappear into Saul's courts. They're taken as servants and never return to their families. We don't know what they're expecting from you or what they're bringing you into."

Hearing the panicked lilt of her own voice, she cuts herself off and forces a ragged smile. She's worried about me, and for a moment I allow myself to feel grateful. She's the only mother I've ever known, and her concern has been one of the few constants in my life. I put my arms around her waist, and she presses her face into my hair, whispering, "I'm sorry. Just come back to me. Promise?"

My laughter is muffled in her arms. "Eema, you do realize that I face much more dangerous things in the pastures than I will in Saul's court?"

"Don't remind me." Her eyes drop to my chest where the claw marks are still visible through the gap in my robe. "Just be careful. There are lions in kings' courts too. And remember, the Lord goes with you." She touches my cheek before retreating inside.

The moment she's gone, the weight settles back in my stomach. The weight I can only take to Yahweh. No one else has answers for it. My father would have us believe everything is behind us. He hopes it is. But it's not. Everything is ahead of us, and it's all uncharted territory.

What if Joab is right, and there's more to Saul's illness than insomnia? And why would he have sent for me, out of all the musicians in Israel? It's unnerving, but it's no coincidence. God has done this, and I can only hope that what He's put in me will help me face whatever is ahead.

I hook my fingers into the sides of my shepherd's vest to steady them. These days, I can't tell if it's the urge to play or the *Ruach* pulsing in my hands. The Spirit of Yahweh has changed locations, pushing into me, whereas before, I would only feel Him on the wind or in song.

I'll never forget the way it felt to have Him take hold of me that day, while the oil dripped down my chest like thick raindrops. I was humbled and battle-ready in the same breath, filled with boldness and a heart-searing joy. To know that I had Yahweh's favor eclipsed everything else. But in a way, I had always known.

I close my eyes and wait for the soft stirring to join my heartbeat, His presence entwined with mine. *You were there before, Adonai. Even before I realized it. Your presence was my shield in the pastures when I faced lions and bears. Be with me now.*

Other footsteps join the silence, and I look up into Shammah's face. He's a calm presence. Eyes like Eema's. Patient wisdom that deals skillfully with all the chaos that follows a family of eight sons. Of all the brothers, he knows me the best. "Are you sure about this?" he asks.

I shrug. "We really don't have much of a choice. Saul must be desperate if he had to come all the way out here for a harp player."

"Who would have thought your music would bring you to Saul before you even joined the army?" Shammah gives me a half-smile, but something heavier waits behind it.

I scuff the dirt with the toe of my sandal. "I've never seen Abba so nervous. He'll be relieved when he finds out they only want me for a servant."

Shammah's smile disappears. His jaw tight, he steps squarely in front of me, blocking my view of the gate.

"Listen, David. Samuel may be forgetful, but the Almighty is not. He knows what He anointed you for, and He's able to bring it about in time. Trust that. Wait for it."

I nod, grateful for at least one brother who understands. Shammah doesn't say much, but when he does speak, he's worth listening to.

His voice drops a few notches. "Still, it's no secret that Samuel hasn't spoken to Saul in some time. Best not to mention the prophet's name before the king. Or that he came here."

I nod again, but this time something races up my spine. Something cold.

"And what if Saul already knows?"

Always honest, Shammah barely hesitates. "Then...we could all die."

THREE

Jonathan

———————◆◆◆◆———————

The fortress walls close in around me as I stagger back to my chambers, holding Samuel's message like a smoking ember. My eyes burn, and I'm struggling to get a breath through the dread that's thickening in my lungs. Once I'm alone, I unroll the parchment again, but think better of it. The message won't change. The prophet's words are seared into me, throbbing in my side like a wound that won't heal.

The God of Israel doesn't change His mind.

I pull in a sharp breath, closing my eyes against the pain.

I can see it so clearly now—the Roeh coming across the plain at Gilgal with anger leaping from his eyes. It wasn't until he'd come within inches of my father that I'd noticed Samuel had been weeping. He'd stood there as immovable as a tree while my father gushed about our success at Amalek, as if he didn't hear the endless bleating and lowing of the animals we'd spared against

God's command. As if he didn't see the terrible finality on the prophet's brow.

Abner's footsteps approach from behind. "My lord…"

I suck in hard to keep my voice from shaking. "Is Eema still out there?"

"No. She's gone back to her chambers."

"Good." I can't imagine how I'll explain this to her. Because it will have to be me. Just not tonight. I feel hollow, as though I'm staring into a dark canyon. We have decisions to make. The Philistines won't wait. But how do we move forward without the certainty of victory?

I mutter, "Send word to my brothers to go secure the towns around Gibeah. Tell them I plan to join them as soon as the king improves."

The shadow of Abner's arm stretches toward me, but I jerk out of his reach.

"Don't touch me."

Groaning, he snatches the parchment from my hands and holds it against the nearest torch. The paper curls in on itself and finally disintegrates. When it's almost black, Abner drops it and stamps on the pieces.

"There. That's the end of that."

If only. "It doesn't change what it said."

He sighs, forcing his hand onto my shoulder. "Please listen to me, Jonathan. Forget about Samuel. Saul is still king, and no one else knows about that message. What difference does one man's opinion make?"

I shrug him off again, my voice breaking. "Abner, Samuel is Yahweh's prophet! He's been the Almighty's voice to Israel for decades! If you're after one man's opinion, he's the one you get! Why do you think I wrote to him?"

"Because you have a hard time letting go of the past." It's a bold statement, but he doesn't retract it, his eyes full of everything we've seen on the battlefield. And in my father's tent. It's timely too, since I have a question for him.

"Abner, what happened at Amalek?"

His initial silence tells me more than enough. The certainty in his face disintegrates faster than the parchment had burned.

"You know what happened at Amalek. We destroyed everything," he mumbles.

I laugh grimly. "No, Yahweh *said* to destroy everything. We left the king alive and took all the best animals as spoils at my father's command. Samuel was furious, or don't you remember?"

He folds his arms. "I remember. What's your point?"

"What happened after that? After Samuel took my father into the tent and told me to wait outside?"

Abner shrugs. "I don't know, my lord. As you said, they wanted to speak in private."

"But Abba told you what happened, didn't he?"

Abner drops his shoulders, his eyes edging away from mine. "Why would he do that?"

I step up closer, rearing over him. "Because he tells me everything, and anything he's afraid to tell me, he tells you." And because he beat me senseless only a week later, emptying himself of some deep rage I couldn't understand. "Out with it."

"All right! All right! You're becoming incensed over nothing." Flustered, Abner uncrosses his arms. "The Roeh gave the Word of the Lord to Saul. Very similar to what you just read. Your father became angry when Samuel tried to leave. He grabbed the prophet's robe and tore it."

I knew it. At least, I'd suspected it once they'd returned to camp. "And who killed Agag?"

Abner's hesitation looks painful now. "Samuel."

"At his age? He killed the Amalekite king?" I'm both angered and amazed.

"Yes. He took your father's sword and hacked Agag to pieces right there. He said he would make Agag's mother childless for all the children the Amalekites have taken from their mothers."

"But Samuel killed him." Not my father who had wanted Agag for a war trophy and was busy building a monument for himself at Carmel. I point at the charred remnants of paper on the floor. "And that's what Samuel said to my father that day? That's why Abba was angry?"

Abner has turned to wood, his face carefully expressionless. "It's possible."

I nod several times because it's all I can do. Everything is clear now. Terribly, horribly clear.

After the battle at Amalek, Yahweh had completely torn the kingdom from my father, just as he had torn the Roeh's robe. Abba had hidden it from me for years, but the truth had eaten him alive, igniting the torment that haunts him now. The darkness that turned him against me. I fold my arms so tightly that they ache, but the trembling won't stop. "Leave me."

"Jonathan…"

"I said, leave me. Get out!"

Abner retreats, and I wait for the shuffle of his footsteps to fade. Once I'm alone, the inner tremors take a fiercer hold. All those years, seeing my father unravel, suffering at his hands. This was why?

My heartbeat blurs my vision, clawing all the way out through my fingertips. I'm seeing red, the way I do in battle cutting down Philistine after Philistine. How are we supposed to fight without the security of Yahweh's favor on our king?

I press a fist against the wall and lean my face into it. "God Almighty, we are nothing without You. You are the lifeblood of Israel. We cannot go on without Your blessing!" I catch a sob before it escapes my teeth. "Yahweh, I didn't choose to walk away from You! Please give me a sign that You haven't fully abandoned us. Can I even ask such a thing? Do you even hear me anymore?"

I picture my father shaking his head in wonder, the presence of the anointing oil heavy between us. "I'm new, Jonathan," he'd said. "Ever since He touched me, when that oil dripped from my brow...I'm new."

But then he'd disobeyed. Continually. Turning from the light to embrace the haunting torment I'd seen rearing over me back then, after Amalek. The memory breaks my control, and I shove off the wall, grabbing the nearest item. It's a curtain, and I go down in its folds, tearing it with me, my inner pain screaming louder than I dare in this house that already has one maniac.

Shaking on my knees, I tear the cloth in two and begin to punch the floor. Until my knuckles are bleeding. But the weight in my chest won't release.

On my feet again, I spin around, looking for something—anything. In seconds, my spear is in my hands. I can't fling it anywhere, not without waking the house, but I clench the wood fiercely, hoping it will break in my hands. Instead, the floor creaks a few feet away from me, and I turn to see the shepherd boy standing in the open doorway.

"Good God!" I jerk back violently, his shadowed shape more startling than it should have been. Gripping the spear harder to make sure it's actually still in my hands, I slowly set it aside and thrust my fingers into my hair. "*What are you doing?*"

David stays silent while I press my hands into the wall, trying to gather an even breath. When I look at him over my shoulder, I swear there's a smile in his eyes. At least the hall behind him is empty.

When the boy starts stammering, I talk over him, exasperated. "How many real weapons have you handled in your lifetime? Not many? Well, here's lesson one. Never surprise a man with a spear unless you're completely out of reach of his aim! Not unless you were going to fight me with that."

David looks at the lyre in his arms and represses a nervous laugh. "No, my lord."

Spent and embarrassed, I rub my face, streaking blood across it from my split knuckles. Wonderful. The boy will have plenty of stories to carry home. Can this night get any worse?

I force air into my lungs. In and out. "Where's my fath— the king?"

"He's sleeping, my lord."

"What are you doing in here, then?"

"You're not." Gentle honesty reaches out from the boy's eyes.

His simple concern is jarring, especially after what he's witnessed tonight. But I can't deal with it until I decide what the motive could be.

"This isn't like him. He's a good man." I didn't plan to say that. But somehow, I'll always continue to believe it, and that sharpens my grief. I never wanted to see this happen to him. "He's the most powerful warrior I know."

David just nods. "I've heard."

"I'll bet you have." I drag a laugh out from somewhere, past the aches. I revered my father even before he was crowned, imitating his actions, practicing his strength. For years, it was my goal to be just like him. Until Michmash, when everything in my life broke apart and then woke up redirected.

David sets his lyre against the wall and walks over to my spear, running his hand down the shaft.

"Pick it up," I encourage him, amused at how he's holding back.

He adjusts his grip several times with one hand, then two, the muscles in his forearms squeezing as he hefts it off the ground and poises it over his shoulder. After several seconds, he sets it down, the crooked smile back on his face. As a shepherd, he probably doesn't fight his battles with a spear. His attempt should make him appear weak, but somehow it doesn't.

I lift it easily, sliding it back into its place on the metal hooks beside my bow on the wall. "The servant from Bethlehem said you were a man of war or something. Frankly, I expected someone who fit that description to be older."

I feel the question between us before he even asks. "Didn't you save Michmash at my age?"

"How old are you?"

"Fourteen."

"Then, yes. Something like that." These days, I can hardly believe I was ever that young. But I was tall for my age and had been training like a madman. Full of zeal and courage, preparing for a lifetime of fighting. I had no idea then how brutal the years would be. If we had spent them walking in obedience, we would be staring into a completely different future. Our ancestors walked through much worse with Yahweh at their side.

I glance at David again, my trained eyes finding the horizontal slices carved across his body from his breastbone to his lower right side. He fought something. "Where did you get those?" I trace the patterns of his scars in the air.

"A lion attacked our sheep. I got my knife into it before it did any real damage."

I can feel a smile edging up into my eyes again at the way he's trying to be modest. But lion wounds are nothing to sneer at. The teeth can strip flesh off bone, leaving organs exposed. There's always the danger of infection. The thought of massive claws tearing into the skinny shepherd is chilling. His scars are deep, and not very old. Up close though, the boy isn't as scrawny as I'd thought.

His frame is slender, but his taut muscles and calloused hands indicate that he hasn't led an easy life physically. Shepherds aren't to be underestimated. They hike great distances without sleeping and have to be able to fend off wild animals and intruders. No doubt his music is what's kept him sane during all that time with the sheep. And now he's in a whole different lion's den.

The untrained passion jumping around in his face opens something in my chest. I've been a warrior as long as this boy has been alive. His whole life he's probably dreamed about fighting beside my father and me. Only to come here and find us like this.

I step closer, looking down at him. "Listen, I know there are many rumors going around about what's happening here. I don't want you to get the wrong impression. It wasn't always like this."

His eyes stay fixed on mine. "I know."

"You do?" I study him again, still looking for some sign that he's sincere. More than twenty years his senior, I'm still too young to feel so jaded. But the king's anointing was supposed to last for generations, sustained by continual obedience and victory. We had so much more to do. How long before Abner's fears are realized, and people know that we've failed?

I'm so tired, I can barely see straight. I sink to the floor, my back against the wall, and rest my arms over my knees. "Why don't you tell me what you know, and I'll tell you how accurate it is."

David hesitates for a moment, wondering if I'm serious, but I can see the sparks in his eyes. "Michmash was your idea, wasn't it? You had no orders?"

I blink. I had expected him to ask about my father. "Yes, I—"

He edges closer, settling on the floor beside me. "You heard Yahweh calling. So, you went."

Moisture pricks my eyes. I've never said that in so many words, but..."Yes."

"And it was only you and your armorbearer?"

"Ezra. Yes. He's been with me for years." But we were only youths then. The image of us scrambling up those cliffs fills me with awe now. Would I be willing to do that today? Launch into battle with only an unction from Yahweh?

David searches my face, his breath coming faster. "People say you killed forty men in the first strike."

I laugh once. "No. Twenty within the first mile. Go on."

He stops to breathe. "Is it true that you told your armorbearer that nothing prevents the Lord from saving, by many or by few?"

My breath hitches. As many times as this story has been told over the years, few people remember that part. I swallow. "Yes. That's true."

"And you believe it?" He looks as though everything depends on my answer.

"I do." The words taste like ash. But I still believe them. Even now. Yahweh's character remains steadfast, regardless of our weakness. All the more reason I wish we hadn't failed Him.

David's smile is real now, filling his face. But I can't look too hard at it. I hate feeling defeated, especially after seeing with such clarity what we're capable of when the Lord fights with us. I clear my throat, trying to deflect the boy's rapt attention.

"So, how disappointing is it, meeting us in the flesh?" It's all I can think to ask, and it comes out more bitter than I intended. But David's answer is like cold water in my face.

"Not at all." He settles onto both his knees, his chest heaving as though he's just scaled a cliff himself. "You listened to the voice of Yahweh over the fears of the army. You inclined your ear, and He met you with His power. The mountains shook before you because He came. And He came because you trusted Him to. You believed He would when no one else did."

He breathes deeply. "And it was the same for the king. King Saul was chosen by Yahweh to lead Israel. When he was anointed, the Spirit of God rushed in and drove him to defeat Nahash of Ammon. Even with the blood of his enemies dripping from his hands, he still proclaimed it as the Lord's victory. He refused to take glory for himself."

The boy hunches forward, his words coming like water tumbling over rocks. "I've grown up hearing these stories, and they taught me that Yahweh was worthy of complete allegiance. Before I even knew Him, I knew He could be trusted. Because of you." He pauses, looking right at me. "You are right. It wasn't like this."

I gasp a little, caught up in the intensity of the boy's words. His fervor is like the physical warmth of a fire, but I shudder when I notice his eyes. It's like seeing someone I've missed for so long. Someone I know well. My heart dances in response to the thin silence that's pouring strength into me, shoving fear away like a discarded garment. And all I want to do is weep. Because I'm sensing *Him.*

The last time I felt this close to Yahweh was the day I'd followed Him to Michmash. I had given myself completely into His hands that day, sensing it was the only safe place I could go. But the only indication I'd had of what God was thinking had come from the mouth of Samuel:

"The Lord has taken the kingdom from you, Saul, and given it to one who is better than you, a man after His own heart. And the Glory of Israel is not a man that He should lie."

It's haunted me for years, what it would mean to be after the heart of God. How would a man accomplish that? But somehow tonight, I feel like I've come closer to it than I've ever been.

"Who are you?" It's all I can think to say. Even though I know the boy's name, it's not what I really want to know.

David just bows his head and reaches for his lyre. Gentle, smiling notes warm the room. The melody is simpler than what he played for my father. When he starts to sing, I almost protest.

I'm not the one who needs this. But the moment I think it, the excuse dies, drowned out by David's gentle praise.

"Bless the Lord, O my soul."

He repeats it softly, over and over, each refrain pushing deeper into my chest.

I close my eyes, setting my jaw. I can't let him see me break like this. But my steely efforts are no match for what's gripping me, wrapping me close. Errant tears slip down my cheeks.

"Bless the Lord O my soul,

"And forget not all He's done.

"He has forgiven all your sins,

"He has healed all your disease,

"He has redeemed your life from the pit,

"Crowning you with steadfast love and mercy.

"He satisfies you with good,

"So that your youth is renewed like the eagle's."

My breath releases, and a sob breaks free. Somehow, he's reached into my heart and dragged out everything I can't put into words, the things I'm afraid to ask even in prayer. If God has heard my cry, then what's the shame in tears?

I wind my fingers in my hair and weep, ashamed at how quick I've been to forget. When we are faithless, Yahweh remains faithful. He is the God of Israel, and He can be trusted. He is the answer to every aching question my heart can hold.

Words of hope from Torah, our sacred Law, run through my mind like healing oil.

Adonai will not keep His anger forever, nor deal with us according to our sins. As a father has compassion on his children, so is the Lord's heart to those who fear Him.

My father's rebellion isn't the end. I can believe it. I can breathe again. And the heavy weight has been lifted from my chest. I'm slumped against the wall with absolutely no desire to move. Too tired to get up, I lie back against the floor, surrendering to the pull of exhaustion.

It's something I haven't done in years—doze off in an empty room with a stranger watching. My grandfather had lectured us in the early days of Abba's kingship when we'd still trusted everyone.

"You can't just carry on as usual, Saul! You are *king*, whether they like it or not. And there are men out there who want to see you dead. You have to guard yourself and your sons."

My position has brought more danger than anything else, but the safest I've ever felt was when I left the stifling shelter of the cave behind and stepped out into the open air with Adonai. My muscles are unwinding, the deep disquiet ebbing away. I release my grip on my sword, my final act of surrender before choosing rest.

Yahweh is here. I will dare to believe it. In spite of everything, I'm still in His hands. He just had to send a shepherd to remind me.

FOUR

David

———◆◆◆◆◆———

Gentle birdsong strokes me awake. I'm halfway onto my feet before I remember I'm not in the pastures, sleeping at the door of the sheepfold. I'm in Saul's fortress in Gibeah, and the first pale breath of morning is edging through the heavy tapestries that choke the windows. Leaning back against the wall, I hold still, my ears waiting for the bird call again.

I'm not used to having to strain through heavy silence to hear it. The twitter and chatter of songbirds is much louder in the open fields, mingling with the restless noises of sheep and the mounting sweep of wind through the trees. The breeze and the birds make their own chorus, filling everything with praises. My mind whispers, singing along.

The earth is the Lord's, and everything in it.

With my eyes still closed, I lean into the thin slice of sunlight, allowing the hint of dawn to touch my face. It's so strange to have walls around me, especially in the warm season.

In Bethlehem, I only sleep inside during the winter months when the sheep are closer to home.

The floor is cold underneath me. Stretching, I tug the sleeve of my cloak back up over my shoulder and tighten my sling around my wrist. I never look at it without remembering the day I'd finally mastered the weapon, shattering a fork of branches with enough force to silence my brothers' taunts.

It was a bittersweet victory. As soon as I could defend myself, Abba had decided I was worthy of exile. I've grown up among the sheep, hidden away to help people forget that I'm not Jesse's full son.

Still, I feel richer in the pastures, freer than I've ever felt in my father's house. The open meadows and sprawling hills make a vast palace out of the countryside I share with the flock. It's become a relief to escape there and release praises to God. Reaching for my lyre, I consider the phrases trying to fit together in my head. The gentle tune from last night still lingers in my mind.

I don't remember when or how I started composing songs. They're more given than written, the overflow of my heart seeking expression. A way to relish the closeness of my God.

For years, my music has been for Him alone. I was cast on Yahweh from my birth, clinging to the God of Israel for the acceptance I couldn't get anywhere else. Out in the fields, giving voice to the praises of God, I feel vindicated, seen by the One who holds my inheritance. Now I know He didn't leave me in the sheepfolds as an oversight. He sent me there, to learn to know Him better. For years, I drank in everything I could about Him—all the stories of the battles He'd won for Israel through men like Saul and Jonathan.

Who would have thought I'd be singing to those same men one day?

The prince is still stretched out on the floor, sleeping. His ragged dark hair obscures half his face, and his knuckles are still etched with blood from the night before. I suppose I should be afraid of him, but I'm not.

The people worship Jonathan, and he has many namesakes in my hometown alone. But there's so much more to him than mere fight. He wears honor like he wears his seal ring, and his yearning for the God of Israel is so evident. I saw the ache in his eyes just before he broke down.

He honors you, Yahweh. Even after all these years, his heart is still yours.

I still can't believe I handled his spear. And said so much. Speaking to him was even stranger than finding him in the midst of a private battle, spear in hand. I kept waiting for him to stop me, but he never did, so I just kept talking, not realizing that it would mean so much to him. The words had poured out of me as though I'd been waiting my whole life to say them.

I shiver when I think of how deep Jonathan's eyes had gone as he'd struggled to figure out how I could speak with such authority about *his* battles.

Who are you?

I know how my brothers would have answered, if they'd been here. I'm just a shepherd-singer, the son my father never looks at. But that wouldn't have been the full truth. Not anymore. I didn't need really to give the prince an answer. He already knows enough about who I am. Because he knows Yahweh.

I smile, gratified that Adonai's presence was the cure the king and his son needed. I've learned that recounting our God's faithfulness is the best antidote for human weakness. Singing His praises over the years has kept my head up, calling me higher while everything around me was a reminder of my lack. And to think all that time, He was lifting me up, planning to make me into something I couldn't even imagine.

I can almost smell the oil running down my temples, dripping over Samuel's knuckles. I remember the way the promise sounded on the Roeh's lips.

Melek Israel. Yahweh sees in you what men don't. He has chosen you for your heart.

Until now, the thought has filled me with joyful awe, but now it knots between my ribs, an unfamiliar anxiety sweeping in behind it. Something heavy waits at the door of my mind, and for the first time, staring at Jonathan, I allow myself to think it.

I was anointed to take his place.

The moment the thought takes shape, I want to reject it outright, but it digs into me like a thorn branch scratching at my skin. Samuel's words flow back, but now I can barely hear them over the turmoil swarming in my head.

I have to get out of here. I have to go to Him. I need to hear Yahweh speak.

Steadying myself, I unfold my limbs and stand, tucking the lyre under my arm. The door is still ajar, so I'm able to slip through it without making a sound.

A few guards linger against the wall a few feet away, but they barely look up. One nods as I pass by. Gripping the lyre at my side, I keep going, trying to make sense of the labyrinth of stone steps and tapestry-covered doors. Working from memory, I try to recall the layout of the fortress from the day I'd arrived, circling around a curve of stairs and pushing through the antechamber beneath the king's rooms. Light pours in from between two curtains at the far end, illuminating a stone floor and a table flanked by cabinets of scrolls and rolled-up maps. Saul's council must meet here.

Sliding between the curtains, I come out onto a stone balcony that overlooks the compound. It juts out far enough from the fortress that I can see all the way to the gates of the city. The path that winds beyond it out to the hills has never beckoned so insistently.

Setting my harp aside, I plant both hands on the railing, fighting the sensation of being trapped. I've never really struggled to find words in the silence, but now I feel like everything is hovering just out of my reach. Closing my eyes, I drag in a long breath, trying to return to a place of rest.

The sky is nearly golden after the night's rains, the persistent smile of the sun slowly melting the heavy wall of clouds. A chilly breeze sweeps up from the king's fields, bringing with it the scent of wet, turned earth. A deep ache spreads through my chest before I can fight it.

I shouldn't want to go home, but I do. The enforced isolation of my life has taught me to lean into peace, to find richness wherever I am. Solitude with my Creator has become a sweet balm to my spirit, strong enough to cover any disappointment or neglect. I remember leaning into my songs whenever I couldn't think past the sheepfolds, when it felt like my life wouldn't stretch any further.

Aaron, the old hired shepherd had poured himself into training me, pushing the sling into my hands until my arms were strong and my aim was sure. Atarah had become my Eema, embracing me when my own father wouldn't. But eventually, I had grown up enough to want more. I would watch my brothers and nephews sharpen their weapons for battles I wouldn't fight. I would follow Shammah, pressing the only brother who would listen, but he never had a satisfying answer.

"Why won't Abba let me learn to fight? Saul could command any of us to battle!"

"That doesn't mean he needs you, David. You're just... you're made for a different life."

"Different, how? I don't understand!"

It hadn't made sense that my father would try to keep me from the battles that were the birthright of every son of Israel.

Yet, here I am, in spite of it all. My surroundings are a clear reminder that nothing will ever be the same. And all I want right now is to escape. Not back to the pastures, but back to the steadiness of the familiar, where I can have more time to…to… just more time. Back in Bethlehem, it was easier to believe that I had a purpose beyond the pastures, and I would find it someday. The hand of God would bring me to it. But now everything feels unreadable, uncertain.

I fold my arms and lean into the wind threading my hair. "Am I doing your will, Yahweh?"

No words answer me. Just silence shimmering in the air.

I fiddle with the cords of my sling, trying to bury my agitation. Not that I can hide it from Adonai. But I'd imagined He would have had more to say. Sometimes the anointing feels like a strange dream. I can't deny the heightened presence that surrounds me, but the other events of that day are disappearing faster than melting frost. I couldn't have just imagined what the Roeh said, could I?

I can't even believe I'm doubting now. After the Lord's presence rushed in on me that day, I thought I would never feel fear again. But now I can feel its breath on my neck, its fretful questions nagging me, as shameful as that is.

It was one thing to embrace the commissioning in the pastures, reveling in Yahweh's acceptance. But now my own eagerness to believe feels foolish. Even dangerous. I'd poured out my music and my admiration for the king and his son as if I wasn't treason walking. As if they both wouldn't kill me if they knew.

The imposing fortress looms at my back, representing Saul's reach, his control over all Israel. The spear-studded walls stare me down as though they're speaking for the king. *It's all mine.*

Saul has ruled Israel for longer than I have been alive. He holds his authority with an iron fist, and Jonathan was burned at the same forge. Even on their knees weeping, they're the strongest men I've ever met. Real men of war who know how to hold onto what's theirs.

Meanwhile, I've never set foot outside the pastures until now. All I know of leadership and defense has to do with sheep. I can feel all the stares of my brothers measuring me again, wondering if Samuel was serious or not. Hoping he wasn't. Their lack of faith hadn't bothered me once Yahweh touched me. God's estimation was all that mattered. But now...

I close my eyes, trying to silence the turmoil crowding into me. Did I even understand Samuel? Am I right to wait, or is there more I'm meant to do? How will I know when it's time?

The wind shifts, and something breathes in it, speaking words over my mind.

How much do you want to know?

"Everything," I respond without thinking, breathless to understand.

Tears jump into my eyes, and I search the sky avidly for whatever sign might appear. My own heartbeat counts down the seconds of waiting. But in the same moment, it's like the deepest canyon is opened before me, one that I can sense without seeing. The future is heavy with significance, but I can sense hesitation also, like the pause of a father deciding whether his child is ready for every disclosure.

Uncrossing my arms, I take a step back. Not yet, then.

"I thought you'd be out here," someone says from behind.

My fingers tighten around my sling, but the man who's walking out across the porch is dressed in the common linen of a servant. His familiar face and manner dance around in my mind, trying to attach themselves to a name. Once he gets closer, something in his eyes confirms it. "Othniel?"

He smiles, spreading his arms in greeting as he sizes me up. "You've grown. I wasn't sure your father would send you, but here you are."

"You were the one who told Saul about me?" I wonder if my parents would feel safer if they knew there was such a simple explanation for Saul's interest. Othniel is the nephew of Aaron, my father's hired hand. He had left Bethlehem years ago to serve as one of Saul's fortress guards.

I laugh, ridiculously relieved to see a familiar face. "Joab was desperate to figure this out. He said the messengers had a lot to say. What did you tell them?"

Othniel's face gleams with satisfaction. "Everything. My family knows you better than most of your brothers do. How do they fare these days? Is Eliab still angry you exist?"

I chuckle. "Unfortunately, yes. Even more angry that I— that I'm here," I amend, snagging back what I'd almost said.

"And how is Abigail?" Othniel winks.

I glance down, unable to control the heat taking over my face. I can hardly believe he remembers that, even if he was a close friend of the family.

Abigail's mother had relatives in Bethlehem, and Abigail and I had met one summer as children, not long after my own mother had died. We would play together every summer she visited, making songs and retelling the stories of the judges of Israel until the feats of Deborah and Barak and Samson were embedded deeper in our hearts than anything going on in Bethlehem. The memory seems to make summer itself come sweeping back.

"She's well as far as I know. I haven't seen her in a year." By design.

Othniel studies me, an unruly smile pushing onto his face. "My uncle always said it made him feel young again, watching you both running through the meadow like two lambs. I had thought perhaps you two would..."

"No." I say it too quickly, my cheeks burning. "I mean, it's not likely."

I can't deny a slight sense of pleasure that at least one person had imagined me good enough for Abigail. But no. Our last meeting had been more than awkward, interrupted by her older brother who'd acted like she'd done something wrong.

"Her father wants her closer to home now." Likely already scouting out possible husbands from the wealthy farmers of Judah's upper pasturelands.

Othniel just shrugs. "Seeing you together brought my uncle great joy. But what are the hopes of an old man compared to the will of a father seeking riches?" His expression tightens. "My own sister went to a man twice her age last season because he blackmailed our father over debts he couldn't pay. I pray Abigail's parents are wiser."

It troubles me to imagine otherwise. Abigail is special. Her exuberance is boundless. I still blush when I think of how she'd release her hair, throw her head back, and sing into the sunlight. As far as I know, she's only done that around me.

"Is she still beautiful?" Othniel probes.

"Yes, still beautiful." But too good for me. Her brothers had made sure I knew that. The image of the princess who'd stared at me last night jumps into my mind, but I push it away. Also too good for me. Mercifully, Othniel changes the subject.

"I hear the king slept."

"Yes. The prince also." I glance toward the door. "I still can't believe they sent for me. My family was baffled that Saul couldn't find anyone else."

Othniel shrugs again. "All of Bethlehem knows there's more to what you do than just music. You have a different spirit about you. The king needs that right now. Though it might not be enough at this point." His expression deepens, something forbidden pushing to the surface. "We all thought his rule wouldn't last, but now it's obvious. Everything is slipping out from under him." Folding his arms, he leans closer, his tone dropping. "Benjamin had no business taking the throne."

I look out over the wall, trying to keep a neutral expression. I know the talk. I've heard it all my life, particularly growing up in Bethlehem. The tribe of Judah has enjoyed superiority since the days of our ancestor Jacob, the father of the original twelve tribal leaders. Saul's descent from the tribe of Benjamin has been Judah's greatest complaint against him from the beginning. Our tribe had received the birthright from Jacob all those centuries ago, and many still believe that gives Judah a greater right to the throne.

Until now, I hadn't really considered that claim. It was more Joab's obsession. Yahweh had chosen Saul, and that had been enough for me.

Harshness edges into Othniel's voice. "He no longer carries Yahweh's favor. He's disregarded the Lord's commands too many times, letting his suspicions rule the people. And he's cast off the prophet, sending spies to report on his movements. He's obsessed with the rumors that Samuel might anoint another king."

"People have been saying that for years." I measure my response carefully, feeling the sting of his words on the back of my neck.

Othniel persists, barely concealing his fervor. "But Saul has declined dramatically *this* year. If the favor of Yahweh has left him for good, it can only be a matter of time. Israel's future won't wait for an apostate king. We have to be ready." The corners of his mouth twitch. "Judah was meant to rule. And we will. One day."

I keep my face turned away, hiding the insistent hammer in my throat. As carefully as we've guarded them, I almost wish no one else had heard the prophet's words—not my brothers, not my father. Joab doesn't know the whole story, but if he finds out, all of Judah will know, and we could be pulled into war against ourselves. The wrong men won't wait for direction from Yahweh. But we cannot run ahead of Him and expect a good outcome.

Othniel's hand on my shoulder is like an iron weight. "Our future is in the hands of young warriors like you."

"Othniel!" Abner's voice strikes the air behind us. I whip around, hoping to God the general hadn't heard anything.

Turning on his heel, Othniel bends into a relaxed bow. "Found him, my lord."

"I see." Abner ignores him, towering over me. "What are you doing out here? You are the king's servant now. Your days of running wild in the fields and writing songs to sheep are over."

"I'm sorry, my lord." Even with my head bowed, I feel like Othniel's whispered plots are painted all over my face. Now that Saul and Jonathan aren't around, Abner's careful manner has been replaced by a tight, closed-off authority. And it's taking every bit of my certainty and scattering it like dust on the wind.

"We will find something else for you to do when you're not attending the king, but you are not to leave the fortress without his permission." Abner's tone grows heavier. "And anything you see or hear within these walls stays within these walls. Do I make myself clear?"

"Yes, my lord."

He's about to walk away, but as he turns, his eyes drop to my waist, and the sternness in his face sharpens into hostility. "What do you need a knife for?"

Abner strips the leather-bound weapon from my belt, yanking me up closer to him. He flips it over in his hands, no doubt annoyed that he overlooked it before. He sizes me up, and I read a dozen unspoken threats in his eyes.

"You were not brought here by my choice, shepherd," he snarls. "You will keep to your place and stay away from the king's family. Now get inside. After last night, you should be sleeping. Othniel, take him to the armory, and make sure he stays there."

Grabbing my lyre, I follow Othniel, my eyes on the pavement. If it wasn't for Samuel's visit and the anointing, Abner's bluster wouldn't mean so much. I would have nothing to fear. Nothing to hide. But there's so much more at stake than I realized.

Abner is just one of many who will fight to the death rather than let Saul be dethroned. He would turn on me in an instant if he knew. I had known that before, but staring him down has pulled the threat of death into the open so I can see its ghastly shape. And it's not just my life that's in danger.

A dozen faces flash into my mind, followed by many more. Anyone associated with me. Will I have to defend them all? How much blood will I have on my hands before this is over? Why would Samuel anoint me now and then leave me with no instructions, no assurance or direction? What was Yahweh thinking?

The lion didn't come to the pastures your first day.

The statement is so jarring that it makes all my uncertainty shudder, shrinking into the corners of my mind to make room for the recent memory.

Lions are some of the worst threats a shepherd can face. Aaron taught me how closely I had to watch for them in the tall grass, how I could sense their presence in the movement of the birds and the sheep. It was a battle my mother hoped would never happen, but when it came, I had been ready for it, my hand molded to my weapon like it was a part of me. I'd dragged myself out from under the animal's bulk, covered in blood, but thankful and alive, with no sheep missing.

Peace trickles back in with the thought, like rivulets of water finding thirsty ground. Yahweh had been my Shield then, equipping me with what I would need and guarding me when my strength failed. Why should I fear another lion?

I almost laugh, remembering my own words to Jonathan last night. He was my age when he took Michmash, and he had no more instruction than I do now. The call of Yahweh was enough for him, and it will have to be enough for me. I clutch the lyre to my chest, reminding myself why I'm here.

Just sing. You're only a shepherd. Yahweh will do the rest.

FIVE

Jonathan

When I wake up, David is gone. The slice of sunlight between the curtains is almost blinding, streaking the floor next to me with a thin band of gold. I move one muscle, and cramps claw at my neck, threading across my shoulders. I wince, rolling over onto my knees. Why couldn't I have made it to my bed? Still, it was the best sleep I've had in a long time.

The sky outside my walls is glaring with the sun at full strength, making me wonder how far into the day I've slept. No doubt Abner threatened the servants and made them leave me alone. I can only hope he didn't berate David for coming in here without permission. Untangling myself from the heavy folds of my outer robe, I walk to the window, a loose board creaking under my feet.

The same moment, there's a knock at the door. Ezra waits on the other side of it, along with a servant holding a cloth and a basin of water.

I smirk at them. "It's about time. How long did I sleep?"

Ezra grins, knowing how much the answer will bother me. "It's past noon, my lord."

"No." I'm shocked. I didn't think I could sleep that long.

"Don't look at me like that. Abner said to let you sleep. God knows, you needed it."

I won't argue. Not when I feel more alert than I have in days. I dip my hands into the water and scoop it up over my face, combing my fingers through my hair. Ezra adjusts my robe and replaces my armbands, barely restraining a smile.

I watch him, curious. "You're in a good mood. What's going on?"

He smiles wider. "I have good news, my lord. Walk with me."

I follow him back into the king's bedchamber, but the bed is empty, the room set in order. Ezra leads me through it to the side chamber Abba uses for private feasts and conferences. Inside, I find a table spread with food. My father is sitting at the table's head, fully dressed in fresh robes, his hair bound back. He's actually smiling at the servant filling his cup, and I'm surprised at how natural the moment feels.

The sunlight from the adjacent window catches my seal ring, and Abba looks up. "Jonathan."

He sets his cup aside and stands, moving around the table with open arms. I have a hard time concealing my shock as he pulls me into a full embrace. I pull back to look at him. "Abba. You're—"

"Rested." He keeps one hand on the side of my face. "You look better too. I hear your exhaustion finally won out over your stubbornness."

I try to laugh, but the look in his eyes is tightening my throat. I can't remember how long it's been since I've been able to stare openly at him without feeling silent threats seething toward me. His eyes are so open, I can actually see the depth of their color. Something shudders in my chest, but I don't want to embarrass my father.

"I'm grateful you're well, Abba."

A muscle shivers near his eye, but he smiles, keeping his voice light. "Of course. All I needed was a little peace. A rest from…everything."

Yes, but it's taken months for him to find that rest. We'd brought in healers and musicians before with no effect. And now the cloud has been lifted from our home with the arrival of a Judean shepherd boy and his harp? Something is missing. I wonder how long it will take my father to recognize it. For now, he just squeezes my arm. "Come. Eat with me."

I sit on a low stool next to him, suddenly famished. In spite of the lingering uncertainty, I can't deny that a weight has been lifted from my body. Abba's servant fills my cup, and I take a long drink. "Where's Abner?"

Abba tears a chunk of bread and hands half to me. "Oh, he'll be here. We have a lot to talk about. He's been wanting me to gather the council, but we will need to speak privately before I have anything to say to them." He settles back against a cushion, unusually relaxed. "Where's that shepherd? The one who played the harp for me last night."

"He's sleeping, my lord." Abner bows from the doorway before entering. "Somehow, he was up at dawn on the balcony outside the antechamber. I had Othniel send him to the armory with Ezra and the others."

My father nods approval. "I like him. His skill is uncanny. I haven't felt so much peace in ages. Send word to his father that he will be staying for a while. He can serve with my armorbearers." His eyes dart to mine over the rim of his cup. "Othniel said he could fight or something, didn't he?"

"Sort of. He's—"

Abba flicks his hand. "No matter. The others can teach him. After all, he's mostly here for his music."

I can't help smiling when I remember how determined David was to lift my spear fully into position, his eyes glowing the whole time. He's definitely a fighter. You can teach a man moves and strategies, but the heart of a warrior is something he has to be born with. And a heart for Yahweh is something else, entirely. I'm not sure where he got that. Every son of Israel knows the stories of how our God set us apart to be His people. But I've met very few men who live like they've been chosen.

"I had to remind him why he's here." Abner holds out a dagger wrapped in leather. "I didn't know he was wearing this when he came to you last night. He had no business being armed in your presence."

"I saw it," I tell him, hoping he can read my expression. *Don't ruin this.* "He played for me last night as well."

Abner's face falls. "Tell me your guard was there also."

"I was there, along with a dozen weapons the boy can't even lift," I say, hoping my blistering stare is enough to silence the general. "Trust me, he's just playing his harp. Exceptionally well. And we should be grateful for that."

"Indeed." My father talks over Abner's growing anxiety. "We should thank Othniel for pointing him out. I would never have guessed anyone from the Ephrath region possessed such skill."

"Yes, I think he writes his own music as well. Abner, sit down." Tired of watching the general shifting from one foot to another, I hold out my hand. "Give it here."

Once he gives up the knife, I angle my head at the table. Rolling his eyes, Abner sits across from me and releases his agitation in a final comment. "You know he's of Judah, don't you?"

Abba chortles. "He's the tamest Judean I've ever seen. Such sweet songs. I've never heard anyone his age sing about Yahweh so...intimately. As if he came from the school of prophets."

Abner fidgets across the table, politics filling his eyes. I raise my brows at him, hoping he understands. Samuel is the last person we should bring up now. I never want my father to know I sent that message to the Roeh.

Before either of us can speak again, the king turns to me. "So, I hear we have a disturbing new problem that you've been keeping from me."

The breath in my chest turns cold until he clarifies, "Achish."

"Oh. Yes." I answer quickly, relieved to be shifting to a subject I understand. "The Philistine prince has only had the throne eight months and already his reputation is ridiculous. There are rumors of him recruiting those demon warriors from Ekron."

I'm careful not to add much more. Not yet. The reports of the *Nephilim* are enough to make anyone's blood run cold. Over nine feet tall, cannibalistic, wearing the skulls of their enemies. We'd thought we were finished with them, but apparently, they've been taking refuge in the coastal cities to the southwest, plotting with our enemies.

Abba's expression tightens. "What do the spies say?"

"It's been a while since the giants have been seen in our territory, but the Philistines have been raiding the mountain towns beyond Aijalon."

"That close?" He sits back, rubbing his hands on his knees. "Why aren't you at the training grounds?"

"Abba, you weren't well. I couldn't leave you."

He tosses his napkin. "Well, now you are going to. I will be fine. The shepherd will continue to play for me when I can't sleep. We must answer these threats while they are still manageable by my own personal forces. We don't want to have to pull the whole army unless Achish attacks with his."

"I sent Ishvi and Malchi ahead of me," I remind him.

Saul's eyes glitter. "Your brothers are skilled warriors, but everyone knows you and I are the ones the Philistines fear the most. We've slain thousands before Achish even got near the throne."

I hide a wry smile. He loves recounting our successes. I'm more concerned with repeating them.

"You will go ahead as soon as you can. Take Ezra and a few others to Aijalon and meet with the elders there. You can send word to me once you find out what kind of threats we are dealing with. I will follow in a few days if there is trouble."

Uncertain, I pick at the leather around David's knife. "Abba, you've barely recovered. What about the shepherd?"

"I'll bring him! He can carry my armor."

I'm torn. Every fiber of my resolve wants to quench the Philistine threat before it grows out of hand. But I hadn't planned on leaving Abba so soon. The plan was to keep him out of danger and away from chaos until he could stabilize. Now we're going to drag both the king and the shepherd boy into possible combat?

"We should inquire of Adonai first, my lord. Before we make any concrete plans." It's risky, but I have to say it. Yahweh may be searching for a wiser king even now, but as long as we still hold the future of Israel in our hands, we have to submit every move to God. Unfortunately, I can't bring that up without reminding the king of his disfavor.

Saul grips the stem of his cup harder, his lips thinning. "Very well. Why don't you send for Ahijah and ask him to bring the *ephod* here? He can inquire of the Lord while you prepare to leave." He scoffs into his drink.

I wince. Seeing him push this aside never gets easier. The kingship was meant to be governed by Yahweh's direction, continuously sustained by His presence. My father's practice these days has been to make a show of acknowledgement while assuming Yahweh agrees with what he's already planned. It never seems to occur to him that God might have different instructions.

But I won't argue. Not when I can't say with certainty what Yahweh's plan is. The closest I've felt to Him lately has been listening to David's music—and hearing the boy recount my battles as though they were his own. That still makes chills race up my arms.

Possibly reading my thoughts, Abba waves his hand. "Have someone bring the shepherd here. His music steadies me more than anything Ahijah has to say."

"I'll go, my lord." I get up without waiting for him to agree. He doesn't like to be reminded of his break with the prophets. And somehow, I always do it.

By the time I reach the door, Abner is already leaning toward him, ready to release every rumor and strategy he's been collecting over the past few weeks.

My father doesn't turn his head. "I'll be out at the tamarisk tree in my fields. Meet me there."

I head for the armory, feeling the strain against my mind again. I have fought beside my father for years, defending Israel against every threat. Our battle successes have won us respect among our neighbors and rallied our fighting men. But we still have so much to do.

The Philistines have been nursing their wounds for too long, and we have far too little insight into their plans. Though I've never confronted one personally, I've seen the damage that the giants from Gath and Ekron can do. How many will Achish recruit to his side? And how will we face them?

In the past few years, I've seen my father's strategy change. He has settled into a troubling self-confidence that ignores growing threats in favor of whatever move will bring him the most personal fame or revenge. He rarely speaks of Samuel's pronouncements except in dreams, but I know they plague him. He's turned inward, fixated on the possibility of enemies within our own ranks—a move that has earned him more than he already had.

His efforts to demand respect and flush out treachery have resulted in higher taxes and the nervous following of a shrinking council, manned only by his closest allies from our family's tribe, Benjamin. He claims things have improved, but only because he's surrounded by men who always agree with him. The Law has been set aside, rarely touched. I have to go behind his back in order to keep a show of respect before the priests. But it's better that way. He hates being told what he's not doing.

All I want to know is how we are to move forward if the king no longer carries Yahweh's blessing. It's more than ironic that on the night I was made certain of my father's loss of favor, I've met a boy who clearly seems to carry it. Why, I still can't say.

Unnoticed for the moment, I linger in the doorway of the king's armory, my footsteps covered by the clatter of bronze. A half dozen armorbearers work over our weapons with polished fervor, and I watch them, my gratitude lifting.

Every piece of metal in this room has been hard won, our supply growing from two swords to a surplus that finally meets our needs. The armorbearers are skilled fighters, but also artisans who inspect every weapon, testing them in mock battles until the weight and swing of every sword complements its owner. Every man in this room is a tested weapon himself, utterly trusted to be an extension of myself and the king. Our lives have been saved by them more times than I can count.

It seems fitting to find the shepherd boy here.

His lyre up against the wall, David sits beside Ezra, their heads bent over one of my bows. Ezra talks softly, winding new fletchings to a bundle of arrows. David watches avidly, holding a sword with the blade resting vertically at his side. I smother a laugh. He's probably forgotten it's even there.

I step into the room, and every man either gets to his feet or salutes from behind a row of spears. David lays the sword aside almost reverently, and I walk over and swing it into my hands, recognizing it.

"This one's not for real fighting anymore. It's crooked. Pulls too heavy on one side." I arc it in the air a few times, demonstrating, then hold it flat against my palms. "You never forget your first one though."

I set it down and angle my head toward the door. "The king has summoned you. He's out in the field. In the warm months, he holds council under the tamarisk tree that faces Ezel. I'll show you."

David grabs his lyre and follows me, relief surfacing on his face.

"Not used to being confined, are you?" Once I realize it, I'm surprised I didn't think of that before.

David shakes his head. "No, my lord. I spend most of the year with my father's sheep."

For some reason, I want to know more. "Didn't I hear that your father is something of an elder in Bethlehem? Fairly wealthy?" For an Ephrathite, anyway.

David's hands tense on the lyre. "He is advanced in years. Highly respected. Descended from Boaz ben Salmon."

I recognize the name. Boaz was a wealthy landowner in Bethlehem generations ago, but his influence extended beyond the small Judean town. His wife was a woman of Moab who had left her country to embrace the God of Israel. As their grandson, Jesse must have inherited their extensive property.

"So, why does Jesse need one of his sons to tend sheep?" I don't really know why I'm asking, but I like for things to make sense.

I let my question hang in the air as we walk through the fortress and out into the courtyard. Once we reach the outer gate leading to the fields of the king, David squints up at me. "It's what he wants."

I can tell the rest of the story is much longer, waiting right behind his eyes. But I'm almost grateful he doesn't offer any more details. We have other things to talk about. If we ever wanted to discuss our fathers, we would need to take a much longer walk.

Still, my answer feels flat. "They do what they think is best." Once I hear myself say it, I scoff. "At least that's what I tell myself."

Even after all these years, it still hurts to remember that my father once sentenced me to death in front of our entire army. Sometimes when I have to disagree with him, I see it in his eyes all over again—the suspicion wondering if he should have gone through with his vow at Aijalon and ended my life.

Shuddering, I arch my shoulders, shrugging the memory off. The sight of the open fields is a welcome relief, stirring the need for battle that I've shoved aside for weeks. My fingers twitch, aching to handle my bow. I fiddle with my sword instead.

"I meant to ask you where you got those songs. The ones you played last night."

For a moment, David looks tentative. "I didn't mean to disturb you."

"You didn't. Don't listen to Abner. I'm the Hassar, and I'm capable of telling you when something disturbs me. In fact, I'm...grateful."

David's smile returns, his shoulders relaxing.

"Who taught you to play?" I ask him.

"The lyre has been in our family for generations. Eema gave it to me when I was six. She would teach me songs of praise, songs for the feasts, everything in the Book of Jashar, until I knew them by heart. I just never stopped."

"So, you wrote those other songs yourself?"

David shrugs again. "In the pastures, I have a lot of time on my hands."

I stop and look at him, raising my brows. Redness creeps into his face, and he hesitates, looking out over the fields. "It's hard to describe."

I just laugh. "You don't seem to have a problem with words."

He shakes his head, grinning. "It comes more naturally in song. I'm just releasing what I know of Yahweh back to Him. And it's strengthening me in turn. There's nothing like it. It's what I was made for."

I'm more than a little impressed. I can't say that I know much of that kind of kinship with the God of Israel. Even if I did, I wouldn't have the ability to express it the way David does. This is exactly who my father needs, and I'm awed by Yahweh's graciousness to send him to us. I have to remember to bring a thank offering before sundown.

I study the young man beside me. He's reaching for something so lofty, and at such a young age. So few men really seek Yahweh as our ancestor Moses did—in friendship. Such a pursuit will change this boy forever.

"It's not a light thing, David…to be able to experience such peace with God." My throat twists around the words.

David nods, absently running his hand over the harp strings. "I'm in awe of Him, my lord prince. I'll never understand why He chose me."

I'm smiling, but I feel the expression freeze on my face. My heart stops midstride, and sudden heat mounts inside me. David? Chosen?

Before I can decide how to respond, a shout pulls my attention back to the fortress. Ezra is running across the field. "My lord!"

I wave and start toward him, with David following. But I'm not really seeing anything that's around me. My heart is beating double-time. Did I imagine what the boy just said?

Ezra takes far too long to reach us. We meet him halfway back to the courtyard. "We've just received word from your brothers. One of Aijalon's military outposts has been attacked. At least thirty are dead. The rest have fled to the city. A few of them joined the princes at the training grounds."

I pull in a breath, planting my hands on my hips to steel myself. Hearing of Israelite deaths is never easy. "How many raiders were there?"

"They don't know, my lord. The messenger said they came by night and used flaming arrows. One of the commanders was killed. Aijalon is convinced they will be the next target. The king has sent word to your brothers to expect us at the training camp in a day or so. We leave at first light tomorrow."

"All of us?" I ask him. "The king included?"

"Yes, my lord."

I shove his shoulder. "Take David to my father. Tell Abner to meet me in the armory."

Ezra bows, and he and David leave me to rein in my thoughts. Fidgeting, my fingers find David's knife in my belt. Flinging it aside, I pull my own blade free and drive it into the ground. My thank offering will need to be accompanied by fervent prayers for *chesed*. Only Yahweh's mercy will prevent more needless deaths. Another war with Philistia is imminent, and only time will tell if we are adequately prepared for it.

At least that battle can be sorted out with weapons, unlike what I just heard from the boy.

Retrieving both my sword and David's knife, I run the rest of the way back. No longer trying to be quiet for the king's sake, every man in the fortress is on high alert, completely scattering the peace from before. I make my way to the armory, moving fast enough that no one stops me with questions. Ezra will take care of packing what I need for a few days' travel west to Aijalon. I will have to find my mother and sisters, deal with their concerns before we leave. And give my youngest brother instructions to secure Gibeah while we're gone.

Music drifts down the hall after me as I pass my father's chambers. David's voice rides the chords, lifting gentle words of praise to our God—the God who promised to choose a man after His own heart to rule Israel. Is it the shepherd boy?

My heart hammers against my ribs as I try to remember Othniel's exact words when he'd told us about David.

"He's the youngest of Jesse's eight sons and skillful in playing the lyre. He is also a man of valor, a warrior of good presence, and the Lord is with him."

Back then, it had sounded like a welcome description, a possible answer to our prayers for my father's torment. Now I wonder how I could have missed the significance of such a narrative. His people called him a man of war, of prudent speech and good repute, even though he was the least in his father's house. Maybe few in his family have bothered to look past the surface. Until Yahweh did.

What's more, some rumors surfaced not too long ago about Samuel randomly showing up to Bethlehem for a sacrifice. The southern elders had talked of nothing else for weeks, but I had made sure that the news never reached my father. Was there more to Samuel's journey?

Either way, this boy is one to keep our eyes on. We have to know more about him.

Ezra jogs up behind me while I'm flipping through my arrows, running each new one through my fingers as I slide them into my quiver. I can't take my chances with any crooked ones. I hand Ezra the weapons as Abner joins us.

"Looks like we won't be able to avoid this after all," the general mutters.

I sharpen my gaze on Abner. "We're not avoiding anything. Achish will pay for every Israelite life he's taken." I turn my back to him, reaching for my bow. "Did my father mention whether he was bringing David?"

"Who?"

"The musician."

"Oh. Yes, the shepherd will be coming. Any other time, I would say it's foolish, but your father needs to stay healthy, and the music seems to relax him."

"Agreed," I mumble, testing the twine on my bow.

"Is anything wrong?" I can hear Abner's suspicion being prodded awake.

"No. Of course not. You should inform my mother of our plans. And tell my brother Ish-Bosheth he will be remaining here to guard the city."

My pulse unsteady, I hand the bow to Ezra, refusing to turn around until I'm sure Abner has walked away. "Make sure the boy stays with the armorbearers. Keep him close."

"Yes, my lord." If Ezra suspects there's more on my mind, he doesn't say.

Even more disturbing than the possibility of an anointing is the thought of discussing it with Abner. It's more than likely I misheard the boy. Or misunderstood. To mention it now would be foolish. Possibly fatal. There will be time enough in the future to find out more.

I fumble with more arrows, sudden numbness prickling through my fingers. The one thing I know is that Yahweh's presence changes everything. The memory of His hand on me is as fresh as though it happened yesterday. And I've never seen so much passion and yearning as I did in the shepherd's face. If David was anointed, he won't be able to hide it for long.

Especially if the God of Israel's armies is on his side.

SIX

David

———◆◆◆◆◆———

When the familiar shade of the forest closes in around us, I feel my shoulders relax. The temporary cover of trees is comforting, even if every step takes us closer to possible battle. We've been riding for two days, following the well-worn trail to the west where Saul's personal forces wait for his command at the site of the latest attack. We've seen no one for miles, but the predations of Philistine raiders are heavy on everyone's mind, and the king's guards keep their weapons within reach.

Saul and Abner ride their mules in the front, flanked by armed attendants, while the armorbearers maintain a tight formation directly behind them. Jonathan keeps to the outskirts of the group, but Ezra stays close, always acting as a barrier between his master and the edges of the trail as we ride into the open. I ride my father's donkey, not really sure where I should travel.

Saul's oldest armorbearer, Gera, is still disgusted at being saddled with me. Every time I get too close, he urges his mule several steps ahead, so I've fallen toward the back where Saul's servants drive the animals laden with supplies. A few guards flank us at the rear, making sure nothing approaches from behind.

It's still so strange being this far from the hills of Bethlehem. Every sound pulls my attention to the south where the landscape lumps into rocky knolls just large enough to conceal attackers. I expected to see some sign of a raiding party by now. But everything is strangely quiet, except for the steady shuffle of mules and the occasional screech of a hawk over the plains.

I shift my weight in the saddle, relaxing my grip on the reins. We might as well enjoy the silence now. Everyone expects it to be broken eventually.

Before we'd left Gibeah, Jonathan had placed my knife back into my hands. "Here. Just keep it out of Abner's sight. He shouldn't have taken the one weapon you know how to use."

"I have this." I had lifted up my wrist to reveal my sling, but Jonathan had simply thrown a heavy cloak over my arm without responding. "This was Ezra's. It gets cold on the road. And that won't suffice." His downward gaze had indicated the threadbare cloak I'd shivered under on the journey from Bethlehem.

I'd thanked him, but he's hardly spoken since, no doubt troubled by what could be waiting for us in Aijalon. Saul's men have talked openly about the latest attack, incensed by the threat it represents. But whatever grips Jonathan is less pronounced than anger.

I've caught him watching me occasionally, something heavy and unspoken in his eyes. Agitation, with a shiver behind it. I didn't expect to find something like that on the Hassar's brow, but listening to the commanders' talk, I understand more of the burden the prince carries.

The new Philistine king has uncovered all the uncertainty we thought Saul had buried in the past. Our enemies line the coast of the great sea to the southwest, and they've been a scourge to Israel ever since the days we came out of Egyptian slavery. Saul and Jonathan have provided us with the most victory we've had against them since judges like Samson ruled.

We used to know Philistia's strength, back when there were battles every other month. Saul's spies would guess their numbers based on the weapons they would pillage. But if Achish has been adding mercenary forces from Gath and Ekron to his ranks, then we might soon find ourselves outnumbered, even if Saul commands every Israelite man to fight. And building our army hasn't exactly been the king's main focus lately. His decline has been more evident to the people than he probably knows. Othniel's grumblings represent so many more voices.

Tightness winds my muscles. If I am to lead Israel one day, I will inherit all her conflicts. There is so much I don't know. But then, I never expected to be this close to someone with so many answers. Perhaps Yahweh intends for Jonathan to teach me. But right now, the prince is encased in some kind of invisible armor that I'm not ready to break into. He's been withdrawn for the entire trip, speaking only in brief snatches before retreating to the same stony silence.

I ride closer to Ezra, and he slows down, dropping a few steps behind.

"Does he always look like he's ready to rip something apart?" I ask him, lifting my chin at Jonathan.

Ezra chuckles. "He usually is."

I smother a laugh, but Jonathan is still wrapped in a cloud of his own thoughts, his eyes drifting over the trees.

"Do you remember Michmash?" I say it as loudly as I dare, already sure of the answer. Ezra had been the only one who'd followed Jonathan that day. He would remember better than anyone.

His eyes change, pride waking up inside them. "I don't think I'll ever forget. I'm not sure what we would have done if the

Hassar hadn't taken the city that day. We were trapped, hiding in that cave in Migron for weeks, losing more men than we could afford to. I have no doubt the Philistines would have pushed us until our army disbanded completely. My parents had crossed the Jordan River to hide in the wilderness. I didn't think I would ever see them again."

"But you did."

Ezra nods, pensive. "I couldn't believe it when they were able to return to their homes. It was a miracle, a victory sent from God. We thought we would spend the next decade under Philistia's thumb, trying to push back into our land. Instead, we sent them running. And stirred their anger."

No doubt the humiliation of being defeated by a fourteen-year-old prince has deepened their rage over the years. Still, it's hard for me to imagine Israel being forced from her land even though it's happened many times throughout our history. Would it ever come to that again?

I clear my throat. "So, this new king, Achish. Is he really the monster everyone says?"

Ezra glances at Jonathan, but the prince keeps his eyes forward, a muscle grinding in his jaw.

"It's possible. Conniving, definitely. An opportunist, as they all are. He wasn't in line to inherit the throne from Maoch, but people followed him without question. No doubt he's been busy the past few years, killing anyone who stood in his way."

And now he's ready to deal with us. "Do you think he wants to answer all the battles from before? Like Michmash?"

Jonathan scoffs flatly, interjecting, "He's been waiting years to have his way in Philistia. I would say he's eager to rewrite history."

"What about these men from Gath that he's recruiting?" I've never seen one of the *Nephilim*, but chilling rumors have slithered through Bethlehem about their Philistine descendants who have the strength of ten men, limbs like the trunks of trees, and a demonic source of power.

Jonathan's hands tighten on the reins. "They've threatened our people one too many times. And yet we know far too little."

He turns his mount slightly, allowing me more room to move up beside him. But I stay where I am, my thoughts drifting. "Why would Achish send raiders to attack one military outpost? Why not push further? They don't need our weapons. And they didn't take any captives."

Ezra shakes his head, his wary gaze still fixed on Jonathan. "It doesn't make much sense. Unless those men moved without their king's knowledge."

I picture the burning outpost, working the evil magic of fear over Aijalon. It seems like a taunt, like all the recent attacks. Small, inviting skirmishes, slowly growing larger and more serious. Threatening to test Saul's strength, which has been in question lately. I can't shake the feeling of being lured into a trap.

"What if there's more of them than we thought? What if they attack Aijalon or amass their whole army in the south?"

Jonathan turns in his saddle. "Then every man will have to fight, in all of Israel. We can't let them uproot us again. We'll stand against them and drive them back so that they cannot return." He doesn't raise his voice, but I can hear the sharp edge sliding into it.

I twist my sling through my fingers. "Can we do that?"

Jonathan hesitates before he answers. "Not today."

Resolve tightens my chest. "All my life, I've wanted to fight for Israel." This much I can tell him. "I will serve the king with everything I have."

Jonathan's smile is grim. "That's good to know. You may not have a choice."

Saul's shout breaks the silence, and several men answer his call from an outpost up ahead.

I tense in the saddle, but Jonathan waves me off. "Relax. It's just my brothers."

In the distance, the outline of a structure edges up from the horizon, and several men approach us on foot, servants leading their mules behind them. Saul and Abner dismount, embracing two younger versions of the king.

I've never met Sar Ishvi and Sar Malchishua, the princes. They stand a full inch shorter than Saul and Jonathan, but they're just as broad and heavily armed. Deeply-colored robes edged with embroidery cover their armor, and their manner speaks of a boisterous confidence that matches their father's—on better days. They're roughly trying to cover everything with hearty greetings, but a deep strain shows through.

While Saul greets his commanders, the princes approach us. One of them gives a short bow before reaching up to clasp Jonathan's arm. "It's about time."

Jonathan dismounts and hands the reins to Ezra. "Shalom to you too. Are you all right?"

His brother shrugs, glancing behind him. "We're fine. The outpost is gone though. Burned to the ground."

"Completely," the other man clarifies. "They even burned the bodies. Except for the ones they left hanging from the gate for our benefit." He lowers his gaze. "We've been busy trying to bury them. We were hoping to be finished before Abba got here."

Jonathan's fingers tighten into fists. "Where are the survivors?"

"Up in Beth-Horon. A few of them stayed with us, hoping to get revenge on the raiders. The men aren't sleeping, thinking we'll be attacked any moment. This one may not end quickly, Jonathan."

"I know that," Jonathan says tightly, his attention fixed on the king.

Uneasiness crawls up my spine. Strange that the Philistines wouldn't have pursued the survivors. Why are they so content with these flash attacks? And why up here? Why not closer to their own land, down south?

One of the princes continues, "I'm surprised to see Abba here. He looks better than usual."

"Yes, that reminds me." Jonathan steps aside, lifting his hand toward me. "This is David of Bethlehem, Abba's new armorbearer. David, these are my brothers, Sar Ishvi and Sar Malchishua, the princes of Israel."

I go down on one knee, but not before noting their confusion.

"Isn't he a little young?" Ishvi comments.

"What does he need a harp for?" Malchi mutters.

"He plays for Abba so that he can sleep." Jonathan lowers his voice. "You know how it is. Now are we going to stand out here all night, or can we get some cover?"

Joined by Saul's personal forces from Benjamin, we ride ahead to the outpost and stare at the blackened skeletons that remain of the fortress walls. The wind is already carrying the ash away, letting the scent of burning linger in the air, along with the stench of rot from the hanging bodies. Sickness winds through me, but I hold myself rigid against it, my feet digging into the earth and my fingers tight around my knife.

No one speaks. The commanders' servants remove the nails from the wrists of the men who perished. It's evident from the wounds on their bodies that they didn't die quickly. Burning digs into my eyes, and I breathe short and fast through my nose to settle myself. The dead men's empty stares fix themselves in my mind while I help the servants bury them.

Saul listens to the survivors' reports in silence, then walks several paces away, draws his sword, and drives it into the ground, kneeling next to it. When weeping breaks through his chest, the soldiers draw him toward their camp, and I follow with my harp.

Jonathan won't take his eyes off the shell of the gate as though some answer is written on the charred wood. Instead of retreating to a tent for the night, he stays by a fire on the outskirts, his sword at his side. Ezra slumbers a few feet away, stretched out on the ground.

Unable to sleep, even after the king does, I watch Jonathan. Something about him stills the apprehension trying to rush back over me. I've been fighting it since I left Bethlehem, the weight of what's been entrusted to me revealing everything I lack.

Until now, I had simply believed in Yahweh's faithfulness and His good plans for Israel. I had trusted that I would have a place in those plans someday, and that Yahweh Himself would direct me to it. But there's so much I need. So much I don't understand. I don't know how to be king. But someone else does.

I can only see half of Jonathan's face, but I can tell that his lips are moving in prayer. I take a step toward him.

"You can show yourself. I'm not holding a spear this time," Jonathan says aloud, without turning around.

Slowly, I step into view and kneel by Jonathan's side. His eyes are staring through the flames, still locked on the charred outline of the fortress.

"Are you afraid, my lord?" I ask him.

He grimaces. "Not the word I would use. Are you?"

"No." But it's really too early to say.

Something lifts the corner of Jonathan's mouth, but it's not a full smile. "Of course not. I wasn't either when I was your age." He spins his seal ring around his finger. "Ever see a man die?"

"No," I admit, sensing something dark creeping between us.

I do remember seeing a handful of sheep torn apart by wild dogs. The helpless look frozen on the dead animals' faces was something I knew I would never forget. If it's anything like that…

Jonathan arches his neck, rubbing the strained muscles. "It's ten times worse when it's one of yours. Someone you were supposed to protect. And instead, they died protecting you." A shaky edge slips into his voice, and he deepens his tone to cover it. His eyes cut to mine, then back to the flames. "After all this time, after everything Yahweh has done, those heathens still look at us like a pack of sheep that they can take one by one."

Something fierce stirs in my stomach, the same tossing I feel every time I hear the war stories repeated. "They know nothing of the God we serve."

Jonathan exhales sharply. "No. But do we? You know our history. Far too often, it's our own failure to believe that keeps us from what's ours. That's what kills me, more than any of it."

Ezra stirs on the ground, and I drop my tone. "Surely that's one thing a king can do for his people. Remind them of what they've forgotten."

Jonathan looks like he wears a thousand weights. "Only if the king himself doesn't forget." His eyes lift to his father's tent. "I used to believe that a king simply rallies his men, giving them the courage to go out and fight his battles. But now I know that a real leader goes in first. He sees ahead and prepares the way so his men can advance to victory and get home to their families— so that Israel will live on. To this day, I still wonder if I have it in me."

I'm gripped by his sincerity. It's one thing to race ahead to personal glory. It's another to set things in motion that will continue after you're gone, to raise up other men who will finish what you began, something the judges of old failed to do after their conquests.

Perhaps that is what Yahweh seeks in a king. A heart that will go after His plans for Israel, plans designed to extend beyond a man's natural life.

The revelation is expansive, and I breathe it aloud. "Building Israel. With Yahweh as the foundation." And the goal. And everything.

Half a laugh escapes Jonathan. "You really are a poet."

"How do we do that?" I ask, ignoring his comment.

He sighs. "I don't know. Usually, Yahweh only reveals one step at a time."

Of course. And I'm waiting for the next one. I look over at Jonathan, aching to tell him everything. Who better to help me sort all this out than the man who's been fighting for Israel his entire life? It won't be long before I have to tell someone. The stirring inside me to fulfill Yahweh's calling has deepened into an intense yearning, but it's also a fearful thing that I want to run from.

Watching the prince, I let myself think the one thing I'd be too ashamed to say to anyone. I'm not ready.

Jonathan's face relaxes suddenly, a strange calm stealing over it. He touches my knee briefly, looking into my eyes.

"Whatever we face in the days to come, there's really no way to prepare you for it. But you'd be surprised what being thrown into the fire can do for a man. If you trust Him, Yahweh will give you what you need."

I'm glad it's dark enough to hide the smile taking over my face. I'm amazed at how the prince continues to answer the questions I'm not asking. It's true. Yahweh's hand is moving already. Simple trust will allow me to see His plans unfolding in time.

Jonathan angles his head at the tents. "Try to sleep. I have a feeling our enemies won't let us rest for long."

I obey him, feeling the pull of exhaustion the moment I stand up. And Jonathan's right. My eyes are barely closed before someone's shoving me awake and light is pouring in through the door of the tent.

Outside, Saul's forces are preparing for the day's ride to Aijalon amidst an uneasy tension. Anxiety hangs heavy on everyone, and it looks like Malchishua was right. No one slept. I eat in snatches, helping the servants cover the fires and pack up the supplies.

Gera taps my shoulder, scowling impatiently. "Go find Ezra. Maybe he can find something that'll fit you."

Ezra doesn't say much when I approach him, but I can tell it's going to be a challenge to find armor for me. He slips an armored vest around my torso and turns me around, tightening the straps under my arms, then retying them when he realizes it's too big for me. Several of the men snicker, watching, but Abner looks concerned.

"Ever been in a battle, boy?" he asks.

"No, sir," I answer simply, figuring that my private battles for the sheep won't mean anything to him.

"He's a shepherd, Abner." Malchishua's tone is laden with contempt. "All he has is a stick, and that toy." He looks askance at my staff and lyre.

The general's gaze darkens at me. "Keep your wits about you, and don't move from your post unless Ezra tells you otherwise.

You have no experience, and the armorbearers have more to do than look after you."

"Yes, sir."

Gera glares at me over the king's mule, muttering as he tightens the saddle straps. "The king has more than enough armorbearers. Now they expect me to train a songbird how to fight?" Several of the men chortle in response.

My veins are humming, heat rushing into my face. My fingers wind through the pouch at my belt, grasping one of the stones I keep hidden there. I slip it into the center of my sling, hearing my oldest brother's protests as clearly as if he were standing here.

"No showing off," he would say.

But I can't help it. *Just once, Eliab.*

I just have to find a target. My eyes skirt the landscape and lock onto a small cluster of sun-scorched pinecones hanging from a branch over Gera's head. Controlling the smile jumping around on my face, I release a short breath, then brace, wind the leather, and send the stone flying. It crashes into the branch, snapping it in half, and every head jerks up.

Gera flinches violently, nearly running headlong into Sar Ishvi. Abner whips around so fast, he stumbles over the banked fire. Jonathan stops midsentence. For half a second, annoyance flickers on his face, but then he laughs through it. "Happy now, Gera? You can stop looking out for him."

The men burst into relieved laughter, and Ezra gives my shoulder a good-natured slap. Gera is still frozen in place, trying to recover. Even the princes look at me with something different in their eyes. The commanders shake their heads, looking almost grateful for an amusing distraction.

Abner is the only one who looks angrier than before. Once everyone resumes their business, he strides over and grabs my wrist. "And by the time your little stone is in the air, the Philistine will have his sword in your chest. Or the chest of someone more important." He yanks me close. "Stay back. That's an order."

A few feet away, Saul stands with his arms out while two armorbearers fuss over the crisscrossed cords of his mail and shoulder plates. Abner shoves me. "Go help them. We don't have all day."

Saul keeps his head straight, but his eyes wander down to study me as I bend to tighten his leg greaves. "You must have sent a few wolves running with that aim," he observes, chuckling to himself. I glance at the others, but they are careful not to look at me.

It must seem ridiculous to them to see a shepherd among Saul's closest forces, but they haven't seen the battles that have found me over the years. "I'm honored to fight for you, my king."

"In time." Hiding a smile, Saul squares his shoulders, testing his muscles under the restricting armor. "It's too tight. Fix it," he tells one of the others. Looking down at me, he jerks his chin a few feet away. "Go help my sons."

Ishvi and Malchishua are entrenched in an argument with Ezra, so I pick up Jonathan's sword and carry it to him. He slides it into the scabbard at his side and tightens the straps around it, his jaw firmly set. He's visibly agitated, more so than the day before. But he's experienced enough to know that whatever simmers beneath the surface has to be pushed aside.

Watching the hills, Jonathan touches his left shoulder, then brings his fingers to his lips in one brief, subtle movement. When our eyes meet, he straightens his shoulders, adjusting his expression. "Just praying for Yahweh to go with us."

"We will defend Israel whether He goes with us or not," Saul mutters staunchly, leaving me chilled by his indifference.

Yahweh can't be pleased with a statement like that, and I don't want to see any of them die in battle.

"Surely you have nothing to fear, my king," I venture. "Yahweh will always stand with His anointed ones. He sets them apart to fight His battles."

Jonathan's head is lowered, but his eyes are fixed sharply on his father. For a frozen second, I fear I've said the wrong thing.

But after a moment of uncertain silence, Saul spreads his arms, releasing a hearty laugh. "The shepherd speaks more sense than any one of us! To Aijalon, Israel! The Lord is with us!"

His armed men roar in answer, banging their shields, the air around us resounding with exuberant cries. "The Lord our God is One!"

Saul touches my shoulder. "And when we return, you can sing of what He's done."

The king and his sons move to the front of the army, and their armorbearers fall into step behind them, carrying extra weapons. I grasp my donkey's lead rope, praying with each step over the uneven rocky path.

Yahweh, please give us favor. You have called us to drive your enemies from this land. Whatever we face today, give us victory.

Anticipation churns in my stomach even though it's not certain that we'll see battle today. We're merely going to Aijalon to secure it, leave some extra soldiers to defend them against the reprisal they fear. Possibly follow the raiders' trail, see where they'll strike next.

But we've barely gone half a mile when the air changes. Jonathan slows, his attention shifting to the rise in the landscape. Several of the animals veer from the path, stamping nervously. I look over at Ezra, the sense of danger hitting me at the same time it finds him. I know the way the air tightens in the open country, promising ambush.

The next moment, a sharp, whining hiss enters the air, and arrows take wing overhead, slamming into the ground all around us, knocking several men from their mounts. My breath lodges in my chest as a frenzied war cry drags all our attention to the nearest hill.

The look on Saul's face tells me this move was completely unexpected. I tense next to the other armorbearers, every defense rising at the sight of dozens of Philistine warriors flinging themselves off their horses, sprawling over the hills like ants. The sun catches the flash of their iron armor and the crowns of red feathers in their helmets. King Saul's answering war cry, mingled with shouted orders from the princes, shakes the ground as their soldiers struggle to charge.

"Stay back!" Ezra commands, shoving me toward a collection of boulders where several of the servants are crowding. "If they seem to be taking too many of us, get out of here. Ride toward Gibeah." He waits for my acknowledgement before leaving my side.

I pull my knife, my heart beating out of time against my armor vest. Even from behind the rocks, I'm transfixed, avidly trying to keep Saul and Jonathan in my sight. They leave their mules almost at the same moment and fight back-to-back near Ishvi and Malchishua, creating a tight perimeter of safety. Arrows stab the ground around them.

Leaping to Jonathan's side, Ezra swings his sword, slashing the throat of a man getting too close. I'm fascinated by how the prince and his servant seem to read each other's movements, fighting as one. The rest of the battle blurs around them, drawing them apart from the others.

The Philistine warriors fling themselves savagely at Saul, six or seven at a time. His armorbearers fight around him, dispatching threat after threat. But it's hard to tell how many of them are being cut down themselves.

I'm losing count, unable to keep Saul's men straight in my field of vision as they're swarmed by the enemy. I strain my eyes, pushing breath through the mounting anxiety. Is there a chance we might not make it out of this? The servants around me are barely armed. What happens when the Philistines turn on us?

The thought is only halfway through my mind when something powerful rushes through my veins, gripping me from head to toe. Suddenly, it's an effort to stay still, every sense riveted on the battle. *Go.*

You mean, disobey?

My skin prickles as I recognize the beckoning from Yahweh, a fierce leading pulling me out of hiding. But where? What does He want me to do? My pulse launches into a full gallop as I glance around, looking for direction. I search for the king first. But he's almost lost to sight between the armorbearers clustering around him.

Every heartbeat has only one answer. Jonathan.

Pulled around, my eyes jump from man to man until I find him, fighting several feet off with Ezra at his side. Further afield, the Philistines are still swarming Saul, and every armorbearer that leaps to his defense leaves his son more alone. Jonathan leans into his sword, advancing fiercely, but his opponent is edging away, his gaze darting to the thin line of trees skirting the hillside.

Clearly distracted, the Philistine fails to deflect Jonathan's next blow and ends up on the ground, blood pooling under him. I leap over a fallen man and break into a run, my mind buzzing. I'm not sure of anything—not what I will do or why I'm doing it. I'm only sure of what's driving me.

Nothing is clear until I'm within a few feet of Jonathan, just behind him. He's standing frozen for a moment, sword in hand, but when he turns slightly, I can see the arrow pushing up under his left side, beneath his armor. He staggers back a step, and another arrow hits him in the shoulder.

The archer darts back behind a tree while another Philistine leaps into view, swinging his sword. Ezra lunges at him, but the attacker rotates, slamming his iron shield into the younger man's head. Ezra staggers to the ground, dropping Jonathan's spear.

The sight sets my blood on fire. In the seconds it takes for the Philistine to swing his sword again, I've crossed the feet between us, fierce, protective anger charring the coldness inside me. Ducking between the prince and the blade, I seize Jonathan's spear from the ground, pivot, and drive it up hard into the Philistine's chest.

Impaled, he barely makes a sound, but his hot blood chokes out onto my arms, and I duck my head away from the man's floundering sword. The weight of his body against the spear shoves sickness up into my chest, and I steel hard against it, digging my feet into the ground. I thrust the weapon forward, and the Philistine falls with the spear, his blood spurting out onto the ground.

Instantly, pain explodes up and down my arms from the sudden movement, and I realize I won't be able to lift another spear for a while. The adrenaline shifts, dragging fire through my limbs, and I stagger backwards, almost tripping over Jonathan. He's braced against the ground, both hands clenched as he tries to stay off the arrows.

Shaken and angry, I drop to my knees and grab his good shoulder.

"David, get back," he rasps. "You have no weapons!"

"I have your sword." I'm relieved to hear him speak, but a thin stream of blood is already escaping from around the lower arrow. The sight drains my strength into my feet.

Ever see a man die?

I drop my chin to my chest for a moment, trying to settle the wildness inside me. Yahweh is with us. They'll need more than a few arrows to take Jonathan down.

Braced against him, I drag breath into my lungs, waves of fight rising and crashing over me until a shrill whistle lifts my head. Mercifully, the remaining Philistines are dispersing, and the princes are ordering their men back. Across the field, Abner looks around wildly, finally spotting us from several feet off.

"Help him!" I call out, but several men are already sprinting toward us.

Jonathan's weight shifts, and he groans through the pain.

"It's over, my lord," I tell him. "We're safe. The king has driven them back."

He doesn't respond, concentrating on getting his next breath. I push my shoulder under his good arm, watching for more blood. The lower wound concerns me the most. If the arrow isn't in a rib, he could easily bleed to death.

Jonathan grabs at my wrist, panting, "David. Tell my father…tell him…"

I grip him tighter, anger flaring through me. "You tell him. You're not dying today."

I move my hands to the lower arrow, trying to stanch the blood. Steadying my fingers at the base of the shaft, I touch something rough. A thin roll of parchment is curled around it, already thoroughly stained. Pulling it free, I unfold it, fully expecting a threat of some kind. But the message staring back at me drains all the blood from my face.

"And so it begins, Melek Israel."

SEVEN

Jonathan

———◆◆◆◆◆———

The shock of realizing that the shepherd boy used my spear is much duller than it should be. But whatever mixture of adrenaline and rage helped him do it, I can't answer it. Most of the words in my head are dying on my lips, broken off with too little breath.

In contrast, David's voice is ironclad, holding back the tremors I feel in his fingers. It's not at all who I planned to have beside me at this moment, but I'm clinging to him anyway, clinging to life. His face jerks, and he grips me tighter, cupping his hands around the lower arrow to stop as much bleeding as he can.

I want to smile, but I have absolutely no energy. I try to look up, figure out what's going on, but nothing in my field of vision makes sense. The Philistines must be retreating, or one of them would have come after us by now.

I release a short breath, and the earth tilts, heavy pain nearly sending me to the ground. I refuse to go down completely, digging my elbow into the dirt, but my entire left side is immobile, paralyzed by pain. One arrow is lodged in my shoulder beneath the spot I always touch before battle. The other went in at an angle, edging up under a rib. Maybe into a rib.

I struggle to breathe, grappling with the waves of nausea crashing my insides. When my breathing returns, it's in short, tight gasps, and I grind my fingers into the dirt, trying to steady the ground. Suddenly panicked, I look for Ezra. But he's been knocked flat next to me, blood dripping from his face.

The Philistines planned this, bombarding my father to draw the armorbearers to his side and expose me. But even as the reality blooms in my mind, I have no strength to fight it. Flames eat up my shoulder, and the rest of it flashes through me in seconds. The upturned sword, the Philistine staggering backwards with my spear buried in his chest. David standing over me. I would've been dead without him.

I exhale around a voiceless prayer. *Thank you, Yahweh.*

At David's cry for help, men surround me, trying to free my robe and sword without jostling the arrows. My father pulls my forehead against his, and I swear I feel moisture on his face.

"We'll finish them," Abner whispers raggedly from my other side. "We'll drive them all the way back to the accursed sea!"

But I can't respond. My jaw burns from how hard I'm clenching my teeth. When they try to help me up, the pain cuts deeper, sweat dripping from my hair as heat consumes my body. I throw all my strength into holding back moans while they carry me back to the outpost where we will have to camp.

Once I'm settled on the ground again, I fade in and out, feeling the hours like days. I'm braced up against something, and my fingers are locked around a thick fold of cloth at my chest, bunched up against the lower arrow. Shapes waver against the sliver of sky that's visible outside my tent. Men murmur back and forth, but their words make no sense, washing up against my mind like muddy waves against a riverbank.

I recognize the voice of Ammiel, my father's physician, arguing with Saul.

"We should push farther east. The Philistines will regroup and be back here by sundown."

"No—he's in pain," my father protests. "We have to take those arrows out now."

"The arrows are protecting him. Once they're out, we're fighting a battle against infection. That's how men die."

Something clenches around me, but it's not my own muscles. There's another set of hands underneath mine, also gripping the arrow. I shift my weight, trying to sit up, and instantly regret it. Nausea twists through me, forcing another groan to the surface. A head leans over from behind, and someone murmurs, "The healer is coming, my lord. He's outside with the king."

My head aches around every thought. "Is the king hurt?"

"No, my lord."

"Ezra...?"

"The healer said he'll recover. The princes are safe too. But there are twenty dead. Several more injured."

Light spears me as someone pulls the tent flap aside. Abner and my brothers crowd behind the physician while he kneels next to me.

The sight of Ammiel is calming even though he'll probably have to hurt me at some point. He's served as my father's army physician since I was a youth, and he's more of a grandfather than anything else. I smirk at the disparaging look on his face. I wasn't supposed to be fighting. Not since he set my ribs after Saul threw me on my back.

"You never have it easy, do you, boy?" Ammiel bends to inspect my side, his smile trapped behind a tight line of concern. He's seen me sick and severely wounded before, but in over twenty years, he's never had to remove two arrows from my body. "I finally convinced the king that you will be well, so let's see if I can save both our lives."

I grit my teeth while he feels all around the lower wound, testing my bones. His eyes lift to mine only once. "I think this one stopped in a rib. It will be hard to remove without causing more damage. I will have to cut around them both."

Ishvi leans over me, whistling through his teeth. "That Philistine was a good shot."

I grimace at him as the pain mounts again. "If you aren't here to help, get out."

Ammiel's expression tightens behind his beard. "We can remove them, but keeping the wounds closed will be of utmost importance. I will have to stitch up the lower one, depending on what kind of damage is there."

I hear every word he's not saying. Infection is the greatest concern. It will be a painful ride back to Gibeah, since we can't stay out here for long.

Ammiel unpacks oil and honey from the bag at his side and unrolls several thick pieces of cloth. "Sar Ishvi, Sar Malchishua, I will need you on either side to hold him down. Abner, go make sure the king is out of earshot, if possible."

Abner's face creases in half, but then his attention shifts over my head. "Shepherd boy, you can go."

Shepherd boy? David's here?

His arms tighten again, and I realize he's been holding me up. "I'll stay," he says.

"No, you'll go," Abner snaps. "You've seen enough."

"David—" Unable to turn my head, I find his fingers around the arrow and squeeze them. "Go to my father. Play for him. Sing something so he doesn't hear." I have to grind the last words to keep from crying out.

My father's stability is tenuous at best. The last thing he needs is to hear me in pain. It's bad enough David had to see this. I grip his wrist. "Promise me you'll stay with him."

"I promise."

David releases me gently, but pain still chews through my side when Malchishua takes his place, shoving his arms underneath mine. Ammiel visits the fire outside and returns with his knife scorched clean and a vial of hot liquid in his hand. The henbane drags a heavy flame down my throat, but it will confuse my senses enough to dull the pain of what has to happen.

"Ready?" Ammiel's expression is closed tight, any emotion buried. I've seen that look many times in the war camp. In my father's tent.

Ishvi grips my shoulders, and I take several slow breaths before pinning my gaze to Ammiel's. "Ready."

* * * * *

I'm lying still, but my head refuses to stop spinning. Even with my eyes closed, dizziness crashes over me in a furious tide as the medicine battles with the pain. I have no idea how long the torture lasted. I screamed when Ammiel removed the arrows, but he didn't have to cut as deep as he thought to release them. After binding the wounds with every conceivable deterrent against infection, he finally left me to rest.

Conflicting scents of honey and oil wrestle with the sharpness of myrrh and elm bark, and I can't decide which to focus on. Impossibly thirsty, I fight for rest, wondering how long it will be before we need to get moving again. Or before I start to burn with fever.

The Philistines won't wait. I'm still amazed they didn't keep after us. The sight of the shepherd boy anointed with blood, gripping my spear, is something that I won't be able to cut from my mind any time soon. Every breath pushes like an angry tide against my ribs, and I focus on holding it back so I can hear the faint music coming from my father's tent. If it wasn't clear before, it is now. Yahweh sent that boy. Whatever else happens, I know that.

The next time I open my eyes, I'm not alone. David is curled in the corner, his head against my saddle. He has to be exhausted, but as soon as I make a sound, he's awake, scrambling to my side. Without being asked, he holds a waterskin close enough for me to drink, then touches my forehead.

"Praise Yahweh, there's still no fever," he exhales. "I don't know who was more frantic, Ammiel or the king."

I try to sit up again, but it still feels like teeth are grinding on my ribs. "It took long enough."

"He had to go slowly. There were two arrows."

"Only two?" I mutter.

"One wouldn't have stopped you."

"Ha. I was shot down almost immediately." A ragged laugh escapes me, and David's face jerks.

"After you sent them running." The boy is hardly blinking, watching me with dilated eyes. For an instant, I wonder at the extra age in his face. But then I remember he killed a man. For the first time.

"Is my father well?" I ask him.

David swallows. "He will be, now that you are."

I avert my eyes, my throat suddenly dry again. "Did I shame him?"

"Not at all."

David's certainty makes me want to laugh again, but it's too painful. "I'll pretend I believe you." I search his face. "Are you all right?"

Before he can answer, Ammiel pushes through the door. "Thank God. You're awake. How do you feel?"

I wince, failing to sit up. "I'll survive, thanks to you. How long have we been here?"

"Only two days since the battle."

"Well, tell the soldiers to pack. We'll be on our way to Gibeah in no time. I should be able to ride, as long as I don't open the wounds."

Ammiel bends over, checking my side. "Patience, my boy."

I roll my eyes. "Not exactly my best trait. David, go to the king and tell him I'm willing to leave as soon as they can be ready." The sooner we get home, the sooner I can recover and get back to work.

David obeys immediately, breaking into a run outside the tent. Where he's getting this energy after all the interrupted sleep, I don't know.

Ammiel's smiling eyes follow him out the door. "That's not your armorbearer, is it?"

"My father's. He's the singer we summoned from Bethlehem."

Ammiel kneels next to me, the containment gone from his face. He's speaking to me man-to-man, not as a healer. "Before you ordered him to attend the king, he wouldn't leave your side. He's been praying night and day over you. You are highly favored to have such loyal men in your service."

Instead of answering, I stay quiet, letting the word take shape in my mind. Loyal.

In only a week, David has epitomized something that we've taken years trying to wrest from others. And for all this time, I've been trying to figure out why. His loyalty goes beyond simple service. He has already exceeded what he was brought here to do, and all without direction or permission. It's as though he came here knowing what we needed before we did.

Everything about him points to something more than meets the eye. It's evident to me that he's been set apart by Yahweh for some purpose. Whether or not it's to rule Israel, that remains to be seen.

The thought bothers me though, and I can't push it aside. It lingers in my mind, uncovering an undefined fear. Why would Samuel anoint someone so young with no direct line to the throne? Why put him in so much danger? Did he know we would summon David here?

As foolish as it would have been, the boy has had several chances to turn against me. And he's done the exact opposite. Instead of hiding for his own safety, he had been there at the exact moment I needed him, shoving my spear between me and that Philistine. If he had waited a second longer…

My side aching, I relax my muscles, too grateful to bother with suspicion. For better or for worse, I've decided to trust him. Time will tell if I've made a wise decision or a horrible mistake.

* * * * *

Back in Gibeah, I battle impatiently with my own recovery, which stretches into several weeks as the lower wound heals under the stitches Ammiel put in place. There's a hole in my left shoulder now too—a reminder that Yahweh isn't through with me yet. Unable to practice with my own weapons, I shove them into David's hands instead.

The first morning after we'd arrived home, I had shaken him awake myself. He's easy to find, usually curled up in the corner of my father's bedchamber with the lyre in his arms. Just like Ezra, he'd followed me without any questions. Almost.

"What's going on?"

I'd tossed him a weapon with my good arm. "We're going to make sure that the next time you have to fight, you can throw more than one spear."

The light exploding in his eyes had made me feel young again. Still, I've had to take things slower than usual.

For the past two weeks, I've held back like an old warrior, careful not to strain my left side, while David spars with Ezra. My armorbearer is skilled enough to give the boy a challenge without hurting him. Occasionally, I demonstrate with a few weapons, trying to build my strength back up.

At first, David looked to me for everything, approval or criticism. But now, he lunges at Ezra without hesitation, finally moving past raw defense. He's careful to remember my advice, willingly adjusting his grip, his aim, or his stance according to my experience. The pride welling inside me makes me wonder if this is what it's like to have a son.

I remember my own father's shout ringing in my ears while I swung swords, hefted spears, shot arrow after arrow until I dropped to my knees, exhausted.

"Get up, Jonathan!" he would rail at me. "You're not finished. On your feet!"

I could be on the ground, trembling, sweat stinging my eyes, but Abba always insisted I had more.

I shake my head as I watch David, full of zeal, drinking in everything he can learn. This is how it *should* feel to have a son.

Gripping a smaller sword, David ducks out of Ezra's reach, shaking his head at me. "My aim is still pulling left."

"We'll work on it," I promise him. He sounds frustrated, but I can sense the undercurrent of pleasure just beneath the surface. He doesn't want to be anywhere else. I lift my hand. "Relax a little. No tension, just zeal. Remember, every movement should flow out of the previous one. Try it with me."

I take the sword from Ezra and loop it a few times, ignoring David's hesitation.

"Are you sure, my lord?"

I just smirk from behind the blade, raising it into position. "Are you?"

Excitement winds itself back up into David's face, and he advances on me, deflecting a blow and cutting close to my side the way I showed him. Ridiculously proud, I decide to try something. When he cuts in again, I drop my arm sharply and stagger back onto one knee, sucking in my breath as though in pain. Dismayed, David drops his sword and bends over me.

"I'm sorry, my lord! I'm sorry…"

Barely controlling my laughter, I swing my arms around his neck and drag him down, pinning him on his back with my blade across his chest. "Left yourself open. Don't let a Philistine trick you like that."

Embarrassed and relieved, David scrambles to his feet, and Ezra claps a hand on his shoulder, laughing. "I should have warned you, boy. He's a fox."

"My lord!" Abner approaches from the fortress, but I don't turn around. I wait for him to reach us.

"My lord, I have a command from the king." He glances at David. "And a message from the boy's father."

David straightens up, and I squint at Abner, confused. What could Jesse have to say? "Well? What?"

His chin and shoulders high, Abner looks almost triumphant. "Jesse wants his son to come home. News of the attacks have reached Bethlehem, and they're anxious to have the boy back in familiar territory."

I almost laugh. "That's ridiculous. David will be safer here than in Bethlehem. Besides, he's part of the king's service now. Tell Jesse he's not thinking clearly."

But Abner is shaking his head, talking over me. "The king has already agreed. He's feeling well enough now, and he wants to begin focusing more closely on the Philistine threats, planning for the next battle season. He said he will summon David when he has need of him again."

"You're serious?" I don't look at David, but I can imagine what's going through his mind.

Abner doesn't even blink. "You both can leave first thing tomorrow. The king wants you to ride through some of the cities in Judah and count their fighting men. So, you can take him more than halfway yourself. And if he runs into trouble after that, he can always use that sling."

Amazed by his pettiness, I give Abner a disgusted look, resisting the urge to fight this one out in front of the boy. "David, go with Ezra, and make sure you have everything you need for the journey."

David obeys without speaking. As soon as they're gone, I press Abner. "Are you sure you didn't put Abba up to this?"

"It's better this way, Jonathan."

I can feel the daggers in my eyes. "You had better not be putting your personal preferences ahead of what's best for the king. He has barely recovered. I don't see why we should be so quick to throw away the best security he's had in months."

Abner holds up his hands. "It wasn't my decision. Jesse asked if he could come home, and the king agreed. There is no evil plan afoot here. Saul can summon him whenever he chooses. In the meantime, the king can focus on the countless matters of state he's been avoiding."

I fold my arms, annoyed at how the heightened frustration is making my side ache. "Admit it, though. You didn't like him."

Abner's mouth curls into a sneer. "I don't need to like a servant. But he has done nothing but disobey me from the moment he set foot in this house. At every turn, he follows the voice in his own head, and that—"

"Saved my life."

Abner's shoulders drop. "It won't always work out like that. We need to know that everyone close to the king is completely loyal, committed to following orders no matter what."

"Even if it kills one of us."

Backed into a corner, Abner glares at me. "I know I'm right about this, Jonathan. I've been around a long time, and I have to trust my instincts. That boy is dangerous." Vehement, he nearly spits the words, amending when he sees my face. "But I pray I'm wrong."

EIGHT

David

———◆◆◆◆◆———

"We've made good time. Bethlehem isn't far. We should be able to reach Socoh before dark."

Ezra's voice goes over my head, and I don't answer. He wasn't speaking to me, anyway. As we've traveled, I've moved to the front of the group, leading the way as the landscape changes and memories start rushing toward me. I pull each one into me, my mind racing.

Behind me, Jonathan watches the thickening tree line, keeping a tight hold on his reins as the path becomes rocky. The few guards who have followed us south scan the forest as though it's a foreign enemy. This isn't their territory.

Judah's land is wilder than Gibeah. Saul has built up the cities to the north, but Bethlehem is carved out of a hillside, her short stone walls dwarfed by the surrounding wilderness. The rolling landscape is stunning, anointed by sunlight and crowned by thick forests, but its gentle beauty hides an undercurrent of danger. The southern woods conceal more than just wolves and bears.

Renegade foreigners and rogue Israelites make their home in the hills, some driven there by crime or taxation, others choosing to live out of Saul's reach. Joab has forged an understanding with many of them, but there are still plenty who aren't above plundering a farmer's flocks or fields. I've been threatened by them before. And they have no love for Saul or his followers. Praying that we won't encounter any trouble, I look avidly for a sign that we're close to home.

I haven't said much during the journey, but the clamor inside me is deafening. Something has been awakened in my veins—a fresh fire that threatens to burst the bounds of my flesh. It seems impossible how much has happened in the past month, but I don't even understand my own actions or how to interpret the recent events. I'm just moving in response to what pulls me, not really sure why I'm doing anything. It's all pent up inside me, trapped, as we head in the wrong direction.

My fingers twitch around the reins. Just a few weeks of training have intensified my yearning to fight, to stay at Saul's side and ensure Israel's continued safety. It's no longer just the dream of a shepherd trying to see beyond the hills of his hometown. It's what I was made for. I haven't slept one full night since leaving

Gibeah. The Philistine king leers at me in the dark until my tangled dreams force me awake. Our enemies are coming. I'm sure of it. With something more serious than we've ever faced to this day.

The slip of parchment I took from the arrows burns against my ribs, hidden under my cloak. I still haven't decided what to do with it. I've memorized the words, unable to shake the feeling that they were meant for me somehow. My thoughts fight back, arguing with me.

No, you fool. Saul is the king. The Philistines meant it as a threat to him, hoping Jonathan would die. Achish doesn't even know you exist.

But Yahweh does.

The weeks in Gibeah have opened my eyes to what is ahead of me, and I can't go back. Not completely. Not when half of me is still on that field facing down the Philistine who put those arrows in the Hassar.

Restless, I get off the donkey to walk. Watching my footing on the uneven hillside gives my mind something to do while the rest of me writhes. Holding Jonathan's spear in my hands has pulled me into something so much bigger than myself. And now, my father wants me in the pastures again? How am I supposed to become a king if I am continually held back?

Even Yahweh's own Name speaks of One whose nature is revealed by His actions. Over the centuries, our God has gone before us in power, the fire of His presence consuming our adversaries as long as we remained obedient to His Word. As our people struggled to stay faithful over the centuries, Yahweh chose men like Moses and Joshua to walk before Him and serve His purposes. Following in their footsteps seems a lofty task, but the anointing of Yahweh must be answered with action. Which battle is going to define who I am? When will it come?

Slowing my pace, I stare into the forest thicket ahead, feeling like an intruder. I've traveled these paths countless times, night and day over the years. Always with the sheep. Always singing. These rocks and hills know my voice. But now they seem to greet me with something like tolerant disdain, like they want me to forget I'd ever left.

Isn't this what you wanted? A return back to the hills you used to hide in? Because you're not really ready for anything more. You're just a shepherd.

Grabbing the donkey's halter, I angle him down to the river where the guards are stopping. The clearest water tumbles over the moss just beneath us, scooped out between dripping rocks.

Part of me might always be a shepherd. But I can't just erase everything that's happened. I was called to Gibeah for a purpose, and it seems too soon to cut it off. My music had touched Saul, giving him the rest that he needed. I had been given access to the king at his most vulnerable, and I had seen his panic and rage dissolve, lifting from him like a fleeing fog as I sang.

And what about Jonathan? I hadn't meant to save his life. But when the time came, I couldn't do anything else. I still shudder, thinking about how insistently Yahweh had beckoned through the chaos. It baffles me what a single moment of obedience had accomplished. But a conflicting voice still grapples with the flame inside me, trying to stamp it out.

What you did on the battlefield was instinct, not skill. Easily forgotten. If it really meant that much, the king would have honored you or at least mentioned it. But he didn't. Because you're still invisible.

My face catches fire. I recognize the familiar shame creeping up my neck, trying to fasten itself there like a chain. It's trying to convince me that I'm still just a hostage, held back from what I yearn to be a part of. It's what I'm used to feeling. But it's not the truth.

Samuel's words, and my songs, and Yahweh's touch all breathe something very different into me. *You're a faithful shepherd, cast on God from your birth. Yahweh's praises live inside you. He sees what men don't see—the heart of a warrior. He anointed you. His favor is the gift on your life.*

My spirits lift, gratitude rushing in. The pleasure of being chosen by Yahweh is something I hope I never get over.

I had felt that same pull of purpose standing in Jonathan's doorway that first night. Without thinking twice, I had gone to his side, pouring out everything I knew and loved about our God, everything I had learned from His faithfulness over the years. Seeing the waking world in the prince's eyes had been worth the risk of speaking out. But watching him sleep the next morning, I'd felt fresh fear cut deep into me. Because we're linked somehow, Jonathan and I. And yet I have to take his place.

We've both felt the stirring of Yahweh's presence, beckoning us beyond the threshold of our courage and abilities. He's probably the only other warrior in Israel who understands what that's like. But he doesn't know me. Not really. And once he finds out, what I did on the battlefield won't matter. One day, I will have to tell him what I've been chosen to do and watch all the faith he has in me burn.

I press my knees into the cold earth up against the river and watch the sunlight winking at me in the current. Yahweh is with me, but there won't be anything easy about the path ahead.

"All right?" Behind me, Ezra fiddles with his sword, something he always does when the prince is out in the open.

"I'm fine." I get to my feet and shake the excess water from my hands.

I expect Ezra to walk away, but he stays, watching the river. The gash in his temple still looks ominous even as it heals. He's been having headaches every other day since the battle. The space between us thickens as he grapples with something unspoken.

"Look, I know I never said anything before. But I know what you did." His eyes lift, and I see the pain on his face. "I didn't have Jonathan's permission to speak of it, and I wasn't sure if he wanted the king to know how much danger he was in. The Hassar is my master, but he's also my friend. If he had died because of me..."

My stomach tightens when I remember the sound the shield had made slamming into Ezra's head. "He doesn't blame you. He wouldn't have anyone else by his side."

Ezra scoffs gently. "I'm not so sure about that these days." His gaze shifts over to Jonathan, several feet away. "I would venture to say you've earned his trust, and that's not easily done. Everyone either wants something from him or resents his position with the king." He studies me, his face changing. "But around you, he talks. Because he knows you'll listen without judgment. And offer solutions if you can. It sounds simple, but he doesn't have many men like that around him."

Unsure what to do with the compliments, I avert my eyes. "Thank you for your patience. I haven't met many men willing to put a sword in my hands."

Gratified, Ezra slaps my shoulder. "Believe me, you'll be back in the court in no time. Jonathan's convinced you'll become something, and he doesn't give up that easily." He's smiling, but I can sense the unrest underneath it.

"How long do you think we have before the Philistines return?" I ask him.

Ezra's face darkens. "Hard to say. Personally, I think they'll wait a while. Maybe regroup next spring. Achish is still dealing with political enemies in his own land. Like every new king."

"They planned that attack. To kill Jonathan." Even without the threatening message, it's glaringly clear. Why else would they have isolated the prince and then fled as soon as he was shot down? The previous raids were taunts, designed to draw us in.

Ezra nods, his jaw tight. "I know. I'll keep a closer watch on him. He needs more help than he thinks."

"Are you two conspiring something?" Jonathan joins us, and Ezra smirks.

"He's just throwing the battle in my face."

Jonathan looks away briefly, his brow pulling. "None of us were expecting that one." He nudges my shoulder. "I haven't heard you sing once these past few days. What's wrong with you?"

I just look at him without speaking. He knows I would rather stay in Gibeah. Even with all the danger that city holds for me, it still carries the pull of destiny. But I'm still subject to the will of the king. And my father.

Jonathan's voice warms. "Don't forget how. The king will want you back at his side before too long. Tell your father that." He glances back the way we've come. "We're well within Judah's borders. How much farther, Ezra?"

"The king has sent word ahead of us to Socoh," Ezra informs him. "It's best we part here."

My stomach drops, but he's right. We're so close now, I can easily go on alone. The main road is overgrown here, winding through the forest and down into Bethlehem. I've driven the flocks farther than this.

"Are you sure you're all right from here?"

Jonathan's concern makes me smile. I can read these hills the way he can read the angle of a sword. "I'm a shepherd. I know my way home."

He nods silently. There's nothing else to say. One of the guards holds out the reins of my father's donkey to me.

"Wait." Going back to his mule, Jonathan unties something from beneath his saddle. "I want you to keep these." He hands me two arrows wrapped in leather, the length of both stained with dried blood. "I'm grateful for what you've done. For me and for my father."

"Thank you, my lord." My throat aches around the words.

I've finally found someone who invites me in rather than shuts me out. Someone who can prepare me for the battles ahead. A hint of the father I've always wanted. And now I have to walk away. Back to the sheep.

Jonathan winds the reins in my other hand, folding his fingers over mine. "Try to be patient. You have many more battles ahead of you. But the life of a fighter is not an easy one. It doesn't stop once you begin, and it will age you before your time. Take your rest while you can. Build your strength. Listen for Yahweh." His smile comes out of hiding for a moment. "And don't jump into battle again unless He's calling you."

Drinking in all the counsel I can, I lift my eyes from the arrows to his face. His expression is warm with pride when he looks at me, and I never want to forget how that feels. "I promise."

"You are the bravest shepherd I know. Don't let anyone tell you different."

With a crooked smile, I reach up to my left shoulder, then bring my fingers to my lips, the way he always does. "God go with you, Hassar."

Jonathan repeats the gesture, his face softening. "And also with you."

His guards wait for him halfway down the road. I watch them until they've disappeared over the ridge, then breathe deeply, allowing the familiar feel of home to settle over me. I'm back where I began, a month ago. Except everything is different.

I consider going straight to Aaron in the pastures. Someone safe to talk to before I face my family. But already, I'm turning toward the river path. My father is expecting me, and no doubt Eema is watching the road like a hawk, waiting.

I can't deny a sense of relief when the gates of Bethlehem appear in front of me.

The watchmen nod over them. They're used to seeing me coming and going, though I'm usually approaching from the hills, followed by sheep. The shadows are already pulling toward evening, so the streets are full of people heading home for the day. Women carry water and herd children down the narrow streets, while laborers haul tools home from the fields.

Several heads lift in surprise when I pass by, and a few soft *shaloms* lift toward me. I smile back, but I keep walking, not holding anyone's gaze. Our family has ignited Bethlehem's gossip over the past month, first with Samuel's unexplained visit and then with the king's summons. Everyone wonders what we've done to attract all this attention. None of them understand.

I'm halfway through town when a voice reaches out from behind me. "Son of Jesse."

I stop, recognizing one of the village elders. They all call me that as a reminder that they know what my father tried to hide for a while. I turn around, bowing my head. "Shalom, adon."

Micah ben Jether is not the oldest of the elders, but he's respected, and his word is law here. Alongside his brothers and a few servants, he studies me with his hands folded beneath heavy sleeves. "You're back sooner than we predicted. We all thought Saul would keep you in his service."

"Yes, sir."

"Why didn't he?"

Seeing Saul's messengers here weeks ago had unnerved the elders. When the king's soldiers come here, it usually means a tax increase or the loss of more young men to the king's service.

"Abba sent word to the king asking if I might come home for a while," I tell them.

"And Saul permitted that?"

"He plans to summon me again if he needs to. For now, he understands that the Philistine attacks have made people nervous."

Even from a distance, I can sense Micah's disdain. He folds his arms while his brothers mutter amongst themselves. "That's observant of him. And what action does he plan to take to alleviate that strain?"

I stiffen, wondering how I should answer. I resent the way Micah's mistrust pushes at me, trying to force its way in. It's part of the air we breathe in Judah, but for some reason, the elder's dislike stings as though he's speaking of a close relative of mine. I lift my eyes. "The king still fights Yahweh's battles. He will not fail to do it again."

Micah picks at his sleeve, flustered. "Of course. I didn't expect that he would tell you his plans."

Yahweh or Saul?

He squints at me. "The king sent you home alone?"

"No, sir. Jonathan and his guards brought me as far as the river." I say it without thinking, and then my neck heats up as the elders start to whisper.

Micah corrects me coldly, "You mean, the Hassar? He accompanied you?"

"Yes…Hassar Jonathan," I amend.

They already think Saul is a strange man. Now they must wonder if he's completely insane, calling a shepherd boy to come play the harp for him and then sending him home accompanied by the heir to the throne. I keep my eyes on the dust, frustration nagging. There's no way for them to know what the previous month has meant to me. Or what Yahweh has called me into. They just see what they see and wonder why I deserve it.

Micah's tone is sharp with irritation. "Go on home. No doubt your father is tired of leaving his sheep with an old hireling."

I turn on my heel and walk away, resentful of their implications. Aaron may be old, but I have no doubt he'd wrestle a lion before any of the elders would. He's been more of a family friend than a hired hand, teaching me more than my own brothers have. But of course, they're right about Abba. I'm sure he's eager to have me back.

* * * * *

Being back at my father's table is more unnerving than I expected. At first, Eema's joyful relief was enough to fill in the discomfort, but now everyone's silence is glaring at me. So much has been laid at our family's door in the past few months, but nobody knows what to do with it. And they're not used to looking to me for answers.

I can feel Abba's gaze across the table, heavy with what he wants to express but doesn't know how. For once, I wish Joab were here. His boisterous confidence always commands attention.

Abba clears his throat. "Saul's guards didn't follow you into Bethlehem?"

"No. They've ridden to Socoh on the king's business."

His brow creases. "The word around here is that you've seen a lot more than you were supposed to. The Philistines attacked?"

"Yes. While we were on the road to Aijalon."

The space between my words is thick with everything I'm not saying. We were ambushed. Jonathan was shot. I killed a man. But I haven't decided how much I should reveal.

One of my brothers speaks up. "Eema was worried that Saul would press you into the army. Make you an armorbearer or something, since you had to be serving the king so closely."

"He did...sort of," I fumble. "I probably would still be there if not for Abba's message. The elders were surprised that Saul granted your request."

Abba grumbles, "Micah should mind his own business."

Eema's eyes lift. "The elders are worried. The Philistine garrisons are much closer to us here, but all the king's attention goes to the immediate threats around Gibeah. Our enemies could rise against us before Saul even hears that they're close. It's best if we're all together while we still can be."

Shammah nods. "That new king of theirs is a vengeful monster. Joab found out that he wants to make an example of one of Saul's sons."

"They tried..." I feel the fire building again.

"What?"

"They tried to kill Jonathan. That's what the raids were for. To draw him into battle."

My mind darts back to the arrows I left among my belongings on the donkey. I have to get them out of sight before someone asks where I got them. The ambush is still sharp in my mind, continually pushing back into view. I can't forget how it felt to have the weight of a man against my spear.

"Are you sure you're all right?" I can feel Eema's consternation across the table.

"Why wouldn't he be?" Abinadab cuts in. "You think Saul would have put a weapon in the hands of a harp player?"

My mother shakes her head, still looking at me. "Well, he did pull you into the middle of a raid. When I heard about the attacks, I broke down."

Abinadab smirks. "She did cry her eyes out. Sort of like you did when we sacrificed that lamb."

I grimace at him. "I was eight." And I knew all the sheep by name. "Where's Joab?" I ask, trying to shift the attention. If he were here, half of this awkwardness wouldn't exist.

Shammah shrugs. "He's started running messages for the elders, so he's always gone. Drives his wife crazy. When he's home, he's usually up in the hills with Abishai and Asahel."

Still meeting with the resistance groups. My stomach tightens. My nephews had wasted no time finding others who shared their hopes for a revolution. So far, their efforts haven't grown beyond spying, but I know their ambitions run much deeper. And darker.

My brother chuckles. "Those three will be running the country before too long."

Abba blinks several times, his face graying. "Let's hope not, for all our sakes. If Saul goes to war, they'll have to put their wanderings aside for a while."

"Surely he won't order every man to fight," Eema worries.

Abba shakes his head. "If the Philistines have doubled their army, as Joab says, he won't have much of a choice."

I nod. "Achish is not going to be content with these raids for long. He wants to take the land. Drive us all out like they tried to do at Michmash."

"And how many years ago was that?" Abinadab scoffs.

My throat thickens. "It's different now. The giants from Gath have joined Achish, helping him recruit others from all the Philistine cities. We have to stop them before they get too strong. Before they're too much for us."

Abinadab laughs aloud. "Listen to the child, talking battle politics like an old warrior. Who'd you hear that from?"

My attempt at an answer doesn't reach him over the snickering commotion.

Defenses rising, I glance at Eliab. He's been too quiet this whole evening, but something has to be coming. I used to think anticipating his blows would soften them. It doesn't.

"So, did you establish your kingdom?" His mockery is so blatant, it paralyzes me.

"Eliab—" Eema reproves quickly. "I thought we had decided not to speak about that."

Ignoring her completely, he raises his eyebrows across the table, daring me to say something.

I refuse to look away, but I'm not going to argue with him, not when I'm feeling Abba's silence like a slap in the face. "No."

Eliab feigns surprise. "You mean they mistook you for a servant?"

"Did you not hear your mother?" Abba speaks without looking up.

"I've heard plenty." Eliab stretches, still speaking directly to me. "Never mind, David. Abba has plenty of subjects for you to rule here. Tomorrow, you spend the day in the pastures."

"As long as you're rested," Eema cuts in.

"He'll be fine." My father's answer to everything. "In fact, he's never looked so well. That isn't yours, is it?" His cursory glance takes in Ezra's cloak, which is a thicker material and a deeper color than anything I've ever worn.

"One of the armorbearers gave it to me." I don't feel like mentioning Jonathan. Everything that comes out of my mouth feels foolish.

My father's look is laden with mistrust. "No doubt you learned much in the court. But King Saul does not deal kindly with those who grow too close to his affairs. Not long term, anyway. It's probably better if you stay in the pastures from now on. Unless he calls for you, of course."

"I'll go now." I don't even know why I'm sitting here. Halfway to the door, my father's voice stops me.

"You didn't mention Samuel, did you?"

"No, Abba." I had tried to forget about the prophecy, afraid that King Saul would read it in my face somehow, but once I'd seen how much the king needed me, I'd relaxed. "Saul was pleased with my music."

For a second, my father's countenance softens, and I want to tell him everything—all about the battle and the weeks Jonathan had pushed me into fights with Ezra, teaching me things only a warrior would need to know. But in front of all my brothers, I feel restrained. It won't mean anything to them.

My father waves his hand at the door. "Good. Go."

Escaping the house, I head across the courtyard, agitation creeping after me. Sometimes I wonder if Eliab spends the day thinking of what he can say that will hurt me the most. And

Abba doesn't help. All he can think of is whether I endangered him with talk of Samuel. Does it bother them so much to think that Yahweh might take me out of their reach? It's still so obvious that they don't trust me.

The outer gate has barely closed behind me when the remnants of a conversation dart back to me, stinging like bits of frost on the wind. It was out in the fields when Jonathan had first asked about my music. Halting in place, I run back over my own words until they catch fire in my mind. *No.*

Had I really told Hassar Israel that I had been chosen by God? Am I that stupid?

I glance behind me as though someone might have seen my thoughts hanging in the air. The more I think about it, the more certain I am that I said it. I'll never understand why He chose me—or something like that.

Unwinding my sling, I grab a stone from the ground and fling it, watching it ricochet off the nearest tree. But the anxiety doesn't subside, swelling like an angry wave in my chest.

I break into a full sprint across the field and up the nearest slope. From the small rise, I can see the sheep spreading out over the lower valley like scattered snow. I slide to the ground against a boulder, push my fingers into my hair, and let my lungs burn.

Abba is going to kill me. If Saul doesn't first.

Unless Jonathan didn't tell him anything. It's possible the prince didn't even hear me. He certainly didn't act like he had. Immediately afterwards, Ezra had brought the news of the attack. And it wasn't like I'd explained myself. All I said was that God had chosen me. But Samuel is constantly on the king's mind. Anything could rouse his suspicion.

Squinting at the sky, I shake my head at the early stars blinking through the evening haze. I should have known it would be like this. I finally meet my childhood heroes, and I have to keep a life-altering secret from them. I press my knuckles into my eyes.

Put it out of Jonathan's mind, Adonai. At least until I'm forced to tell him.

How long will I have before everything is exposed? Abner already looks at me like I might have something to hide.

"David?"

My head jerks out of my hands, but it's only my father's servant Jehiel approaching with the donkey in tow. "I brought your things. I didn't unpack any of it."

All the better. "Thank you." I scramble to my feet and untie everything myself, careful to keep the arrows hidden until Jehiel is halfway back to the compound. Shrugging the packs onto the ground, I feel inside them for the arrows, considering what Ezra had told me.

It's probably best that Saul doesn't know what I did for Jonathan. If he knew that I'd saved him, he might start looking too deeply, asking questions that don't need answers right now. He might have wanted to press me into the army, elevating me beyond my skill level, something Jonathan seems wary of.

As kindly as they were spoken, the prince's words had felt like a warning. *Once you begin a life of fighting, it never stops.*

If I'm not elevated now, there's a reason. Whatever Yahweh is keeping me from, it's for my own protection and preparation. I close my eyes, releasing a slow breath. Yahweh's favor is honor enough, and I can live freely in it. His presence seems to be the only thing I can really stake my life on.

I undo the straps binding the arrows in rolls of leather. When I pull out the stained piece of parchment from the Philistine king, something rumbles inside me, a much deeper rage waiting to be ignited. They had gone after Jonathan, but they'd found the tip of my spear instead. I crumple the paper.

Let them come. Yahweh's plans for this land go beyond anything Achish could ever conceive.

Right there, I realize I've decided something. Whatever I face in the future, I won't kill either of them—Saul or Jonathan. My hand will never be turned against them, either to advance my own kingdom or protect my own life. I won't touch them unless I have a direct command from Yahweh. A command I pray never comes.

I pull the arrows out of their casings, intending to conceal the message inside. I will keep these safe in the pastures, hidden like me. But when I unfold them, another slip of paper catches the breeze and flutters to the ground. When I pick it up, the first thing I recognize is the Hassar's seal at the bottom, right beneath these words:

"My trust is rarely misplaced. And Yahweh's never is. You, son of Jesse, have both."

NINE

Jonathan

———◆◆◆◆◆———

When the path forks ahead of me, sloping up to Samuel's town, I hold up my hand. "Stop."

Ezra reins in his mule next to mine, confused. "My lord, it's too early to camp, isn't it? We're only a day's ride from home."

"We have one more stop to make before we return."

Ezra follows my gaze up the road. The path is clearly marked, skirting Gibeah and leading to the gates of Ramah, the town of the prophets. Ezra's concern creeps toward me. "My lord, please leave it alone. You already know everything he's said…"

"Not everything. Not yet." I turn and face him once. "I'll return quickly. If you can't keep this between us, then ride on ahead and follow the guards to Gibeah. Otherwise, stay here and wait for me."

Ezra sighs, reluctant. "He may not see you, my lord."

"Then I'll be back even sooner."

I shove my heels into the mule's sides and leave Ezra to his thoughts. Let him think I'm still obsessing about the past. There's something else I need to know. If the Roeh will tell me. I can't be this close and not try.

Ramah is quiet in the cool of the day, with no one in the main streets. The gates open to me without a word being spoken, and my ears catch a hint of music trailing the breeze down from the hills. My heart bends around the sound. My father had told me how the prophets of Ramah had met him on the road, singing and worshipping, the day Samuel anointed him king. Heaviness tugs at my throat.

I dismount in the center of the prophet's outer courtyard, anxiety awakened. The weight of Yahweh's presence here is so heavy, I can feel it like I feel the robe around my shoulders or the sword at my side. A honeyed sweetness fills the air, breathing deep peace around me, but my trembling is involuntary. It's what happened to me the first time I saw the Ark of the Covenant. The ancient golden chest flanked with angelic images has represented the presence of Adonai since the days of Moses, and the brooding power hovering over it also follows Samuel.

Unbuckling my weapon, I set it on the ground. There's no sense in appearing before the Roeh armed. I'm still bending down when one of Samuel's younger students approaches through a side door.

"Jonathan, son of King Saul." He says it calmly, with no malice or astonishment, as though he's been expecting me. Which, of course, they have. No doubt, Samuel knew about my journey before I'd even decided to make it.

I can't stay long. The king's business took me to the southern cities of Judah, and Abba knows exactly how much time it takes me to travel anywhere. In another day, he'll start expecting me to appear in Gibeah.

"I am here peaceably," I tell the younger prophet, but he just nods, his eyes fixed on the ground between us where I left my sword.

"You are here to see the Roeh." Again, it's not a question.

"I am. I understand if…"

"Come with me." Just like that. As if there had been no rift between us. As if I was the son of someone who respected Samuel.

Startled, I follow him through a narrow door into near darkness, and we climb a winding set of stairs. Trailing incense follows us to an upper room where Samuel sits by an open window. He doesn't turn his head when we come in.

"Here he is," the student murmurs before disappearing.

The moment I'm alone with the Roeh, my heart stumbles over its own pace, and my eyes begin to burn. It's been years since I've seen Israel's beloved mentor, and it might be years before I see him again. Questions and explanations rush into my mind, demanding release, but I have no right to give voice to any of them. That's not why I've come. Kneeling, I drag my gaze to the floor and keep it there.

"So, you've come." Samuel's voice is heavy, but completely lacking the hostility I'd imagined it would have.

"The king doesn't know I'm here. And anything you say will be for my ears only."

My heart is deafening inside my head. I didn't inquire of the Lord before coming. Should I even be here? I bow lower. "I know you have no reason to trust me."

Samuel keeps his face turned toward the window, but I can hear the smile enter his voice. "If I couldn't trust you, Yahweh would not have permitted you to come."

My cheeks grow warm. I feel honored and foolish at the same time. Of course, Yahweh's eyes are always on me. He knows the hearts of men. And Samuel trusts that. Another reason why he might have seen something in David. But now that I'm here, I don't know how to ask what I want to ask.

Samuel finally turns his head, never losing any of his composure. Peace is cemented into his countenance. "Speak, Jonathan."

I wince. Now that I'm about to, it sounds presumptuous. Why would he reveal anything to me? But I never expected him to tell me I have Yahweh's trust. That is more than enough to stand on.

I flick my eyes up. "You have spoken of someone who would replace my father as king of Israel. A man after God's own heart." My heartbeat digs into the scar over my rib. Until the shepherd boy, I had never met anyone who fit that description. "Is it David?"

Samuel doesn't respond, but his silence fills the space between us. I bow my head quickly so he won't misinterpret anything on my face. Then again, God could unfurl me like a scroll before the prophet if He wanted.

"Thank you, Roeh. I will leave you in peace." I stand up, feeling numb. I still don't know the truth. Not in so many words. But I also feel like I've received what I came for. It's better like this. If the king asks questions, I won't have to lie.

"Hassar—"

I pause, surprised to hear the royal title from the Roeh. Of all the people who doesn't need to address me that way...

Samuel's gaze seems to uncover the deepest parts of my mind. "That boy is a gift to Israel. Whatever you do with David will return to you."

I see the battlefield all over again, and David running to protect me. "I know."

"Yes. You do." He smiles faintly before the shudder is back in his voice, like clouds threatening rain. "Not everyone will share your vision. Use it well."

Honored by this much acknowledgement, I stare openly into Samuel's face, trusting he will see my heart. Trusting Yahweh will see.

"I give you my word."

* * * * *

A Year Later

Twists of smoke curl around the priest's shoulders, and the heat from the burning sacrifice battles with the damp coldness pushing at my back. I'm right behind Ahijah, close enough to feel the sting of the fire, but the forest breathes sharply at us, keeping my arms and shoulders alive with chills.

We're back in the southern wilderness, between Socoh and Azekah, and the tangle of Judean woods only adds to my discomfort, closing in on us with every hour of uncertainty.

When we'd heard that Achish had crossed into Judah with his famed army, I'd expected to feel relieved. After months of sporadic violence and conflicting reports, we could finally take decisive action, and remind the people that Israel will never bow to Philistia.

With the threat of Abba's nightmares behind us, we organized army units, drafted men from every tribe to the king's ranks, and marched south. Our commanders are confident of victory, believing this battle will be a repeat of Michmash, a chance to strike Achish with a blow that will send him staggering. The entire year has been building to this moment.

But with every step into Judah, I've felt dread pulling at me, deepening into a dull ache that keeps me cold. Something's wrong.

His back to the king, Ahijah finishes the offering and steps away from the altar with a careful shrug in my direction. My father watches like a predator, his gaze heavier than the humidity in the air.

Since leaving Gibeah, we've sacrificed every other evening at my request. But once again, there's been no clear direction from Yahweh, and Abba can't stand the hesitation he knows I'm feeling. The disturbance pulls at me like an injury, giving me the sensation of walking into battle unarmed.

Half a mile away, the armies of Israel wait for our command; every fighting man I'd registered last year is trusting us for solutions and strategies. The Philistine king who tried to have me killed is waiting for blood only a few miles south of Ephes, along with thousands of handpicked warriors, each sharpened to take as much of it as they can. The years since Michmash have kept Philistia at bay, and Achish is seething.

This is the battle we've been preparing for, and we'll need more than a cursory acknowledgement of Adonai's existence. We need His power riding out with us. Yahweh's breath has parted seas on our behalf, flattened wicked cities beneath heaps of sulfur and salt. Only His presence on our side will guarantee our victory.

But so far, every offering feels like an empty ritual, and every prayer falls flat. Maddeningly, the only semblance of a plan has come from Achish. Only a day ago, he'd sent word that we were to meet in the valley to "discuss options." My adamant refusal had nearly knocked the messenger off his horse and drawn me into an hours-long argument with the king.

"Abba, after all the Israelites they've killed and hung from their walls, now they want to *talk?*"

I couldn't believe my father would even consider a give-and-take with the man whose people have been harassing us my entire life. Not long after Michmash, Philistine scouts had tried to capture me in the forest outside Geba. I still remember how wildly I'd fought, determined to die rather than let them use me to extort my father. Shortly after Abner showed up, I'd passed out from blood loss, and the deep leg wounds had taken months to heal. I knew what they wanted to do then, and I know what they want to do now.

"They didn't spend the past decade burning our threshing floors so that we could have a discussion. We came here for war, and that's what they're going to get."

But in the absence of any other clear direction, my father had been adamant that we listen to whatever Achish has to say. "It's still possible he didn't sanction the attacks around Aijalon. Maybe they'll offer reparations. Either way, they were the last to attack. And no battle plan will satisfy you without a word from Yahweh. So, we have to try to use this to our advantage."

So today, we're ignoring Yahweh's silence and gathering Israel's armies in the valley of Elah to meet our greatest enemy. To talk. And I'm not hiding my displeasure as carefully as I'd thought.

Moving around the altar, Abba grasps my breastplate where it meets my neck. "Whatever Achish suggests, I will determine our answer. This is not the time for heroics. You will hold your position in silence and wait for my word."

His brows lift, and I incline my head slightly. "My lord."

Unconvinced, he shrugs me off, moving down toward the camp.

Agitation simmers inside me. It's actually the perfect time for heroics. Instead of attacking, Achish has kept to his camp, his troops maintaining a tense formation behind the hills. He has to be planning something. Unfortunately, we're not. And the creeping pull of humidity mingled with inaction is really starting to annoy me.

I wait for my father and his officers to disappear into the thicket ahead, and then turn to Ahijah. "I'm almost certain this is a trap. Achish doesn't want to talk. He wants to lure my father out into the open so he can kill him."

"Or you, perhaps." The priest's wrinkled face wears extra shadows. With a furtive glance down the path, he touches my wrist. "Yahweh communicates more with silence than men do with words."

The statement strokes chills along my arms. I lift my eyes, but only Abner and Ezra have stayed behind, and they both know better than to report on me. Ahijah and I plot nothing.

Still, I turn my back so they can't see the desperation in my face. I don't want to watch my father die, but for the first time, I'm reading that possibility in Samuel's final message. The one Abner burned the day I'd met David. If Yahweh's protection has departed along with His favor, then the least I can do is keep my father from being drawn into a doomed battle.

"What can I do, Ahijah? Is there something I should tell my father? Is there an offering I can give?" Some way to find out what Yahweh wants of me.

"Hassar..." Ahijah's sigh rattles in his chest.

He knows I'm a man of war who hates feeling powerless. I can think of twenty things I could do in this moment—definitive strikes we could make against the enemy. But what's the point if they're not commissioned by the Word of our God? Ahijah's eyes hold the answer in layers of sorrow.

This silence is due to my father's break with the Lord. It was a choice he'd made without me. And there's nothing I can do.

I feel Ahijah's pity reaching out to me while I fight to regain composure. He knows how hard I've tried over the years to maintain my father's good standing with the priests, only to watch the rift widen the more Abba chooses to see them as traitors. My position in the middle made my life torture until my father had burned so many bridges that he had to trust me again.

Once I've muscled most of the struggle out of the way, I squeeze Ahijah's shoulder, still not able to meet his gaze. "God bless you for your continued service to my father."

Even though we're marching into battle blind.

I head back to join the others, my stomach sinking. I'm astonished that Saul still claims so much loyalty after the chaos of his reign. Abba's confrontation with Samuel was only known to a few, but the rumors have spread like a disease over the years, and now distrust and resentment have grown up with the next generation, bearing unruly fruit among the Judeans. I wonder how much longer we'll have an army once people discover the depth of the king's apostasy.

This is the moment I've dreaded since receiving the note from Samuel. We cannot defeat our enemies without Yahweh's clear guidance and protection. It's the common thread uniting all our nation's stories: victory with God, defeat without Him. We've managed to hold our position since Abba's fall from favor, but if we want generational progress that will solidify our nation for years to come, we'll need a king who will follow Yahweh like Abba did when he was first anointed.

I can't forget how he was back then, when the *Ruach* took hold of him and made a warrior. But I was also there for the slow degeneration that followed.

Now, according to Samuel, there's another man somewhere in Israel who better represents the heart of God. I'd hoped that if I could discern who it was, then I could know how to steer Israel in the right direction, possibly secure a better future for my family. We can still serve Yahweh's purposes, even without the throne. For years, I've carried that hope in silence, afraid it was crazy. Why should I look forward to a replacement? But meeting David was all it took to rekindle my faith.

I still can't explain it. The shepherd boy's heart fits the prophecy the way my sword molds to my hand. David's songs had tugged my heart back into alignment, reminding me what we fight for, and where we get the strength to do it. Battles merely advance our position in the land our God gave us. But the real journey is knowing Him, as our ancestor Moses did. As long as men seek the face of Yahweh like that, hope will live.

But that doesn't illuminate much for the present. And I can't imagine explaining something like that to my father. If he ever finds out I went to Samuel, it won't matter what I say. Treason is such a fine line sometimes.

In the center of camp, Ezra slips into my tent behind me and hoists the rest of my armor into place without speaking. He hasn't mentioned a thing about Ramah since I went there. I'm almost relieved that Samuel didn't answer my question directly. I'm not even sure my convictions about David are safe in my own head.

Jesse's three oldest sons and three grandsons are among the warriors of Judah, but David has only been summoned to Gibeah a few times this year, and only to attend my father briefly before being tossed back in the pastures. I don't need to be a prophet to imagine how the prolonged isolation must be wearing on him.

I fidget under Ezra's grip. He's lacing the greaves too tight, allowing the leather of my armor vest to sit snugly against the closed wound in my shoulder. I push him off. "It's fine. Ammiel said it won't open."

Ezra's mouth slants. "Just use the other side."

"I'll use whatever I have to." I try to laugh at his concern, but all I can see is David covered with blood the day he'd saved us both. I have the shepherd boy to thank that Ezra's still at my side. Another thing my father still hasn't guessed. I adjust my shoulder under the armor, wondering if I should have told him what happened.

It wouldn't make sense for my father to summon David to battle when he's never really seen him fight. But I've witnessed the boy's zeal firsthand. I'd recognized the flames stirring behind his eyes after Aijalon. It was why I'd pulled him into training, polishing his youthful exuberance so that the next time he faced the Philistines, his strength would continue past one kill.

Watching David eat up my instruction had fueled my own fervor. And then he was gone, drawn back into the country life he's been outgrowing for years. Was I wrong to think he was meant to be a part of this battle? My own youth had ended at his age. Perhaps it's too soon for David.

Arrayed in my scarlet robe and armed as heavily as possible, I tighten the cords around Ezra's breastplate and find the familiar resolve in his eyes before handing him my bow and quiver. He won't hesitate to take action if anything threatens me or my father. I reach over to grasp my left shoulder and touch my fingers to my lips before we step out into the eerie forest light.

A low hum builds as we move into the valley, the heartbeats of every soldier wound up into one steady rhythm. Sweat builds on my forehead as my father signals for us to stop and steps out from the cover of branches, alone. I move up beside him, resenting all this restraint. I shouldn't be standing here without an arrow ready. But my father anticipates me. When I reach him, he places a hand on my shoulder, the pressure unmistakable.

One hand behind my back, I signal for Ezra to be ready, forcing steady breaths as our enemies begin to show themselves. Line after line of ironclad Philistines appear along the opposite side of the valley, so closely structured that it's impossible to count them. All I can see is the red flash of the feathers adorning their helmets and rows of armored shoulders undulating like a stubborn wave refusing to come ashore.

After months of dealing with handfuls at a time in surprise attacks, seeing their full might unwinds something in my chest that's been held taut for years. I adjust my weight, steadying my grip on the ground, my muscles grinding under the bronze. *Preserve me to fight, Yahweh.*

A sharp clap of iron strikes the air as the lines of Philistines begin clashing their shields, their voices rising in a carefully-controlled shout. They part to allow a man through their ranks, and even from a distance, I can make out the pale robe and golden armbands. Achish.

He's shorter than I expected, but his voice stains the valley with a mocking boldness that I instantly dislike.

"Greetings, sheep of Israel. I see your prince still lives. Eager to shed more Philistine blood."

My heartbeat bursts into flames, but my father's hand clamps down on me. Achish is almost bored with confidence, dressed in royal robes instead of armor, a relaxed smile stretching above his braided beard.

Nervous energy rumbles through his ranks, but Achish laces his fingers together as though he's meeting us in court. "But the time for raiding is past. I daresay I have a more efficient solution."

My father shouts, offense darkening his tone. "I am king of Israel, and you are the invader who comes to take what is mine. What makes you think I will agree to anything you suggest?"

The chortle tumbling out of the Philistine makes my skin crawl. Achish lifts his hands, retreating off to the side. "Don't then. Take it up with my champion."

Their army shifts again, drawing back like a wave about to crest. At the edge of the forest, a tree moves, bending enough to send a burst of crows into the air. My heart stops midstride as the tree becomes a man, his shadow dwarfing Achish as he steps into the valley. My eyes expand to take in all of him, and the fear racing through our ranks is tangible enough to heighten the chill in the air.

This is one of Gath's giants—every demonic rumor fully fleshed out in nearly ten feet of armor and muscle. A jeweled belt adorned with skulls. A heavy bronze helmet snagging every bit of weak sunlight from the air. A coat of mail that I suspect could crush me, and a gleaming javelin slung between his shoulders like a tree limb, its shaft as thick as a weaver's beam.

His iron shield walks separately, carried by an armorbearer who can scarcely see over it. But it's the giant's face that kicks my heartbeat into full gallop. Glowering hatred. Serpentine smile. Absolutely no light in his eyes.

"Paying attention now, Israel?" Striding past Achish, the giant advances, his bellow deflating every lung in our army.

"Why have you come out for battle? We all know I'm a Philistine, and you are servants of Saul. We can decide this here and now." He shrugs his spear from his shoulder to his hand, completely comfortable with its weight. "Choose a man for yourselves, and let him come down to me. If he is able to fight with me and kill me, then we will be your slaves. But if I prevail against him and kill him, then you shall be our slaves, and serve us."

Behind my back, our commanders murmur feverishly, shifting in place. I finally pull my gaze over to my father, but he's not moving. The coldness in his face tightens my veins. I've seen rage tossing in him like a fiery cauldron. I've seen grief tear him in half. But I've never seen fear like this. Our enemy's disdain seethes across the valley.

"Have you no real warriors in your ranks? No one worthy to fight Goliath of Gath? Not even your God?" He spits in the dust, and anger leaps in my chest.

The giant paces, his bronze leg greaves shifting over his muscles. "I defy the armies of Israel this day—find someone who can fight with me, and you will win the respect of Philistia."

My body clenches, anticipating his threat.

"Fail, and your bodies will decorate Dagon's temple. Every last one of you."

Everyone's frozen, incapable of movement, but when Goliath tosses the spear to his other hand, my father flinches, awakening my instincts. I can feel the flames stirring inside me, trying to melt the ice. In my mind's eye, I see myself stepping forward, rotating my spear into position to accept the blatant challenge.

Go on. They're waiting for you. It's always you.

My father tenses, and his fingers find my wrist again. He's afraid I'll move. I'm afraid of why I can't. I've fought for years, but not with darkness openly laughing at us. Not with all the confidence drained from my shoulders. I won't go like this.

The giant holds his weapon aloft for a moment, then drives it into the ground at his side, smirking when everyone steps back. "Go gather your courage. I'll wait."

* * * * *

Back in my father's tent, I listen to the cacophony of the war council, refusing to comment until I have something useful to say. It might be a while. Abba's commanders and generals have found their tongues, tossing out flustered opinions. And numbers.

"He has to be over nine feet tall."

"I'll wager that breastplate alone is more than four thousand *shekels* weight of bronze!"

"There's more of them too. Goliath has brothers back in Gath."

I wince as their voices get louder. Within the false security of Abba's tent, they've all regained a semblance of wits. Even I had felt my muscles relax once we'd returned to camp. But it didn't take long for the relief to disintegrate into humiliation that burns my stomach.

We just stood there, exactly like the sheep he'd called us. Like prey staring at a lion. In a few minutes, he's done more damage to our morale than combat would have. I rotate the hilt of my sword while my nerves scream. If it was just me and my brothers, I would vent my frustration at the top of my lungs. Maybe throw something. But it's the war council, and we have to find some way to salvage this, or we will lose the battle we desperately need to win.

One of Abner's nephews speaks up. "What if no one comes forward? We can't very well command a son of Israel to fight that monster."

"Condemn him would be more like it," another scoffs. "The giant wouldn't even have to use his spear to kill most of us. That sword was thicker than all five skulls in his belt."

My father's shout breaks up the aimless discussion. "All right! We all saw him. I called you here to offer solutions, not chatter like children." Pushing sweat from his forehead, he singles out my brothers. "Ishvi, Malchi, what do you think of his challenge?"

He already knows where I stand.

Malchi grimaces, trying not to look at me. "Total surrender, to the point of slavery, over one man? Why would we risk something like that when we would have a much better chance with our armies?"

Abner mumbles nervous agreement, tapping his elbows while staring out the door of the tent.

Ishvi sits forward. "He can't be serious. He's baiting us. If he really believed we had a man who could defeat that giant, he wouldn't be risking this. Achish doesn't want to see one man die. He wants to engage in combat."

"Then why would he do this? Why not just attack?" Abner asks.

"He wants to kill our courage first," I interject, heat surging up my neck when everyone faces me. "You saw what happened out there. Every bit of fight evaporated like frost on a warm day. He wants to weaken us with intimidation. If he can draw us into battle like that, he'll have already won."

My father bristles. "He hasn't won anything. All he's done is strut like a peacock." He shoves back from the table, squaring his shoulders. "This is merely a setback. The men will recover. But I have no intention of feeding anyone to that giant for Achish's sport. I am king of Israel's armies. When we fight, we fight together."

Abner's brows lift, unsteady relief cooling his face. "So, we just wait?"

"Exactly."

"Wait for what?" The cold edge is back in my chest.

"For them to drop this charade." My father pushes roughness into his voice, but I can tell what he's covering. "Give it a few days. In the meantime, tell the men to save their energy. Achish will get tired of dragging this out and try to attack. When he does, we'll be ready to meet him in a fair fight."

I spread my hands. "And what about Goliath? He's not going to disappear. Someone will have to face him."

My father looks beyond me, carefully controlling his expression. "Not today."

Everything in me wants to protest. The gray resignation settling on the commanders has a sickening permanence to it. I don't think it's likely that another few days will do much to stoke their courage. And if the men can't see their leaders armed with solutions, who will be inspired to take action?

Michmash glowers in the back of my mind. A hundred stragglers hiding in caves, afraid to leave, afraid to stay. Scores more deserting. Philistines pushing closer, taking ground. Everyone who didn't understand what happened said it was desperation that made me do what I did. Maybe it was, partially. But God used it. I'd awakened that morning arrested by a powerful unction outside of myself. I don't feel anything like that now.

And my father is the king. So, we wait. While Goliath shouts and hurls spitting insults across the valley. All day.

By the time the afternoon stretches into evening, I'm ready to shoot anything in sight. But we endure another day. And the next. Then, a week.

My father's "not today" stretches into a month of torment as Goliath's mockery turns more vehement. His rage is like a twister cloud, slamming into the valley and tearing us asunder with threats that are all the more terrifying for their accuracy.

"Godforsaken cowards! Is none of you able to fight a real Philistine? What good are your weapons? What good is your faith? Go back to hiding in caves while we consume the land."

I toss and turn through each night, and pace away the days, unwilling to believe I'm trapped in this nightmare, forced to listen, unable to escape.

What galls me more than the insults is the disrespect Goliath flings at Yahweh. The Philistines know what our God has done. He decimated their temples in the days of Samuel's youth, shattering the image of their god before the Ark of the Covenant, which they had stolen from us. For weeks afterwards, they'd been plagued by diseases. Yahweh's power had trembled the mountains on the day I'd attacked Michmash. And they've all heard the stories of the Red Sea parting on our behalf as we'd fled Egypt centuries ago. Our God is a Warrior, unmatched in battle.

Goliath came forward expecting a fight at least. But now, each day of inaction foments his violent disdain for our armies and our God.

"You're not sheep, you're dogs! You boast of your mighty God who brought you out of slavery. And yet you will be slaves again!"

At the back of the camp, hidden by trees, I shoot arrow after arrow until I'm exhausted. But I'm accomplishing nothing. I can handle the rush of adrenaline in battle, but to sit here and fight with an unseen enemy? I could lose my sanity to this.

Each day drags us deeper into a torturous quicksand that expends the energy we should be throwing into battle. No one is sleeping, and the dark cloud is growing around my father again, making him inapproachable. His daily council meetings have turned into vapid weekly appearances, producing nothing except rewards designed to entice the men to fight. But no one responds to the incentives.

Over every meal, I have to watch the taut anger in Saul's expression deepening into a haunting emptiness. I'm afraid the torment is trying to return, but the king hasn't said anything about summoning David. He wouldn't, not with things so volatile.

On the evening of the thirty-ninth day, I stare at my father across from food that neither of us is going to touch. All my stomach wants is relief from the turmoil that's bound it in knots. I feel hoarse even though I haven't really been speaking. I've been turning the same thoughts over in my mind so much that they feel stale.

His head in his hand, my father glares at me through his fingers. "If you have something to say, just say it."

It's long past time. I lean forward, hoping my father's desperation has opened his ears. "You know how they've been saying that Achish has an unbeatable army? That he's been amassing so many that he could take us over? We've been hearing it for the past year. But I don't agree."

Abba rubs his forehead. "No?"

"No. Achish is a new king. He should be eager to prove himself against you, especially if he has such a large army. Instead, he's letting Goliath take the glory? It doesn't make sense. I think they've been lying to us. I think he's being forced to throw all his hope on this giant. He knows the reputation these monsters have, and he's been letting that simmer for the past few years, trusting that the rumors have run so wild that everyone will flee from them, and not lift a finger to..."

"What's your point?"

My fists are clenched against the table's edge. "We have more than a chance to end this. To deal them such a blow that they will live under *our* jurisdiction for the next decade! Abba, Achish is terrified."

The king turns his head as Goliath's roar reaches the tent.

"He doesn't sound terrified."

"He's letting Goliath do the shouting for him." I'm barely controlling the anger in my voice. I cannot believe we've let Achish do this for so long.

I can see doubt tugging at my father—the conflict between the part of him that knows I'm right and the uncertainty that's plagued him since breaking with Samuel. His eyes darken with the struggle, and I know the moment he chooses a side.

"You're wrong." He shakes his head, his jaw flexing. Veins appear in his neck, and he rubs his knees. "It doesn't matter who I send out there or how we attack. He's not coming."

"Who?" But the moment I say it, I know. He's afraid to face what he can't win without Yahweh. But surely there's something we can do. If my father was willing, we could send for Samuel one more time. Proclaim a fast. We should've done that already, petitioning Yahweh for mercy while we work a plan.

For a moment, the anger on my father's face shifts, dropping down into such hopelessness that my chest hurts.

"Are you sure I shouldn't send for David?" I venture.

His head comes up. "Who?"

"The harp player. The shepherd who's been serving you for over a year."

"All right, all right. I forgot his name." He flicks his wrist as though waving off a fly. "Do you think I need his songs to remind me what I've lost?" Bitterness crowds back into his face, blocking me out. When he edges his chin toward the door, I know he's done listening.

Back in my tent, I pace, refusing panic. There has to be something I can do.

Maybe there's something beneath the surface we've missed. Sparring in the forest, Ezra and I have analyzed every inch of what we've seen of the giant and his armorbearer, always coming up with the same conclusion. Goliath is fearsome. But he must have a weakness. Every man does.

Clenching the tent post, I drag breaths in and out, fighting the grip of confinement. How can this be happening? We're the people of God. Yahweh has sent our enemies running before with just a breath! He has sent fire on our behalf, routed whole armies with worship, sent women to lure tyrants to their deaths. It's what David recounts in his songs. Our nation's identity, bound up in Yahweh's victory.

And now the Name of our God is being dragged through the dust while we watch and listen, refusing to show Goliath any different. The accursed *Nephilim* needs to see more than the servants of Saul, the sheep of Israel. He needs to see Yahweh. But how can he if we don't?

Part of me is desperate for the answer. I want to stretch out on the ground and fast until I get it. But more of me is furious that we've waited this long. I'm tired of guessing, wondering if I'm offending Yahweh by asking questions. I'm tired of puzzling this out, trying to decide why the challenge feels so heavy. With my next breath, my endurance breathes its last.

"Ezra! Get in here."

"What's wrong, my lord?"

Everything. I hand him my sword, keeping my eyes on the blade. "Sharpen this as much as you can, and bring me one of the king's spears." I let my instructions take shape in his mind. "If no one comes forward by tomorrow, I'm going down there myself."

Ezra halts in place. "You're going to fight the giant," he repeats. The uncertainty in his voice makes me shudder.

"I'm the Hassar, Ezra, not some cowardly dog who lies down and takes a beating." I set my teeth as Goliath's curses tear through the valley again. "I've heard enough."

"Then I'm going with you." Ezra's expression sharpens, cutting into me.

"I wasn't asking you to."

He stiffens, fierceness joining the glimmer in his eyes. "If you die, I die."

I look away, hating the thought of leading him into death. I know the tendency of armorbearers to kill themselves if their masters die in battle. But Ezra's resignation troubles me more than I want to reveal. "You're so sure Goliath will win?"

Ezra tries to smirk, but his face wears it like a grimace. "Is it like Michmash? Is Yahweh calling?"

I swallow tightly. "No."

I hate the answer, but I have to be honest. Every day for the past forty, I've waited for a sign, a dream, a rush of courage. Instead, I feel nothing but a lingering dread, burning hotter every day like a persistent fever.

What are we if not the armies of the living God? I know my father has fallen from favor, but we still have a mandate to drive out our enemies. I've never known Yahweh to place a challenge before us without unfolding a plan. We've known that it would probably come to this, and yet we're paralyzed.

"You're afraid." Ezra barely breathes the words. Like he can't believe them.

After the first jolt of denial, I let my shoulders drop. "I am. I don't know why."

Ezra's face pulls with helpless compassion. "You are the crown prince of Israel," he finally murmurs. "God is with you."

Is He? Shame chills me the moment I think it. Our God does not abandon His people. And yet, I'm hardly the crown prince. Not anymore. So, who am I? What does Yahweh want from me—with so many of our people still looking to me for leadership? I should know. And yet I don't.

I touch Ezra's arm, nodding for him to leave. He obeys, taking my sword with him, but his manner screams with hesitancy. We're both willing to die for Israel. But is it time?

I'm exhausted, but I can't sleep. Hour after hour, I lie there watching the lamplight's reflection catch fire against my sword. Am I really meant to go down there tomorrow and fight that giant? Should I believe I can win because Yahweh has strengthened me in the past? Or am I dooming Israel by risking defeat?

The questions return unanswered with the daybreak, and I feel my desperation mounting, crowding out any other consideration.

Change must come today. Goliath will be in the valley before sunup, and God help me, he's going to see at least one Israelite who believes.

I fumble with my robe myself, not wanting Ezra to see how my hands are shaking. Reaching up to my left shoulder, I head out into the sunlight.

Yahweh, if I'm wrong, forgive me. I have to do something.

TEN

David

───◆◆◆◆───

Two months ago

"Are you certain?" I'm breathing fire, barely able to contain myself.

Aaron's deep-set eyes smile at me from his turban. "I'm certain. The messenger from Gibeah said the fighting men are to leave at dawn."

A shout slams into my chest, and I barely wrestle it back. I've felt the hum of anticipation growing louder over the past month as my dreams of the Philistine king have intensified. And now he's amassing his army within Judah's territory!

The old shepherd laughs at me, leaning into his staff. "Easy, boy. They're not at our gates."

I grab his wrist, almost shaking him. "But you know what this means, Aaron! This isn't going to be a regular battle. You know what I've told you."

"Yes. I know." His eyes are full of it.

Over the months of traveling back and forth between Saul and the pastures, Aaron's been the safest person to talk to. I've told him everything I should have told my father—about Jonathan's injury and the Philistine I'd killed to save him. About Saul's response to my music and my dreams about Achish. The only thing he doesn't know is that I've been anointed. He still believes Samuel merely came to sacrifice that day.

He'd grinned when I'd told him how I could barely lift Jonathan's spear, and he'd laughed out loud when I'd told him how adrenaline changed all that in battle. He knows how I long to fight for Saul, but his patient steadiness has kept me sane over the past two seasons, always encouraging me to trust the timing of the Lord.

"Yahweh will not overlook the flame that's in you, boy. He put it there."

But now the spark that was ignited almost a year ago has been swept into a full blaze, and I'm almost dancing in place, more certain than I've ever been.

"Yahweh is going to deal our enemies a blow that will send them reeling for decades. And with Him on our side, there's no competition!"

The lines in Aaron's face deepen, and he sighs, assessing me over his staff. "I wonder what our dear king would say if he knew that the bravest man in Israel is a shepherd boy."

Something in his tone reaches deep and uncovers my hidden fears, reminding me how much the king doesn't know about me. I'm sure he wouldn't be pleased. But I don't have time to consider Saul's reaction. I've been too focused on what Yahweh will do. The gentle presence that I've known in the pastures has grown into a powerful leading that I can't ignore.

"Time will tell if you believe Him," Samuel had said, and I'm yearning to prove that I do.

I believe, Adonai. Command me!

It won't be long before I have clear direction. I can feel it.

And so can Aaron. I can tell by the way his eyes burn when he looks at me. He knows how much I've changed in the past year, and how much will change when I leave. If I can convince my father that I'm ready. Even with Jonathan's training and counsel, I'm still just a shepherd to everyone else. They didn't see the fire that was sparked in Gibeah, and how it bit deep into me, changing everything.

I can feel the change in Aaron, the air between us thick with understanding. Over the years, he's been one of the few willing to search diligently for the source of my strength and draw it out. Now it's time for it to be sharpened, tested. And everything will change.

"Go on home and speak to your father," Aaron says. "I'll take the flocks down to the fold."

I stop to look at him before turning toward Bethlehem. There's no way I can repay him, no way to thank him enough. The gentle pride warming his face is something I've only seen on one other man. It rests on my shoulders as I turn away.

I quicken my pace through my father's side gate, trying to settle my fervor before facing anyone. The illusion of peace that always lives in the pastures is completely absent from Bethlehem. The town is twisting inside out with the reality that our enemy is encamped only a few days' ride to the east. I'm probably the only one in Judah who's glad to hear it.

After almost a year of anxious waiting, grappling with conflicting reports and local raiding parties, we're finally going to face the Philistines and answer their threats once and for all. Yahweh will glorify Himself again with our armies. And this time, I will see it with my own eyes.

I slow my step a little once I reach Abba's compound. Maybe I should circle around to talk to Joab first. It isn't likely that my older brothers will want to listen to me. But once I reach Joab's house, I find Eliab standing outside, along with two mules and half a dozen packs lined up on the ground.

Beside him, Joab shouts toward the open door. "I can't take all of this, Deborah. I need room for *weapons!*"

His expression changes when he sees me, and Eliab looks away, grumbling.

"What are you planning to do? Chase Achish off with a stick?" Joab's teasing sounds halfhearted. He rubs the back of his neck, studying the mules instead of me.

"How about you let me borrow a sword? I've seen the ones you've stolen lined up in your huge stone cellar that fools no one."

Joab's eyes dart back to the house. "It's fooled my wife for two years, so keep your mouth shut."

"Just ignore him," Eliab advises tightly. His eyes cut to mine over the mule's back. "Besides, what makes you think we would give you a sword? You ever fight anyone? Any *men?*" he specifies, tightening the mule's saddle.

The broken Philistine impaled on Jonathan's spear jumps into my mind. But Aaron is the only one who knows about that.

"I can hold my own."

Joab chuckles, keeping his face turned away.

I fold my arms. "If you don't believe me, go fight beside someone else."

"What makes you think you're coming with us?" Eliab snaps.

I'm utterly caught off guard. The air is snatched from my lungs in one winded second as though Eliab had punched me in the stomach.

"What?"

Joab aims a hard look at my brother before trying to placate me.

"Only your three oldest brothers are following Saul. He might summon more if things get bad enough but…" He sighs sharply, glancing over his shoulder. "Did you really think your father would let you go to war? You're half the age of the king's soldiers, and you know nothing about combat. Even Saul isn't that stupid."

He stalks inside the house, leaving me to grapple with the assault of my own assumptions.

Heat jumps into my face. Did I really think everyone would accept the idea of me fighting? Maybe I hoped that Saul or Jonathan would speak for me. Either way, I hadn't really thought it through, and now shame is building a furnace inside me. I should have spoken to my father months ago. I'd just never guessed that he would keep me here after the way this battle has been built up over the past year.

On the surface, it makes sense. My father looks at me and sees a shepherd. He always has. But he doesn't know what I've seen and heard. He doesn't realize what burns inside me. How can I expect him to if I can't bring myself to look him in the eye and tell him?

I'd rather not look at Eliab either. His expression tugs uneasiness into my stomach. But there's more than mockery in his face. He's aghast.

"Good God," he mutters. "You believe it, don't you?"

"Believe what?"

"What Samuel said." He yanks the straps on the saddle, anger darkening his sneer. "Melek. You."

My chest tightens. I'm shocked that he would bring that up. "That's not why I…"

"Yes, it is." He comes around the mule to stand over me. "You think that because of some prophecy, you can fight one battle, and Saul will hand you the kingdom."

"Don't—" I glance at the house, but Eliab just scoffs.

"What? You think Joab will believe it? What are you afraid of?"

"What are *you* afraid of?" I counter. I turn and head for home without waiting for him to answer.

He's resented me forever, and now jealousy is eating him alive. He hated watching Samuel single out the one son he's treated like a servant. But I'm tired of him baiting me over it. I don't understand why I was chosen, but Yahweh's will is enough for me. Why isn't it for them?

Across the courtyard, my father comes out of the house. The moment our eyes meet, his shoulders drop, visible weariness sweeping over him. He starts to turn away, but I walk around him, planting myself in the doorway. Eema is a few feet behind him, but I don't care. She'll have to hear it.

"Why are you doing this?" A tremor curls into my voice.

His expression closes. "David, this is not the time."

Not the time? "Abba, the Philistines are in Judah! They've amassed their entire army against us." I gasp as though I've been running. "This is the war we have feared. The one we have to win. Why don't you understand?"

He frowns. "What is there to understand? Saul has been fighting the Philistines for decades. He doesn't need a shepherd at his side in order to win this."

"I've been to Gibeah. I've learned things. I need to be there now. Abba, I can't stay here. Not anymore."

The words bite my throat. Now that I'm being honest with him, I realize how much it means to me. It's my birthright. It's Yahweh's calling. And the shaken apathy in my father's eyes is more daunting than the reports of impending war.

"David, you're not going to change my mind about this. You were in the court as Saul's harp player, and that does not qualify you to fight."

He tries to edge away from me, but I turn with him. "Did they tell you that I was carrying Saul's armor when we were ambushed outside Aijalon? That I was there when Jonathan was shot? I killed the Philistine that attacked him."

My father's expression freezes. "With what?"

"Jonathan's spear."

A sharp sound escapes my mother. Abba's face slants as he tries to decide whether to believe me. He buries a long sigh in his hand, rubbing his face. "That's hardly what he summoned you for. If Saul wanted you fighting, he would have commanded you to come. The king would resent being responsible for you at a time like this. You're staying here."

"Are you afraid of what I might do? What Yahweh might do?" I raise my voice higher than I've ever dared with him, but my father isn't deterred.

"Don't bring His Name into this. You're *my* son, and I've made my decision."

"*Your son?*" Unexpected hurt cuts into my tone. "You don't even know me."

I break away before he can respond. Before I can see him not respond. I hate that I lost control, that I had to break open like that in order for him to see something real.

My feet take me the long way back to the pastures, climbing up through a tangled hillside in order to avoid being seen. My vision is blurring, and I don't want to run into Aaron. Fortunately, he's at the far end of the pasture, herding the rest of the flocks toward the folds. Several of the sheep scamper in my direction, recognizing me.

I shove my hands through my hair, trying to decide what's happening to me. Am I delusional, like Eliab seems to think? How crazy is it to believe the word of Yahweh's prophet?

What are you doing, Adonai? Why anoint me for something I don't even know how to pursue? Did I misunderstand? Should I leave?

Some of the sheep scatter, signaling the approach of someone else. I half expect it to be my father, but of course it's not. He never comes out here anymore. Not since his heart started bothering him.

Eema stops by one of the sheepfolds and leans against it, her presence reaching out to the agitation crackling around me.

I turn my back to her, my voice straining against emotion. "If Abba's trying to punish me, he's doing a good job."

"He's not punishing you. You've done nothing wrong."

I pick up a stone and roll it around in my hand. "He doesn't trust me. He thinks I'll make some mistake and bring shame to him."

Eema moves closer and touches my hair. "He doesn't know you very well."

"None of them do. My brothers, Joab. They think I look at this like some kind of game. It's not." I look at her. "I'm meant to do this, Eema. I'm meant to fight."

She inhales, forcing a smile. "Yes, you are. I may not like it, but Yahweh has been watching you. Long before Samuel came."

I shake my head, looking over the hills. Why anoint someone whose own family despises him? "I don't know what I'm supposed to do."

"Nothing, for now. If Yahweh has put something inside you, He'll have to be the one to draw it out. And He will not fail to do that. I just never thought things would change so fast." Eema breathes deeply, looking out over the fields, and I can feel it. She's about to change the subject. "You know that it was fifteen years ago, almost to the day?"

"What was?"

"The day Yahweh chose our house in another way we didn't understand yet. The day of your birth."

Of course. She never forgets. Without her, I'm sure I wouldn't have half the memories I do. She's the only reason I have any information about the woman who bore me, since no one else will talk about her. Shiphrah was destitute when she met my father, and after she became pregnant by him, he'd allowed her to remain in his house as a servant. She'd died of fever when I was five years old. Everything before that is a blur—the few years when Abba really didn't know what to do with me.

Atarah was the one who made sense of my childhood. It was her voice that taught me songs and spun stories. Her soothing grip that held all the emptiness back. The night my mother had died, Atarah had found me in the separate rooms by the stables, lifted me into her arms, and told me to call her *Eema*. Mother. Not long after that, she'd given me the lyre, and between her and the music, I didn't feel lost anymore.

Abba refused to look at me for a time, afraid of the shame connected with claiming me, and several of his sons followed suit. But Eema encouraged me to look to Adonai for the acceptance I craved. And out here in the hills, alone with Him all these years, I'd actually found it.

I look over at Eema. "Why did you want me? Abba shamed you too—with what he did."

She puts her arms around my shoulders. "I'm a mother. And nothing was your fault." She smiles pensively out at the hills.

"Do you remember when that ewe wouldn't take her lamb, two seasons ago? He would sleep beside you, and you wouldn't let him out of your sight until he was strong enough to join the others? If a shepherd can do that for a lamb, a woman can do it for a child. A child who is infinitely more worthy."

I start to scoff, but she stops me.

"Don't laugh. You know it's true. I saw it then, and Yahweh has always seen it. Be willing to trust Him, if no one else. Your father is just trying to protect you."

"No, he's not." I don't know what he's protecting, but it's not me.

Eema rubs my shoulder. "Then trust that Yahweh is. Be willing to wait for His Word. You say all the time that He is your Shepherd. So, let Him lead you. When He calls you into battle, no one will be able to stop Him. And all of Israel will know that He is the Lord."

I can't resist the faith reaching out to me from her eyes. When she looks at me like that, I would do anything. I start to answer her, but the words die half-spoken, and danger leaps into my chest.

Over Eema's shoulder, the sheep are scattering, their usual anxious chatter turning to panicked confusion. The bulky shadow emerging from the trees is already lumbering after them, heavy claws reaching for one that's stumbled.

Pushing in front of my mother, I'm halfway to the bear before I've planned what to do. "Get out of here!" I shout, flinging a stone. "Get back!"

Usually, a little bluster is all a bear needs, but this one is out for blood. Rearing up, it slams its clawed feet down over a lamb, guarding it. Dazed and terrified, the lamb shudders on the ground, making no effort to escape.

I sling a stone this time, then another, and both bounce off the animal's sides, angering it. Rearing up again, the bear bellows at me, tossing its head, preparing to charge. The next stone has to kill it or at least injure it. *Adonai, help me.*

"David—" I hear Eema several feet behind me, but I don't turn around. I have to protect her as well as the flock. Fitting the stone, I breathe, letting Jonathan's advice settle into my mind. *No tension. Just zeal. Yahweh is with you.*

Gripped with confidence, I sling the stone, and it smashes into the bear's head. The animal jerks back, shaking its huge shoulders, then staggers off several paces, each effort slower than the last. Pulling my knife, I break into a run and overtake the bear as it stumbles for the last time. Grabbing hold of the coarse fur where the predator's head meets his neck, I sink my weapon as deep as it will go and hold on until the unsteady thrashing stops.

Finally able to relax my grip, I just stand there looking at it. Rather than sinking into my flesh or taking the sheep, the yellow claws and teeth are resting against the ground. Energy buzzing inside me, I step over the bear, pick up the lamb, and carry it to the fold so it can collect its wits among the others.

Thank you, Yahweh.

I turn back to find my mother. She can't speak, too many emotions struggling on her face. She wept when she saw me after the lion attacked. But she's never seen me kill a predator in person. After a few pointless seconds of restraint, she releases a sob, and I hold onto her while she gasps and cries.

"It's all right. We're safe. Yahweh is with us." When I say the words, passion leaps inside me, and I pull back to look into Eema's eyes. "If He's delivered me from lions and bears, what are a few Philistines? I have to fight for Him."

Laughing through her tears, she cups my face, holding our foreheads together. "I know. And you will. You will show the world what you can do with the help of your Shepherd."

* * * * *

Back at home, my father has been staring at the bear's carcass for ten full minutes, his arms wrapped around himself. Eema's uneven breathing is the only sound in the room, except for the hum of adrenaline that's taking forever to leave my body. I've said very little, allowing the bearskin to tell its own story, but now I feel compelled to speak.

"I didn't mean to disrespect you, Abba. But I'm not just a shepherd anymore. Yahweh is with me, and He's taught me to fight. All I want is the chance to follow Him. I want to know where He will lead me, and I am going to find out."

My father's eyes travel the length of the bear and finally find my face, respect and annoyance wrestling on his brow. "Thirty days."

Hope stabs my chest, but Abba lifts his chin, keeping his voice stern. "Saul boasted that his armies would rout Philistia's in thirty days. And Eliab promised to send us word before then. If we don't hear from them in a month, you can join them in

Ephes. *But,*" he holds up a hand against my reaction, "you will not look for trouble. You can carry some food to your brothers and bring something back to let us know they're safe. But you will not shove yourself into battle where you are not needed. Do you understand me?"

I nod once, willing the tension from my shoulders. I'll take it. If I press him too much, he might change his mind.

Abba shudders, pulling his gaze back from the bear. "Get that thing out of here." Before walking away, he touches my chest with one finger, allowing me to see all the misgivings in his eyes. "Don't make me regret this."

* * * * *

Thirty days later, I'm up before the sun, standing next to the mules my mother has packed with provisions. We still haven't heard from my brothers, and the silent strain is starting to wear on my father. I can't help a shiver of pity seeing him watch the road, shadows creasing his face.

"This isn't like them," he mumbles, troubled. "You would think they'd at least send some token to let us know what's happening."

He's right. Joab's brother Asahel is the fastest runner in Bethlehem. He could have easily made it here and back in a day or two with news, unless something is preventing them from coming. Maybe the Philistines have them trapped, which could mean danger for all of us here. It's not normal for us to be so close to the battlegrounds and not hear anything, one way or the other.

"I'll find them, Abba," I promise him.

"Come home as soon as you have word." He studies me longer than he ever has, trying to uncover something before turning away.

Eema holds me longer than usual, urgency pulsing in her eyes. I want to promise her I'll come back, but I feel restrained. It's not my place anymore. Not since the anointing. Again, Eema seems to understand what isn't being said. Touching my face, she whispers, "Follow your Shepherd."

My stomach twists as I walk away, but I don't look back.

It's a shorter journey than the ones I've made to Gibeah, and navigating Judah's territory is no struggle. I approach King Saul's encampment from the woods, not wanting to be stopped by enemy sentries. I'm fully expecting to find signs of battle—a busy war camp with wounded soldiers being treated and armorbearers sharpening weapons. But the tents are deserted by all except a few servants. Wandering near Saul's tent, I run into Othniel.

"David! What are you doing here? Did the king summon you?" He says it over my shoulder as though expecting to see someone else.

I shake my head. "My father sent me to find my brothers. Where are they?"

Othniel is wound tighter than the strings on my lyre, and he's aged since I saw him last. "They're lined up in the valley with the army. Like every day."

Every day? "Doing what?"

Othniel rubs his face. "David, you shouldn't be here. Just go home. If your family can get out of Bethlehem, they should. Go to Moab for a while. Just get out while you can."

His words pluck the ends of my heartbeat. "But why? What's happened?"

Still breathing heavily, he glances over my head toward the edge of camp. "Just go home. Now."

"Not until I've seen my brothers."

Relenting, Othniel pulls at my shoulder. "Fine. Come on. Just be quick."

He leads me to the valley of Elah, where the armies of Israel are spread out in battle formation. Othniel disappears almost immediately, but I don't even notice. I've waited so long to see all of Israel's fighting men assembled like this. But it's like entering a dream. Everyone is motionless, staring straight ahead without speaking or moving. Barely noticed by the soldiers, I duck between the battle lines, looking for the men of Judah.

I spot Shammah first, but he's never looked so disturbed. "David. What are you doing here?" Rather than greeting me, he holds back, agitated. "You shouldn't be here."

I frown, following his hunted glances all around. "Why shouldn't I? Nothing's happening."

"No…" Exasperated, Eliab buries a curse under his breath.

Noticing me at the same moment, Joab flings a triumphant laugh into Eliab's face, slapping his arm. "I knew it! Didn't I tell you the songbird would show up here?"

I roll my eyes. "I'm not here to sing. Just tell me what's going on."

Joab leans on his spear. "Well, we've been…detained."

"What does that mean?" I press him.

"Nothing. It means nothing," Eliab barks, shoving him.

Abinadab tugs at his breastplate, sweat trailing his forehead. "Remember the giants we've heard about? The Philistines have one of them fighting on their side. He's almost ten feet tall, and every day he comes out and curses our armies, challenging one of us to fight. We've been waiting for someone to answer his charge, but not even the king's rewards have enticed anyone."

"You've been waiting *forty days* to fight?" I can't wrap my head around it. All this time we've been worrying in Bethlehem, and no one has even lifted a spear?

Shammah sighs heavily, sounding decades older. "David, you don't understand. Saul can't just send someone out there. Goliath is massive. He's a ruthless killer."

"He's just a Philistine. Surely the king can fight him. Or one of his sons."

"The king won't risk it."

"So, what do I tell Abba?" I'm cut off by a rumble traveling the length of the valley.

"Israel!"

I whip around, shocked at the way our country's name is hurled across the field like a curse. The army shudders collectively as the biggest Philistine I've ever seen strides into view, thundering threats that rumble through his armor.

"Are you spineless thralls ready to kneel before your new gods? Tell your precious Yahweh He's run out of time to save you from my hand. Dagon will have every last one of you between his teeth by sundown!"

His hatred rushes toward me with the fury of a hailstorm, eclipsing the army until it feels like he's looking right at me— every bit of darkness in him raging at the light that's surging and tossing in me like a wild tide. Even from a distance, I can see what the giant wants to do. Murder half of us and enslave the rest. He doesn't see the people of God. All he sees is a handful of sheep. I clench my fists, my veins gripped with fire.

Eliab pushes me, and I jolt as though I'm waking up from a horrible dream. Except the monster is still in the valley.

My oldest brother is trembling. "All right? Now you've seen him. Go back and tell Abba that things are slightly more complicated than we expected."

I gape at him, unable to hide my shock. He must be joking. I'm going to leave now and wait in Bethlehem to hear about Israel's defeat? "Why is it complicated?"

"What?"

"Who does this Philistine think he is, that he can defy the armies of the living God?" Shuddering from the sweep of fury, I barely get the words through my teeth.

Eliab's eye twitches. Abinadab's gaze travels down to the giant and back to me. "I'm pretty certain he thinks he's stronger than us."

"He's not stronger than Yahweh," I remind them, my fingers shaking.

"Are you saying we should send a priest to fight him?"

"No." They're not hearing what I'm saying. "Didn't you say the king promised to reward the man who fights the giant?"

"Yes, but..."

I turn to the other soldiers lined up nearby. "What did the king promise to do for the man who kills the Philistine?"

"Well, he mentioned tax exemption," one man mumbles. "Riches. And his daughter in marriage."

Another scoffs nervously. "But what good is a reward if you're dead?"

I restrain a smile. "None of you plan to win?"

Eliab groans aloud, his angry gestures strangling the air between us. "Can't you ever just be quiet? Why did you even come down here? Did you leave those few sheep with anyone, or did you just run away?"

"I—"

"This is a place for *men*, David. Soldiers." He rears over me, cords writhing in his neck. "This is a very serious situation, and now you come down here hoping to see a battle and lecturing us because we're not giving you something to gawk at. Don't pretend you thought this through because I know you didn't. Abba's tried to knock it out of you, but you're too full of pride and arrogance to hear anything but your own voice."

I fold my arms, standing my ground. His public outburst would be humiliating if I hadn't just heard a Philistine curse Yahweh's army to their faces. "I only asked a question, Eliab."

He turns away, pulling at his hair while Abinadab takes over. "David, I know you would like for things to be simple, just a big battle and it's over. But this man is too strong for that."

I shake my head. "No. No, he's not."

Standing here arguing with them is pointless. They don't understand. They haven't seen what I've seen. Felt what I've felt. There's only one way this is meant to end today. Turning back toward the camp, I start scanning the tents for the right one. At the edge of Judah's battalion, I spot two guards who nod in my direction, and I approach them.

"Where are you going?" Eliab calls after me, but I keep walking.

I'm done answering to them. I'm going to find someone who will listen. And believe.

ELEVEN

Jonathan

———◆◆◆——

"What do you mean, you're going out there?"

My father's expression is fierce enough to melt iron, but I can see the panic waiting just behind it. Stormy shadows hang beneath his eyes.

I hold myself rigid, refusing to let him see the fear tossing inside me.

"It's been forty days, Abba. Someone has to put a stop to this."

Grinding his teeth, my father grabs a stool and hurls it across the tent. "I *know* how long it's been! I've been counting too. Or don't you remember?" He holds his fingers in front of my face, listing. "On the tenth day, I offered riches. The twentieth day, I promised your sister in marriage. Then tax exemption...."

"And we're no closer to action than we were forty days ago! You can't buy this kind of victory." I step closer to him, allowing the shudder to slip back into my voice. "Abba, if I don't do something, I will lose my mind. I came here to fight, not sit in a tent listening to that monster rail at the armies of the Lord."

My father winces, turning his head as though my voice hurts him. "The Lord, yes. You always remind me. The armies of the Lord. And yet, where is He? Does He send us a champion, offer us solutions? No! He leaves us to this."

"He expects us to take action and do what we've been called to do—defend Israel!"

"How will sacrificing my son make us any safer?"

I clench my hands, my chest scalded with pent-up fury. "I would rather die with my sword in that Philistine's chest than with a spear in my back from running away." Suddenly, I'm struggling to see. "They're coming, Abba, whether we're ready or not. They want to push us into the wilderness, lay siege to our cities, and leave trails of blood behind them. I will *not* let that happen."

Just thinking of what my mother and sisters might suffer makes my anger run so hot, I can hardly think through the flames. Achish will march into Gibeah over my dead body.

My father blinks several times, shoving his arms within one another to hide his unsteadiness. "Just go choose someone else. Anyone. Find someone you think can come close to…"

"Abba, no one has come close!" I groan aloud. There's no one in our army who can match the giant's size or boldness. But there he is, in the valley, waiting. "We are the leaders of Israel. We can't run from this."

A sheen of moisture surfaces in my father's eyes. For a moment, I think he's going to break. Maybe send for the priests, proclaim a fast, inquire of the Lord. Something that gives us a chance. Still clenching his arms, he stares me down. His answer is hoarse and exhausted, but unyielding.

"I. Am. King. I do not answer to you."

Faced with a stone wall instead of a solution, I'm the one who breaks. Anger and frustration grab hold of me like wild things, and I storm from the tent, nearly running headlong into Ezra. "Get my armor."

My voice is harsh, but I can't control the tremors taking over the rest of me. You would think just this once, my father would have said something meaningful. When I could be going to my death. I walk faster, letting my fury build. The least I can do is unleash it on the giant.

Ezra jogs to keep up with me. "My lord, wait—"

"What?" I turn to him.

He points backwards. "You left your sword in the king's tent."

I have to go back in there? Swallowing a dozen curses, I pivot and make my way back through the camp. "Go get the rest of my weapons."

"Are you sure about this, my lord?" Ezra is frozen in place.

No. But— "I'm sure of what will happen if I do nothing."

I keep walking, hating how everyone cowers, hiding their faces from me. These past forty days have been a torment. The mightiest of Israel have become men who huddle inside their tents, polishing weapons that aren't being used. Even when the shouts from the valley die down, there's the endless chant of mockery in our heads. We've been given a clear chance to send the Philistines running, to deal them a potentially-fatal blow. Instead, I've watched the smoldering breath of fear sour into the stench of humiliation, and I'm sick of it.

I clench a prayer between my teeth. "Yahweh, what do you want from me? Do I stay? Do I go? This isn't how I planned to die."

I march into my father's tent ready for anything except what I find there. One of the soldiers from Bethlehem is waiting inside, along with… "David?"

The young shepherd turns around and bows to me, but not before I see his face. He's flushed all the way down his neck, and his eyes are burning so hot, their rich brown color is eclipsed.

My father wears a baffled expression while his commanders hide embarrassed smiles. "You remember…Jesse's son?" Abba waves a weary hand at the boy, then returns to rubbing his temples.

I just stand there, looking from one to the other. How can Abba keep forgetting David's name? And why is he here? Does my father think his harp playing will charm the giant away?

In the moment of awkward silence, Abner pushes into the tent, locks eyes with David, and almost curses. "In the name of…"

"Quiet, General." I take the edge of his robe and elbow him into a corner. Whatever this is, I want to hear it. But it turns out none of us are prepared.

David looks my father straight in the eye, his countenance crackling as though he's on fire. "Let no one's heart fail because of this Philistine, my lord. I will fight him."

"You…?" I feel all the air leave my lungs. And the room.

My father winces at me, raising his arms in the helpless gesture that's become all too familiar. "Say something," he mutters over my shoulder. "Help me get rid of him."

But Eliab's doing a good enough job there, trying to pull David toward the door while bending at the waist. "My lord, please forgive me—him. He's a zealous child, eager to fight, but he had no business coming here."

"Indeed." Abner moves to do something, but I tighten my hold, keeping him back. My heart is crashing fiercely, pushing up into my ears. It's as though the boy's zeal is leaping onto me.

My father lets out his breath in a single sharp exhale, his shoulders dropping. "It's bold of you to offer, my boy, but you can't go against that giant. You're only a shepherd. And a youth, for that matter. Goliath has been a brutal warrior since he was your age."

"Yes, of course, my lord." Eliab yanks on David's shoulder. "Get outside, now!"

"Calm yourself, Eliab." I wave him off, still trying to reconcile the image of the country youth playing music in my father's chambers with the fiery presence in the tent now. Even what I saw from him that day in Aijalon doesn't come close to this.

Undeterred, David appeals to my father again, passion exploding from his gestures. "It's true, your servant was a shepherd. When I was tending my father's flocks, a lion and bear came against them. I took hold of both, and killed them. The Lord God Almighty gave me His strength and delivered the predators into my hands." David's fingers shake, opening and closing involuntarily. "The same thing shall happen to this Philistine, for he has defied the armies of the living God!"

Barely restraining a shout, I turn my head to hide the inexplicable smile taking over my face. It's absurd, but this is the rescue we've been waiting for. David is the one whose spirit has been ignited by faith. Even in the midst of our cowering unbelief, the God of Israel sent us this boy, to see if we really want victory.

David stands tall, using every inch he has. "My lord, after today, that Philistine bear in the valley will never trouble the sheep of Israel again. Yahweh delivered me before, and He will do it today. Nothing stops the Lord from rescuing His people." His eyes touch mine. "By many or by few."

Oh, God.

I can barely see for excitement, but somehow my hand finds my father's wrist. When he looks at me, I make sure my eyes say everything I can't. *Let him go.*

My father sighs deeply, giving in. He lifts his hands and brings them down gently on David's head. "Then go. And may the Lord be with you."

Thank you, Yahweh. I'm consumed with amazement and gratitude, but my father's statement startles me out of it.

"You can't face the giant empty-handed, though. Abner, get him into my armor."

What? "Abba, *Ezra's* armor would be too big for him." I would laugh out loud if he wasn't serious, but my father's silencing glance speaks volumes. He's trying to make a point, convince the boy that this isn't a good idea.

"Let me handle this," he mutters.

For the next several minutes, it's a challenge for me to keep quiet. I don't know what's more ridiculous—the image of David lost to sight under my father's chain mail or the look on the king's face when he refuses to wear it.

David's more agitated than embarrassed, unbuckling each piece and tossing them onto the ground one by one. "I can't go in this. I'm not used to it."

I don't even try to repress a chuckle.

"Exactly." My father spreads his hands at the discarded armor. "This is what you would need in order to face Goliath. In addition to years of experience."

"I have all I need." David's fingers are wound around the strip of leather that always hangs from his wrist. I remember the way he'd made the stone fly through the camp last spring, crashing into the branches over Gera's head with enough force to break them.

"Let him go, Abba." I make sure my father is looking at me before adding, "The Lord is with him." Relief is crashing over me, washing away my doubt. Everything I was trying to apprehend last night is resting on this boy.

My father's mouth twitches as though he can't believe his own decision. But mercifully, he relents, his voice barely above a whisper. "All right."

"Thank you, my lord." David disappears without bowing, leaving an openmouthed Eliab to stumble after him.

As soon as they're gone, my father turns to gape at Abner. "What was that? Who is this boy?"

Abner's face is gray. "As you live, my king…I don't know."

"Find out, will you?" A familiar shadow is edging up into Saul's face, something I've seen far too often since Samuel left. And it chills me to my bones. Reaching behind him, I grab my sword and strap it on.

Saul turns around, flustered. "What are you doing?"

"Getting ready. One way or another, we're going to fight today." I'm finally ready to, and I can't tell him how good it feels. My weapon secure, I leave the tent without waiting for another word.

David is already halfway down into the valley, and his haste astounds me. Extreme confidence, level gaze, no hesitation. When was the last time I saw that on a man, for reasons other than mere battle exuberance? This is different.

He doesn't need my father's armor. He came here already possessing something, already knowing that whatever he'd find here would be easy for Yahweh to defeat. All those wasted days in the camp, arguing about what to do. With David, there was never a question.

Summoning Ezra and my brothers, I order the commanders to assemble with their thousands, ready to fight. I position myself at the front, keeping the shepherd boy in my sights.

Stopping by Elah's brook to collect stones, David stays on his knees only a moment, then straightens, turns, and salutes me. I return the gesture, my lungs burning. This is what we've been missing. Yahweh, Israel's true champion is down there with that boy, and I'm breathless in His presence.

TWELVE

David

———————◆◆◆◆◆———————

I kneel by the brook and watch the thin trickle of water slither between an assortment of rocks. Taking my time, I feel around in the moisture for the smoothest stones and weigh them in my hand, dropping five into the leather bag at my side. An undercurrent of awe runs beneath the passion in my veins.

So, this is why I needed to come here. Why everything was pulling me toward this battlefield. It's what Jonathan had told me to wait for. Yahweh's call.

I lift my head and fasten my eyes on the giant. Goliath isn't speaking yet, but his anger fills the space between us. I feel the surge again, white-hot yearning gripping me from all sides. Closing my eyes, I let prayers run through me, lifting from my mind like incense.

"Adonai, you have always been my Yeshu-hah, my deliverance. I sing for joy in the shadow of your wings. Give me this Philistine's life, and I will give you the rest of mine. You are the one and only Melek of Israel. Take back the honor that is due to your Name today, and let Israel glory in you again."

My face warms, sensing the *Ruach*. Yahweh's Spirit flashes past my shoulder, one word tangled up in a jolt of lightning. *Go.*

A rumble meets my knees from deep in the ground, traveling the width of Elah like thunder. I get to my feet and follow it into the valley.

Goliath doesn't notice me at first. He shifts his weight, repositioning his spear. He shields his eyes, squinting. Looks at his armorbearer, then back at me.

The darkest laugh I've ever heard starts deep in his chest, building until it erupts over my head in an explosion of mockery. He drags the king's name out, flinging it over the valley.

"*Saul!* Now I see what a coward you are! Sending a boy out here to run me off with a stick. What do you think I am, a dog?" Finished laughing, he drags his venomous gaze over my body. "At least your shepherd is willing to face his death head-on."

He advances a few steps, swooping his spear in circles that send bursts of air pushing toward me. "Did you come out here to challenge me, pretty boy? Come closer, and I'll give your flesh to the birds. The first of many sacrifices to Dagon."

The sound of the pagan god's name sends anger crackling through me like a shock of lightning. "You—" Heady with zeal, I choke a little, my voice slipping into the higher register I've been fighting for three years. Snagging it back, I clear my throat, making sure my words will carry over the field.

"You come to me with your sword and spear and javelin, but I come to you in the Name of the Lord of Hosts, the God of Israel's armies, whom you have defied. This day, Adonai will deliver you into *my* hands. I will kill you and cut off your head, and the armies of the Philistines will be food for the birds and the beasts…" I pause to breathe, the air singing in my chest, "…that all the earth may know that there is a God in Israel. And that the Lord doesn't need swords and spears to save His people."

Goliath scoffs, swirling his spear into position. "You obviously don't understand battle, Israelite."

I smile. "No. *You* don't. The battle is the Lord's, and He will give you into our hands." I can hardly contain what's pouring into me, filling me up. It's the fiercest certainty I've ever experienced.

Goliath's smirk fades, all the mockery sucked down into a pit of hatred. "Come to me then." He lifts his spear and takes two steps, half the valley disappearing under his stride.

I break into a run toward him, a stone already tucked between my fingers. In seconds, it's in the sling, and I flick my wrist into the series of spinning circles that snag momentum from the air. I squint, locking my eyes onto Goliath's forehead. I'd rather do it in one shot, but I have other stones if necessary. This giant will die today.

Adrenaline building with each twist of the sling, I lean into the breeze, sensing the shift in its direction. *Now.*

Leaping forward, I unfurl the sling with a snap, nearly going to my knees with the throw. The stone slices the sky, lodging perfectly in the center of the giant's forehead. Goliath's angry yell breaks off mid-breath, his helmet knocked askew as his head goes back.

Before the man can raise his spear another inch, it's slipping from his hand. His armorbearer crouches beneath his shield, barely avoiding the tree trunk as it drops. Goliath sinks to his knees, then collapses, shaking the earth under my feet with his fall.

The exuberant cries exploding behind me catch fire in my lungs, but I barely waste time breathing. Sprinting across the field, I reach the fallen giant in seconds, his nine-foot frame stretched out on the ground. His massive limbs are bent around him, and his breathing is shallow and labored. But nothing else is moving.

My foot braced in his side, I yank at his sword with both hands until the blade pulls free. I climb onto his back and hoist the weapon into position over his neck, my breath bursting out of me in wild gasps.

Releasing a shout that splits me down the middle, I bring the sword down on Goliath, throwing my whole weight into severing his head from his body. Once it breaks free, I stumble from the giant's back, the mighty cloud of vigor lifting off of me.

"Thank you, Adonai. Thank you. Thank you." I keep saying it, pain and power crashing into each other in my body.

Shaking on my hands and knees, I fall back against the ground and listen to the exultation of Israel.

THIRTEEN

Jonathan

———————◆◆◆◆◆———————

I know a victory cry when I hear one. The sound that explodes from David's lungs echoes what's inside me, and I roar with him. "The Lord our God is One!"

Israel's armies answer the cry from all sides, shaking the hills with their shouts. The lines of Philistines shudder, fear rippling through their ranks like a fin through water. Our thousands charge while our enemies scramble to escape, frantic and disillusioned. Even as I launch into battle, I'm almost swept to my knees by the gratitude coursing through my veins. Our God has not forgotten us!

I shout when I find David on the ground beside Goliath, trembling for all he's worth. "On your feet, giant-killer! The Lord is with us!" I loop my arm around his, pulling him up. David's chest heaves up and down, his eyes turning amber in the sunlight. I point at the fleeing Philistines, dropping weapons as they run. "Grab what you need and fight, my brother! God has given us the victory."

We pursue the Philistines west all the way to the gates of Ekron, where Achish disappears into hiding. Looping around through the Judean forests on our way back, we pounce on their camp, dragging away as much plunder as we can carry. Our warriors are exultant, their energy hardly expended even after a full day of battle. Back at our campgrounds in Ephes, the men rejoice, breaking into spontaneous worship. It's as though Israel lives again.

Watching the explosions of joy from Judah's ranks, my mind keeps pulling back to the small upper room where I'd knelt before Samuel. What he wouldn't clearly tell me then is obvious now. The God of Israel has taken David as His own. Yahweh's radiant power is unmistakable, fueling the boy beyond his natural strength, helping him do what everyone else wouldn't. I'll never forget the way David's eyes looked when he assured us of Yahweh's protection. If anyone is after God's heart, it's this Judean shepherd.

Now...what to do about it? Samuel had said not everyone would share my vision. Does that mean others won't notice who David is? Or that men will turn an evil eye on him? Before I can puzzle it out, I hear a disturbance inside my father's tent. Abba's voice is straining through the canvas walls.

"I don't care what you know, Abner! You need to find out more. I want to know whose son he is, in every sense. I want to know about his brothers, his cousins. What their ambitions are, where their loyalties lie..."

I push inside. "What's going on?"

"That's what I'm trying to figure out." My father paces, confronting something unseen. "He's a shepherd. He's *fifteen!* What kind of shepherd boy leaps into battle with no hesitation, like he knew what would happen?" He rubs his face. "I want to know more about this one, Abner."

"Of course, my king. I will find him at once."

I fold my arms, resenting the chill eroding my exuberance. "He's right outside, Abba. He's bringing the giant's armor."

Saul eyes his general. "Get him in here."

Abner pushes past me, and I face my father, incredulous. "Are you aware that we won?"

"Yes, we won. By the hand of a shepherd boy who plays the harp!"

"And?" Of course, he's choosing to be suspicious of the bravest man in our ranks. My father's twisted reaction to Michmash tickles the back of my mind.

Abner pushes David through the door and onto his knees, but the boy doesn't really need the shove. He's visibly exhausted, still clutching Goliath's head by the hair. My father struggles to produce a smile, but it's not making it through the lines of mistrust on his face. He leans back into the chair behind him, folding his hands over one knee.

"Israel's champion...a boy."

David's expression is frozen, unreadable. "Yahweh is the champion, my lord. He gave us the victory."

Just like that, the gate slams shut on my father's emotions. "Leave us, Jonathan. And take that with you." He points at Goliath's head, grimacing. "Go deal with the giant's armor. And tell the boy's family that he belongs to me now."

"My king...?" I hesitate.

"Go." Saul waves me out the door.

The hesitation in David's eyes makes me shudder. As I predicted, he's been thrown into the fire with little except his trust in Yahweh to prepare him. Whether or not he realizes it, everything is going to change. All of Israel will be watching him from this day forward.

Even though he fought for his God and his country, jealousy and false assumptions will still chase after him, trying to shred his confidence. Judah will turn David into a hero, while Benjamin will interpret the slightest hint of pride as rebellion. People will try to entice the boy with rewards in hopes of undermining the king. He'll gain false friends and fierce enemies, and most of the latter I could see coming from my own house.

Ezra appears on the heels of my thoughts, balancing Goliath's leg greaves under his arm. "Ever feel anything as heavy as this armor?" He tosses it on the ground, wiping sweat from his brow. "What's going on?"

I grimace. "David has given my father and Abner a lot to talk about."

"All of Israel will be talking. It was a miraculous victory. I expect we'll hear nothing else for a long time."

I search Ezra's face, but there's no hint of malice. Just relief. And some exhaustion. I touch his arm. "Go get some rest. I'll deal with this. We have to prepare for the journey home."

When Ezra's gone, I heft Goliath's sword into my hands, gripped by the image of David bringing it down on the giant. Heavy memories push over me. My own first battle, though glorious, had enlisted me in a lifetime of struggle. The road is never easy, but Yahweh remains faithful.

Breathing deeply, I feel gratitude returning. Our God sent us a warrior who will fight His battles and win. And that's a cause I can give my life to. We need this boy to remind us what we're fighting for—and the One who goes before us. If we can hold fast to that, we might have a chance to become all we were meant to be.

Once I have the giant's armor stowed in a tent, I remove my heavy scarlet robe and hang it over my arm. I collect my bow and my sword, and go to look for David. I finally know how to help Israel, even from a throne that's no longer mine. I can offer myself in friendship, give him the knowledge and favor of my position as long as I have it. I'd do far more after what he did today. I'll stand at his side, even if I'm the only one. But something tells me I won't be.

I find David kneeling outside my father's tent like a prisoner, fiddling with his sling. Head bent, shoulders caved in, he looks as though he's taken a beating, though not physically.

I stop in front of him. "What happened?"

"I don't know." David speaks stiffly, trying to comprehend his own words. "I'm not returning to my father's house. I'm going with you to Gibeah. And I'm forbidden to leave. The king has taken me into his service. He made me swear an oath of loyalty."

I frown. Slaying the giant should have been proof enough of that. It shames me to imagine my father berating the boy after he'd just saved us all.

"I can't even send messages to my parents. The king wants to see any communication between us." David is still avoiding my gaze, twisting the sling around his wrist. "I don't understand."

I clench my teeth, hating the words I have to say. "He's afraid."

David's eyes lift to mine. "Still?"

"Yes. Still. When it's a way of life, David, fear is no longer based on logic. It seeks to poison everything. He doesn't understand what happened today, and that frightens him."

"But what does he need to understand? Yahweh was my deliverance. He gave me the strength to kill Goliath. That's all. *You* see it, don't you?" David's voice shakes, slightly hoarse, and he blinks back the glisten in his eyes.

I stretch out my hand. "Follow me."

David pulls himself up and falls into step beside me, his eyes edging over to the pile of belongings under my arm. "Why are you carrying all that? Did Ezra quit?"

I chuckle. "No. These are for you."

"What?"

"Here." I hold the door to my tent open and nod for David to enter. Lining everything up on the ground between us, I drape my red robe over his shoulders and double-knot the cords in the front so that it will fit him.

David searches my face. "What are you doing?"

"Making you a king's son." I place my hands on David's shoulders. "You are now my brother. These gifts will be a sign to everyone that when they look at you, they should think of me, and treat you with the respect you always deserved. It's the least I can do for the one Yahweh has honored with His presence."

David gapes at me, his eyes flooding. Barely breathing, he stares at the armor on the ground. But I'm not finished.

"There's more." I straighten, releasing a slow breath. "I want to swear an oath of loyalty. To you. I would pledge a covenant with you." I hold out my hand. "Brothers. Before God."

David's head comes up, and I can see the fear enter his face. He knows what I'm requesting, and it's a serious move. The bond of brothers is an oath of surety, based on the actions of our ancestor Judah, who had offered up his own life for his younger brother centuries ago in Egypt. It's deeper than blood, a vow taken before God. It would bind us together, requiring us to protect each other with our own lives, and be accountable to Yahweh for the fact.

David fumbles with the fringe on the robe, his pulse shoving wildly against his throat. "My lord…"

"Jonathan."

A smile darts across his face, but he shakes his head. "Jonathan, you don't…there's something you don't know, and I…I need to…"

I hold up my hand to stop him. "I know all that I need to know, David. There will be plenty of time to talk about everything else Yahweh plans to do." Samuel's words burn in my mind. "But for now, this is what *I* have to do. And when it's clear what action I must take, I don't like to waste time. Brothers?" My hand is still open before him.

David blinks, shaking off hesitation. "Of course, my— brother," he laughs, stumbling over the words. "Jonathan."

I clasp his arms, feeling Yahweh's cords tightening around us. "Before Adonai, I promise that my hand will never be raised against you."

"Nor mine against you." David squeezes my forearms, and I see the fire wake up in his eyes again.

I turn him toward the door. "We'll offer sacrifices before heading back to Gibeah. I've placed Goliath's armor in your tent."

"My tent?"

"Where else would I put it? It's rightfully yours. Just think, for years to come, you will be able to carry that sword into battle and mock Achish with it."

David laughs. "That reminds me." He reaches into his shepherd's bag and pulls out two gemstones that burn with a deep red hue. "These are for you."

I take them, weighing them in my hand. "Where did you get these?"

"From the jeweled clasp around Goliath's belt." He hands them over with a crooked smile. "For the two arrows."

Emboldened by gratitude, I laugh out loud and crush him in my arms.

FOURTEEN

David

———◆◆◆———

L ong before we reach Gibeah, we're met by exuberant crowds. Men of Benjamin and families from the neighboring cities run ahead of us to Saul's fortress, waving branches and banging tambourines. By the time we've entered the city, the roar of Israel's exultation is deafening. The soldiers' joyous shouting mingles with the broken, tearful sounds of reuniting families. Children are lifted onto shoulders, screaming to be heard, and women dance openly in the streets.

I take it all in like I'm peering through gates that have been locked tight for so long. But a strain of caution pulls at me beneath all the wonder. The same festivities will erupt in Bethlehem when they hear the news, though they won't be quite as lavish. But my family will feel the same trepidation that's edging my shoulders when they hear that Saul has taken me. Everything will be different now.

Saul's tight, cautious manner is more receptive now that he's home. He spreads his arms wide, grinning at each person who screams his name. Watching him and Jonathan, I feel pride rising, as though I'm following a father and brother. This isn't the first time they've returned in triumph from battling our enemies. Saul's kingship has turned our army into an impressive force. But it wasn't our armies that sent Philistia running. Not this time. *Praise your Name, Yahweh. The Victory is yours.*

I'm grateful to be riding. My mount seems to be the only thing keeping me from being pulled apart by the crowds. Heat climbs my neck when I catch my own name being shouted right alongside Saul's. Pressure builds, shoving pleasure aside as I pull certain words out of the noise. They're calling me a champion, and their praise carries a strange presence, introducing sensations that I never had to consider in the pastures.

Does everyone think I deserve this? Or are they putting on a show for the king? How much have they heard about what really happened? Jonathan called me a king's son. But from what I've seen of his life, that role carries more danger than privilege. I've never had to grapple with any of this before, and it's troubling.

Somehow, Jonathan's voice reaches me over everyone else's. "You'll get used to it."

I relax my grip on the reins, adjusting my expression to match the prince's. I wonder how long it took before this became commonplace for him. Michmash had made Jonathan larger than life even though he was only fourteen and following the Lord. As hard as it is to believe, there was a time when Saul's family wasn't used to being honored.

The story goes that when Samuel announced Saul as king, Saul was in hiding, hesitant to assume a role of leadership among the people. He'd refused praise, even after his massive victory against Ammon united Israel under him. But years later, after his campaign against Amalek, Saul had ordered a monument built in his honor even though he hadn't fully obeyed the Lord. Samuel had refused to come back after that, and the men of Judah say that was the breaking point, the moment Saul's respect for God fell away. Was it fame that had done that to him? A yearning for approval?

My stomach tightens when I hear the women's songs, ascribing tens of thousands to me, and only thousands to Saul. In the pastures, focus on Yahweh was easy. Here, I'm going to need to sharpen it like a weapon every day if I don't want to lose my footing.

The fortress walls drop welcome shadows over us, holding back the heat, and Jonathan grips my shoulder. "Welcome home, brother."

I return his smile, baffled by Yahweh's kindness. After being ignored by seven brothers for fifteen years, God has given me friendship with the king's son.

As we dismount, Saul lifts his hand to three women standing on the balcony over the courtyard. Saul's wife Ahinoam touches her lips and waves back. Her relief is evident, even from a distance. The two others are Saul's daughters, the Sarrahs of Israel.

The princesses are older than I am. I'm told Jonathan's youngest sister Michal is almost nineteen, but she acts much younger. When she sees us, she lifts up onto her toes, waving wildly.

Jonathan laughs. "We'd better go to my sister before she takes flight."

His hand on my shoulder guides me through the crowds like a boat plowing through water. We've barely made it up onto the porch before Michal throws her arms around her brother's neck, squealing. "I knew you would do it! The best victory we've had in ages!"

Jonathan shrugs her off, chuckling. "Easy, Michal. David killed the giant, not me."

Barely out of his arms, she grabs my shoulders. "Praise be to Yahweh for your courage." She kisses my cheek, barely deterred by her mother's voice.

"Michal! Contain yourself."

Saul's wife is flushed with embarrassment, but I can tell everything in her wants to react the same way. "Welcome home, my son."

She hugs Jonathan regally, burying her immense relief into his shoulder. Her older daughter does the same, whispering through a serene smile. "Brother."

I've dropped behind Jonathan, grateful to be invisible for a moment. In all the months I served the king, I'd only seen Saul's wife and daughters once or twice. We'd definitely never spoken. When the queen's attention shifts, I kneel on the pavement, but Jonathan pulls me back up.

"Eema, this is David ben Jesse of Bethlehem. The killer of Goliath."

Ahinoam's eyes expand, her polite calmness dropping away. "Your father sent *him* to kill the giant?"

"Adonai sent him." Jonathan puts his arm around my shoulder. "He's Israel's newest champion. And my newest brother."

A dozen emotions surge into his mother's face, and the last one to enter is the most serious. "You mean…before Yahweh?"

Jonathan nods. "Before Yahweh."

Her eyes shift down to Saul, deep in conversation with their other sons in the lower courtyard. "Does your father know?"

"Not yet."

"Will he mind?"

"I'll find out."

I can tell Jonathan's answers aren't completely satisfying his mother, but she hides her misgivings in a wide smile. "You are very welcome here then, David."

Merab narrows her eyes at me, clearly not as comfortable as her sister. Michal leans up to Jonathan's ear, excited conspiracy dancing in her tone. "You're bolder than I thought. Make sure you tell Abba in front of everyone, that way you're safe."

Jonathan shrugs her off. "I'll tell him when I tell him."

Michal smirks. "Suit yourself." When she aims it at me, her bright smile pulls heat into my face. "Welcome to the strangest family in Israel."

I smile back, but I feel more nervous in front of her than I did on the battlefield. She's friendly and welcoming, but I doubt I'll ever be able to talk to her.

I'm relieved when I finally make it into an empty room—one that's now mine. No more sleeping among the king's weapons, Jonathan said. I manage to keep a neutral expression, but eventually he'll figure out how strange this is for me. It'll be the first time I've slept on anything besides the ground, the first time I've owned something other than my lyre.

I watch in silence while the prince orders people around, bringing in clothes and armor and spreading it all on the bed. Once I'm left alone, I stand there staring at all the gold pieces the king sent in. How do I belong here?

I remember my first day in this fortress, feeling trapped and uncertain, wondering if I would ever know what Yahweh expected of me. Facing Goliath, I was filled with faith, and the accompanying power was exhilarating. Everything I've ever dreamed of had been bound up in one moment. Now what?

Trust your Shepherd.

The faith stirred by my mother's advice eases the reality that I won't see her for some time. I know the separation will be hard for her. Hopefully the rest of my family will hold their peace and not interpret these events as license to reveal anything. I'm still Saul's servant, and he has to see me that way.

Keep me in your will, Adonai.

I'm still standing there when Jonathan returns. "The feasting will begin soon. I'm pretty certain you'll have to be there."

I turn around. "I'm ready."

Jonathan just laughs. "No, you're not. Here." He reaches for a gold medallion, a pendant with the face of a lion at the end of a thin chain.

I lift my brows. "I have to wear that?"

He slips it over my head and follows it with a ring on my finger. Then he slides a thin gold band into my hair. "These are gifts from the king. He will expect to see them on you."

No doubt to remind me that I'm his.

Jonathan stands back, assessing me. "How does it feel to be a prince of Israel?"

I shrug. "I feel like a shepherd wearing your clothes."

Jonathan's face changes, but I can see that my honesty doesn't bother him. "You're Yahweh's warrior. That's what you've always been. Don't worry about everything else. You're in His keeping. And mine."

I sigh, glancing out the window where that ridiculous song is still filling the streets. "All this commotion for something that we could never have done without Him."

His smile returning, Jonathan leads me to the door. "You'll have to teach them better songs. You brought your harp, didn't you?"

"Yes." I rarely go anywhere without it.

On our way to Saul's lavish banquet hall, we're joined by the king, leading his wife by the arm. Their sons and daughters follow, flanked by servants.

Saul barely greets Jonathan before his attention cuts to me. "Quite a transformation."

I bow all the way to the ground. "You do me too much honor, my king."

Satisfied, Saul motions for me to stand. "I know how to reward raw courage. It's something my kingdom needs more of. You'll be a valuable asset in time. But don't worry. You'll always be a shepherd."

When the king looks away, I glance at Jonathan, wondering if I should read a double meaning in Saul's words. But the prince is completely distracted, his gaze drifting over his sister's servant before snapping back to the floor. It's the first time I've seen Jonathan unable to look someone in the eye. The servant girl doesn't stare openly at him either, the way most women do. Her attempt at a smile disappears as quickly as it bloomed.

"Someone you know?" I whisper once everyone is moving again.

Jonathan waits until the king is several steps ahead. "She's the sister of Ziba, one of my father's servants."

"Is that all?"

Jonathan's face tightens. "By order of the king, yes. That's all."

That night's feasting stretches into the next day, with plans for a weeklong celebration to follow. Saul keeps me by his side, recounting the battle in detail and watching carefully for people's reactions. I say very little except in song. Ascribing honor to Yahweh fills me with fresh purpose, reminding me I'm His servant first.

The only person who ignores me completely is Saul's youngest son Ish-Bosheth. Still much older than I, he rarely follows his father into battle. When I ask why, Jonathan rolls his eyes. "He's grown up a prince. He's the only one of us who exalts pleasure over purpose, and he's the only one who can get away with that."

Perhaps because it's unlikely that he'll ever rule. He is Saul's youngest.

Eliab's old taunts follow the thought, winding their way through the excitement.

Melek. You?

I've barely seen my brothers and relatives in the past week, but whatever their opinions, I know I have to put them aside. The next king of Israel is God's choice, not mine.

At one point during the second day's feast, Jonathan leans over to whisper in his father's ear, and the king's eyes fasten themselves on me, his face tightening. He continues to watch me all evening from behind glass after glass of wine, shadows gathering in his face as the night drops darkness outside.

Finally, Jonathan touches him. "Get some rest, Abba. It's been a long day."

Saul inhales sharply, sitting up, and Jonathan takes the cup from him. Several servants approach, but the king waves them off. "David will assist me."

I know what he's asking. The torturous buildup to the battle followed by the drive of the celebration is likely wearing on him. Reaching behind me, I grab my harp and follow the king into the dark.

Unsteady, he leans heavily on my shoulder, his words labored. "You know what you've done, boy? You've brought Israel back from the dead. And you've secured their affections forever. They all love you now."

I keep silent. The people's praises are overblown, but Jonathan assures me that's typical. Surely the king knows that the favor of the masses is fleeting at best. We fight for something much greater.

The shadows are long and sharp in Saul's chambers, the shapes of his swords and spears wavering in the torchlight. The king eases onto the edge of his bed, a hoarse laugh escaping him. "Tens of thousands…you've barely fought one battle."

Still not answering, I help the king with his cloak and then kneel on the floor, my harp propped securely against my body.

Saul blinks, focusing. "That robe…it's Jonathan's."

"He gave it to me, my lord."

The king makes a soft sound. With the torchlight flickering on his face, it's hard to make out his expression. "He told me he's made you his brother. He's...something else."

He's not pleased; I can tell. Something lurks between us tonight, hanging on the edges of the room. I can't decide what I should say, but it also feels wrong to stay quiet.

Saul's eyes keep drifting, turning darker, but every few seconds, he'll blink, as if waking up. He leans his head back against a cushion. "Just play. I'm tired."

Leaning over the harp, I can feel my heart humming anxiously into the wood. I try to relax, wondering if the king will be able to sense the caution in my playing. Aaron's words come back to me, laced with warning. *What if the king knew the bravest man in his kingdom was a shepherd?*

Alarm elbows its way into my thoughts. *You can't charm away anger with notes and chords. A king's wrath is worse than a burning city.*

But with the first note, I remember. This isn't the time to fear. Goliath is dead. The victory was from Yahweh, and He will be praised. The king will not suffer disquiet—not if I can help it. Breathing deeply, I play past the discomfort, stringing words of quiet praise and hope into the music.

"The Lord is enthroned on our praises. In His mercy, He grants peace to His king, and to His anointed forever."

I picture the wide expanse of the pastures, where praise has always held back the dark. The battle against fear is one I know well. Yahweh has taught me how to fight it.

Several moments later, I catch myself awake, grabbing the lyre before it can slip from my hands. Surprised that I dozed off, I glance at the patch of sky out the window. The faint stars signal twilight, but it's not dark enough to see them clearly yet. I should leave before the light is gone. I uncurl my legs, feeling immediately how long I've been sitting. I wonder if I should head back across the fortress or try to find my relatives among the soldiers camped in the fields outside.

I look up, and my heart stops. Saul is awake, staring at me from his bed. My muscles lock around the lyre, resisting the sudden sweep of danger rushing over me. I had thought the king was asleep. He still might be, even now. But his eyes are open, silent scrutiny seething straight through me.

"You..." He blinks, and I realize he's moving. Slowly, almost imperceptibly, muscle by muscle. Like a lion stalking. "It's *you*...?"

My fingers bite into the harp's wood as a gripping cold takes over, ice riding every heartbeat. I didn't feel anything like this facing Goliath. *He's dreaming. Please be dreaming.*

Saul's dark shape moves across the floor, avoiding the shaft of light from the window. I can't tell how close he is until he knocks the harp from my hands and grabs me, his huge hand locking around my neck. "It's you!" Lifting me off the ground, he slams me into the wall, nearly spitting in my face. "*You're* the one Samuel anointed! The one with such a pure heart—*aren't you?*"

I stumble to the ground against the opposite wall, trying to force full breaths up into my aching throat. Saul rears over me, his eyes blacker than the night. "You dare to bring treachery into my house? You lying messenger of evil!"

Grabbing my hair, he hauls me forward, slamming me into the wall again. This one has a door in it, and my face connects with the metal lock. Moaning, I drop to the ground, every instinct screaming at me to fight back. *God, God!*

I don't want to fight Saul, but I can't win against the king unless I use his own weapons against him, something I'd vowed I wouldn't do. I have to get out of this room.

Ducking away from his attacks, I throw myself across the floor, seize my harp, and stagger to my feet, only to look back into two eyes of pure hatred, two hands clutching a spear. In a frozen second, I know I've made the wrong choice. I should have grabbed a weapon for defense, not my harp for escape. Saul has plenty of room to impale me, and nothing to stop him.

I barely restrain a scream as Saul hefts the tree trunk over his shoulder. "I'll kill you!"

The air groans around the heavy weight of his weapon as he flings it across the room. I drop to my knees, and it crashes into the wall behind me, sending a shudder through everything. Panting, Saul looks around wildly as pieces of dried brick and plaster come loose, crumbling to the ground on either side of me.

"David?" He blinks, barely able to breathe my name. Before I can force myself to move, Saul crosses the room and grabs me again. "David!"

"My lord, please!" I struggle against him, terrified. "Whatever Samuel said, it's not a matter of life or death! If I offended you, I'll go, but please…"

"No! No—David!" Saul takes my face in his hands and holds it close in front of his own as if he can't see me clearly. The anger in his eyes is dissolving, a sorrowful tide taking over. "David! David!" Shaking violently, he touches me all down my shoulders, my chest, my face, checking feverishly to see if anything is broken on me.

"I'm sorry! I'm sorry—I didn't know!" He crushes me against his chest. "I didn't mean to hurt you! It's Samuel! I raged at Samuel! You mean me no harm. It's the anointed one who means to, but—you're no harm at all." He breaks down into wild weeping. "What have I done?"

Groaning, he lets me go and collapses fully onto the floor. "Why must I suffer like this? Why won't he come back? I deserve respect for all I've done. But he will take vengeance on me, kill my sons, destroy my honor! He will take my throne and give it to..." His words cave in, and he looks at me again, deeply, dragging sobs in and out. I grab his sleeve before he can decide to attack again.

"My lord, you have nothing to fear. You are the king, and I am your servant. I won't leave you." I say it through my own fear that's twisting me inside out.

Saul's face shudders. His empty eyes remind me of a wounded animal, too anxious for trust. "You won't leave me?" Clinging to my arms, he begs, his words jumbled. "Jonathan didn't. I tried to kill him, but he—he wouldn't leave. He's my son. I love you like that. You won't leave, will you?"

He tried to kill Jonathan? My stomach is tossing, and I want to be anywhere else, but compassion pushes through my fear, and I kneel in front of Saul, holding his gaze. "No, my king. I will not leave you."

Another deep cry splits him in two. He presses his head against my chest, and I hold him while he sobs, a powerful ache settling into my heart. All this suspicion and torment is so unnecessary. It threatens everyone he loves and holds him back from the God who could give him comfort if he would only repent and stop fighting. No crown, no dynasty is worth this.

After a while, he staggers to his feet as though he weighs a thousand pounds. "Go," he says to me. His voice is flat, all the strength drained out of it.

I push off the floor, resisting the urge to run.

"Wait." Saul stands there, sucking in shallow breaths, gazing at the spear in the wall. "Don't tell Jonathan about this."

Setting my teeth against my own wild breathing, I nod once. "I promise."

"I didn't mean to hurt you. You know that?"

I'm not sure at all. But I just nod again. "Yes, my king."

Saul's shoulders heave up and down several times. "You can go." As soon as I turn my back, the king's voice changes. "When the traitor does appear, I will not miss."

He's made my decision for me. Panic building, I make my way through the fortress, hoping to avoid Abner. Once I reach the outer gate, I break into a run, and the cool night air rushing toward me steadies my nerves. My eyes search the banners frantically for Judah's, and I approach the camp, trying to settle myself. Most of the tents are dark, but one man is crossing between them, adding wood to a large fire.

"David!" The moment our eyes meet in the firelight, the smile drops from Joab's face. "What's wrong?"

"I'm just—I'm staying out here tonight. Is that allowed?" I walk to the other side of the fire, hating the way my voice is shaking.

Joab shrugs, angling his head at his two sleeping brothers stretched out on the ground nearby. "We expected you earlier. Where have you been?"

"Saul wanted me to play for him." I crouch by the fire and close my eyes against the smoke, hoping the warmth will kill the deep coldness gripping my bones.

Joab can feel it though, even from two feet away. He snorts, making the same sound he always does when Saul's name is mentioned. "So, you save Israel, and now Saul owns you?" He kicks a salient branch deeper into the flames. "One of these days that fool will have to make do without you."

"And one of these days, you'll have to learn some respect for the ones God has chosen." I stretch out on my side, leaning into one elbow.

Joab sits down next to me. Too close. "You know I only speak the truth that everyone else is afraid to."

"Sometimes a little fear is good." I look over my shoulder at him. My first mistake.

Sparks ignite his eyes. "What happened to your face?"

"Nothing." I'd forgotten that there would be a mark from where Saul had slammed me into the door. And probably bruises around my neck too.

Joab rears into a sitting position. "I saw you after the battle, David. And for seven days afterwards. You weren't bruised then." His voice turns to iron. "Did he hit you?"

"Of course not!" I push away from him, resenting the anxiety pulsing in my throat. "Please, Joab. I came out here for a little peace."

"David!" Jonathan's voice jumps in my chest. I get to my feet before he can step into the light.

Joab looks up without moving. "What do you want?"

"Joab!" I turn on him, disgusted. "He's the Hassar, not some little brother. On your feet!"

"My apologies, Great One." He stands and bows, but the gesture is full of disdain. "I wasn't aware we would see you again tonight. Is there more the king wants from David?"

My fingers itch to punch him. I roll my eyes at Jonathan. "Don't pay any attention to him. He's probably drunk."

Jonathan clears his throat, his face tight. "Forget it. What are you doing out here?"

"I just needed to be outside tonight."

"Are you all right?"

For the first time, I wish Jonathan didn't see so much. "Yes. I'm just tired."

"You're tired," Jonathan repeats, unconvinced. "And that's why you haven't looked at me once since I came out here?"

I sigh and lift my head, praying half of my face stays hidden. "I'm looking at you."

The moment our eyes meet, Jonathan's face changes. Without breaking my gaze, he pushes my lyre into my hands. "I found it in Abba's bedchamber. Across the room."

Which means he saw the spear. The ice creeps back into my chest.

"Please, Jonathan," I whisper. "Not tonight."

Everything in his face wants to argue, but instead he lifts his chin. "All right. We'll talk tomorrow."

I watch him walk away, then wind my fingers in my hair. How foolish of me to think I could keep this from him. Why would I promise something like that? Does the king think his son is completely unaware? I return to the fire and ease back onto the ground. I still have to deal with my nephew. I can feel the wheels turning in his head, picking up speed.

"David, do I strike you as stupid?" Joab asks, his voice hard.

"No." Unfortunately.

"Then why do you think you can hide so much from me?" His eyes are burning the side of my face that the fire isn't. "You think I haven't noticed that everything's been completely different since Samuel came to Bethlehem?"

"What do you mean?" I try to sound bored, but my heart is racing. "That was a year ago."

"Exactly. And in that year, you've been transformed from a shepherd boy into the kingdom's most famous warrior while Saul's face gets darker and darker. He looks at you like he wants you dead!"

I shift on the ground. "Joab, that's ridiculous. He's tense after the battles. You know that. It's why I play for him."

"Don't be a fool. That wasn't tension seething from him at the feast tonight. That was hate I saw in his eyes, David!"

I keep my eyes on the flames, willing myself to forget the rage I'd felt in Saul's fingers. "You only say that because you've never liked him. Why would he hate me, Joab?"

"You tell me." Joab moves around in front of me, bending so that our eyes are level. "The Roeh came to Jesse's house only a couple days before Saul's men showed up."

"Yes. Samuel came to sacrifice to the Lord."

Joab nods. "That's what your brothers told me. And it doesn't add up. Everything changed about you that day."

I swallow, my eyes filling. "He brought the presence of the Lord, Joab. That does change everything."

Joab's eyes spark. "And what *specific* change did His presence bring, David?"

I close my eyes, rubbing my forehead. Why does he have to be so smart? I can feel it the moment it hits him.

He pushes off the ground. "God above! He anointed you, didn't he?" He grabs my shoulder, forcing eye contact. "David ben Jesse—it's *you?* You're the next king of Israel?"

Jerking from his grasp, I clap my hand over his mouth, but it's too late. It's all catching fire in his mind, and the flames will be burning for a long time.

"For God's sake, keep quiet! You can't say that out loud, especially here."

He grabs my wrist, freeing his mouth. "But it's true. You're the king Yahweh chose over Saul! He has given the kingdom back to Judah!"

"Not yet! In case you haven't noticed, Saul is still on the throne. It might be years before…"

"Don't say that!" Joab shakes me, excitement coursing through him. "You have Yahweh's blessing—it's obvious. Everyone saw it in Elah. And you have private access to the king." He leans closer. "You can free us as soon as you choose."

Immediately, I can feel frustration insinuating itself into my fear. He's known my secret for two seconds, and already he's advising me to assassinate Saul. And if I don't, he just might. *Yahweh, hold him back. Put a shield around Saul and Jonathan.*

I study my older nephew, a thousand thoughts running through my mind. All my life, he's treated me like a little brother who can't take care of himself. But if he's going to be burdened with this secret, he's going to have to see me differently.

Roughening my voice against tremors, I focus everything into the forbidden excitement in his face. "Joab ben Zeruiah, if you believe that Yahweh has anointed me king, then listen to me now. Before I faced Goliath, I vowed that I would never harm Saul or Jonathan. For now, I am content to fight the Lord's battles beside them. Other than that, Yahweh has not revealed what I am to do yet, and I refuse to step ahead of Him."

I catch a breath, continuing, "If you or anyone else takes it upon yourself to force this into the open, people will die. I refuse to be responsible for needless bloodshed or for the curse of casting off Yahweh's instruction. We will keep our heads and *wait on Him.* If you touch Saul or Jonathan without my permission, I will never see your face again. Do I make myself clear?"

Joab studies me, his face glowing like the embers next to us. He's still barely controlling himself, but at least he's heard me. He breathes, his tone full of awe.

"My God. Now we're getting somewhere."

FIFTEEN

Jonathan

———◆——

I cross the threshold of my father's antechamber, resenting the apprehension crawling after me. The last thing I should be doing is preparing to confront a battle within my family. We should be rallying our forces on the momentum of David's victory, planning our next move. News of Goliath's death will reach all our enemies and strike fear into their hearts. For the first time in decades, we have the chance to become a superpower in this region—if we stop seeing enemies in our own ranks.

But as usual, my father is taking another path.

Oil lamps and torches glower around Saul. The king's gaze is piercing the unfurled maps trapped on the table between his fists, and it takes every shred of my control not to confront him here and now. A spear in the wall of his bedchamber can only mean one thing. He tried to kill David. He tried to murder a defenseless boy who was playing the harp. Israel's champion, no less. The senselessness makes my blood burn.

Abner enters the room from the other side, his manner strained. "You sent for us, my king?"

My father's breathing is labored. "I need your opinion before I announce anything to the others." He lifts his eyes, but not his head. "Abner, what have you found out?"

Abner hedges, picking at the edge of the table. "It's not ideal. He's of Judah, which means he's been raised among ambitious men. There's no open talk of rebellion among his family, but he has three grown nephews who are very likely spies for the resistance. You know their presence is stronger in the south."

"If you're talking about those tax evaders who hide out in the hills, that's nothing to worry about." I'm struggling to keep an even tone. "I've come across them before, and believe me, they're nothing but stragglers, malcontents. They don't have any real leadership."

"That doesn't mean we should rule them out as a threat." Abner's glance weighs a thousand pounds.

"What does that have to do with David?" I ask.

"Everything." My father's whisper cuts through the warmth in the room, and a chill slinks up my arms.

Abner's voice tightens. "Also, there's rumors all over Bethlehem that he's a bastard son. Born to Jesse of some servant girl."

I don't believe what I'm hearing. We were farmers from the smallest tribe in Bethlehem when Adonai anointed my father. "How much does that matter now? Jesse claimed him, didn't he?"

Abner shrugs. "Apparently, but for years, he's kept the boy in the pastures, hidden away. It's something to consider."

I turn from the table, threatening to leave the room. "This is nonsense. You're wasting our time with all this. If you want to see some real threats, go to Gath. There are plenty more where Goliath came from. We should be strengthening our allies, not picking them apart with suspicion."

"Watch your tone, Hassar." My father's rebuke is like a fist. Still. I've learned not to flinch under his gaze, but I still hate when he looks at me like he's sighting an arrow.

Saul leans into the table. "You gave that boy your robe and weapons and then announced at the feast that you've taken him as your brother—all without consulting me. What do you think David will do with all those gifts?"

"I think he's going to wear them." My attempt at a smile withers under the king's stare.

"Don't play at words with me. You know what I'm saying."

I squint, trying to find something reasonable in Saul's face. "He's Israel's champion. Did you expect him to arrive in Gibeah in the same clothes he wore into battle?"

"He could have borrowed something from his brothers. You treated him like royalty, and the people can't unsee that."

I fold my arms. I hate not knowing which version of my father I'm going to talk to on any given day. "He's part of our family now. You gave your word at Elah."

Abner gapes. "You can't seriously think your father is going to give one of your sisters to him!"

My father rears back, affronted. "Offering Merab was an incentive to encourage one of the men to fight. No one expected that shepherd songwriter to show up."

I smile into his agitation. "But he did. And Yahweh gave us a great victory."

Abner comes around the table. "A victory, yes. But now all the kingdom's attention will be on a shepherd boy instead of their king, and such overnight favor with the people cannot be controlled. They'll start expecting the king to elevate and reward him—Judah, especially. And who's to say he can be trusted with that? What made him think he could pull this out of our hands?"

"The same thing I was thinking at Michmash. Yahweh called, and I obeyed. End of story."

The minute I say the words, I wish I hadn't. It wasn't the end of the story. The king had tried to get rid of me that day, just like he'd tried to kill David. The chilling irony eats through my certainty like frost.

I look past Abner to the king, forcing calm respect into my tone. "David is under my protection. I didn't make him anything he wasn't already."

After a few baffled seconds, my father relents. "Fine. You want him? You can have him."

Abner starts to interject, but my father holds up his hand, his tone lightening. "No, my son is right. The people were pleased with the way we embraced David. He's a bold fighter, and we could do much worse than try to harness that potential. If his ambition is expended fighting my battles, it won't have cause to reach anywhere else."

He directs a command at me, his eyes sparking. "When you reassemble my forces against Philistia, you will take the boy with you. Train him. Make him serve under Abner, but don't shield him. Let him get a taste of what real fighting is like." His direction shifts to his general. "And watch him. Make sure he intends to fight for us. There's only one way to determine if God is really with him, and that is to let him prove it. In combat."

My mouth is dry. "When, my lord?" It's almost Passover, one of our most sacred feasts commemorating when Yahweh brought us out of Egypt.

"The Philistines who fled the battle will likely try to regroup somewhere in the south once they get orders from Achish," Abner ventures, watching my father closely. "It would be wise to strike soon, take more ground while our enemies are in disarray."

Saul nods, slapping the table in my direction. "You will go as soon as possible. Take my forces and your brothers' thousands to the training grounds and prepare them."

"During the feast, my lord?" I venture carefully.

Saul groans, rubbing his forehead. "Observe Passover and then go. As soon as you find out where the Philistines have regrouped, strike there. If you're successful, you can be back before the firstfruits of the barley harvest."

I'm torn. It's a clear chance for David to prove himself, but will he perform the same way under a different kind of pressure? "My lord, are you certain that…?"

"Of course I'm certain! He wants to fight, doesn't he?" My father sounds a step below frantic. "I want him out of my sight, Jonathan. I can't have him sitting here playing that harp and reminding me…" He pauses to breathe, his knuckles white against the table. "Just get him out of here until I can figure this out."

A new desperation writhes in his face. He's not calling out for help anymore, for someone to come sing praises over his fears. He's asking for us to leave him in them, and take David out of the way. Otherwise, who knows what might happen?

I'm about to mention the spear when something stops me. Inexplicably, my muscles relax, calm remembrance spreading over my concern.

Samuel had said that David is a gift to Israel. Which means he's under Yahweh's protection. It's so simple, I'm actually ashamed of my anxiety. David needs no greater shield than Yahweh Himself, the One who guarded him against both Goliath and Saul. If God proved His favor once, He'll do it again.

I bow deeply, closing any more discussion. "As you wish, my king."

Leaving the room, I try not to look as triumphant as I feel. Fear is pointless. Even if it's trying to take my father by storm, it won't follow my brother and me into battle.

SIXTEEN

David

———◆◆◆◆◆———

I pull myself sharply to the left as Malchi's sword swings past my ear and over my head. I can hear the air hiss against the blade when it loops back around to connect with mine. Blunted or not, the training weapons can be as deadly as the real thing, especially in the hands of Saul's sons.

With experience and age on his side, Malchi is a formidable foe. And I'm sure he's dying to teach me a lesson. He parries and cuts faster than I can swing my arm around, only missing me because I'm quick on my feet—and because his brother's watching.

"Guard that left side." Jonathan's urgency tightens my resolve, and I remember his earlier advice, shifting my attention to the way Malchi moves on his feet. He steps before he swings.

Jerking out of the way, I not only avoid a blow but deflect it, causing the prince to stagger off balance. In the half-second that he's vulnerable, I cut in, jabbing his ribs.

Encouragement erupts around me from the soldiers watching, but I barely hear it over Malchi's blistering stare. His amusement is replaced by the same half-rage, half-embarrassment that I've seen on the king's face. The princes can't be happy that I've invaded their territory yet again, this time as a soldier. Before Malchi can react, Abner steps up closer to him.

"Finish it. We have work to do."

Iron jumps into Malchi's eyes. Flinging off restraint, the prince leans into his weapon, advancing with a ferocity that shows me just how much he was holding back before. I duck out of his way, but he rotates his wrist and slams the hilt of his sword into the side of my head. It's not full force, but the blow still rattles my teeth, and I drop to the ground, pain exploding in my temples. Everything blurs momentarily, and I close my eyes until the rushing recedes from my ears, letting me hear the end of Abner's excuses.

"We have more to do than watch them spar." He turns from Jonathan to the rest of Saul's commanders. "Assemble your forces for orders. We'll reach the garrison by dawn, and I want every man ready to take it."

I resist listening while the men disperse, muttering opinions over their shoulders. Malchi blocks the setting sun with his shoulder before stepping over me. "You'll have to be faster, Slingshot. Hatred will make the Philistines come at you harder than I just did."

Ishvi smirks agreement. "Maybe we should use that. Send him out to lure Achish in." It's meant to be a jest, but Abner doesn't miss a thing. His assessing look still chills me.

"Get some rest, giant-killer," the general mutters. "We have plans to make."

I hide my wince until Ishvi's back is turned. The name had sounded noble coming from Jonathan, but Abner makes it seem like an insult, meant to remind me that I have no excuse for weakness. Ever since Goliath, I've thrown everything I have against every obstacle, desperate to prove I can do more. I've kept up with the army, straining through every mock battle until I nearly passed out. But I can see it in Abner's face. Not enough.

The king has to be doing this on purpose, pushing my strength to the breaking point in order to prove something. Like he'd tried to do when he'd offered me his armor.

Closing my eyes against dizziness, I shove off the ground and try to feel it again—the valley filled with the light of Yahweh's presence. It's still on everyone's mind, but the talk has dwindled, leaving Saul's commanders measuring what I have left. In the war camp, it's harder to think about anything except what's before you. And prepare for what's coming.

Back in my tent, I take a long drink then pour water over my head. The sting in my hands makes me catch a sharp breath. My fingers are calloused from field labor and plucking the harp strings, but I'm not used to the cramps that come from gripping weapons day and night. Between the dried sweat and thick blisters, releasing my sword is a painful process. I grip a wet cloth with both hands, resting my forehead against them.

We're less than a mile from the southern garrison at Shaaraim, where we've learned the Philistines are storing extra weapons, cutting Judah off from acres of prime farmland in retaliation for Goliath. Tomorrow will be a long day of fighting, and the weight of what's expected of me battles with the clamor of my body.

Everything hurts. My hands are torn open. My head throbs where Malchi hit me. Keeping up with the others is taking everything I have. Jonathan's brothers have been careful where I'm concerned, keeping most of their opinions to themselves. But I can tell that they've sided with Abner in suspicion rather than with Jonathan in friendship.

They all heard the king before we'd left for the training grounds. Praising my courage, telling them that if I'm valiant enough, I'll soon have a command of my own. Saul's sons had kept their expressions neutral during their father's speech, but I'm sure they've been secretly laughing since then, baffled that they have to cater to Saul's shepherd boy.

Jonathan pushes into the tent, his shrewd smile reading me like a scroll. "Stop thinking what you're thinking."

He kneels next to me, and I twist my face into a wry smile to hide whatever else is there. "It's what *they're* thinking." I lift my chin out toward the camp. "A shepherd half their age handed a position because he fought a giant? Some of these men would die to have that kind of favor with the king."

Jonathan's brows lift. "I didn't hear anyone offering to die when Goliath showed up." He adjusts his weight. "Listen. My father's armies are made up of valiant men. But many of them remember when I led the charge at Michmash. They were there when my father made me a commander, and they all saw what that meant."

My head swims. "It meant you were thrown into the fire."

Jonathan straightens. "Exactly. If anyone thinks you don't deserve to be here, he can go down to Gath and fight the rest of Goliath's family."

My laugh feels forced, pushing through a lot of misgivings in order to break the surface. Jonathan has worn a target on his back ever since Michmash, and I can already feel mine dropping into place. I try not to wince when Jonathan slaps my shoulder.

"We'll get them. Every last one of those monsters will fall before Israel in time."

I try to rub the ache out of my temples, grateful for the way his enthusiasm stirs mine. "What about Achish?"

Jonathan sits back, sharply dismissing the king's name. "He's the least of our worries. He's a coward who hides behind giants. I wouldn't be surprised if he's assassinated by one of his own before we get to him." He reaches inside his vest and pulls out a vial. "Give me your hands."

The heavy scent of oil awakens my mind while Jonathan anoints my palms and wraps them in strips of cloth. "They'll toughen up before you know it. You're stronger than you think, David. We've all seen it."

My gaze finds Goliath's sword across the tent. "Your father has men who are stronger."

"Brute force isn't what I meant. I've seen that rise and fall, coming on strong one minute only to evaporate like dew the next. Lasting strength lies in staying connected to the source of it."

I lock eyes with him, understanding. "The *Ruach Hakkodesh.*" We both know Yahweh's Spirit is behind every victory our people have won, even before we became a nation. The scent of the anointing oil pulls the truth of it into the room.

Jonathan nods, gentle awe softening the years in his face. "We saw His presence with you in that valley. My father knows that's how you did what you did."

Something lodges in my throat. "Is that why he—?" I drop my gaze. It's going to be a while before I can close my eyes and not see Saul rearing over me, his huge hand clamped around my neck. In all my life, I'd never felt anything so wild as that hatred, and the panic that had reared up against it.

Jonathan's certainty pulls me out of the memory. "I told you. He's afraid. But we're going to show him that there's nothing to fear. He won't touch you again."

I drag a long breath through my lungs. Whether or not Saul will try to hurt me again, I don't know. But the fact remains. He doesn't trust me. And that hurts more than I thought it would. That's why I have to push through the pain, the exhaustion— everything. The urgency that's been sharpened these past few weeks goes beyond self-preservation. I'll do anything for Saul's acceptance. I have to prove his suspicions wrong.

I get up, steeling myself. "Let's go find Abner. We have plans to make. God's enemies have harassed Judah long enough."

Jonathan grins. "Agreed."

We move to the center of camp where the commanders have their thousands waiting for strategies. The princes' smiles glow with disdain.

"Feeling better, Slingshot?" It's impressive how Malchi manages to insert an insult before Jonathan can hear it.

I turn away from him and face Abner instead. "I'm fine. But Judah won't be if they're kept from their fields much longer. It's almost the feast of firstfruits. We have to destroy that garrison and take control of the weapons they have there."

Abner blinks, startled by my tone, but I keep my eyes trained on him, even when he chuckles, shifting his attention to the commanders. "Unbroken youth is a miraculous thing. Since the boy is so zealous for the king's battles, I say we send him in first."

Amid the nervous jesting that ensues, Jonathan protests, "Abner, be serious."

The general doesn't blink an eye. "I am being serious. The boy is Philistia's greatest enemy right now, and every commander hiding out at that garrison wants to prove himself to Achish. They will jump at the chance to kill David, and we can use that to our advantage. Sar Ishvi was wise to mention it."

"I was kidding." Ishvi shrinks slightly when Jonathan looks at him.

Abner straightens. "Nevertheless, it's a good plan, one that will please the king. Saul said the boy is to have as much opportunity to fight as anyone else."

"And what is this great plan that would give him so much opportunity?" There's an extra layer of steel in Jonathan's tone, and Abner's the only one ignoring it.

"If we send David out to draw the attention of the fighters, they might think he's trying to attack alone. If they're smart, they'll follow him, try to capture him. But he'll lead them back this way, where the princes will be waiting with their thousands to engage. Meanwhile, the rest of us will take the garrison and finish off whoever remains there."

"That's absurd. You're assuming far too much. What about the archers on the walls? They'll be the first to attack. And they're not going to send everyone they have after him." Jonathan half-turns away, dismissing Abner. "We can think of something else."

"Preferably something that doesn't endanger your new little brother."

Jonathan's expression is sharp enough to split rock, but Abner doesn't flinch. I can almost see the sparks between them.

"Perhaps if we inquired of the Lord, you'd feel safer," Abner suggests coolly.

Jonathan hardens his tone. "It's hardly a matter of feeling safe, General. The armies of Israel do not fight without Yahweh's direction."

Abner spreads his hands. "Then we agree. Ezra, tell Ahijah to bring the *ephod*. Quickly. We march at dawn."

I try not to look at anyone while Abner explains the situation to the priest. Ahijah looks uncomfortable, his restive glance unwinding my courage, but he obeys. Spreading the sacred linen cloth and gemstones out before the Lord, Ahijah prays and waits to see which stones will be illuminated in answer. It's not long before he looks up. "The boy will survive."

The lilt of his voice indicates there might be more to it, but Abner talks over him. "There. Let the Word of the Lord satisfy you, Jonathan. There is no reason to hold David back. Unless you're trying to shield him."

Again, I see what passes between the general and the Hassar, and I raise my voice over it. "I'll do it."

"See?" Triumphant, Abner drapes his arm over my shoulders. "He's not afraid at all. He's been waiting for this chance ever since the sheep pastures, haven't you, boy?"

I manage not to cringe. I still have to convince Jonathan. The prince is looking through me. "You're sure?"

"Yes," I promise him.

I'm sure of the Lord's protection at least. But even as the commanders disperse, I'm already feeling doubt sliding into view like a hairline crack in armor. Seemingly unimportant. Potentially fatal.

I fold my arms, staring at the fading glow of the *ephod* stones.

Abner's manipulation affronts me. No matter what Saul wants me to prove, this isn't about either one of us. This is about Israel defending her inheritance, taking another step into her future. Proclaiming Yahweh as King. *That* was my dream in the sheep pastures. That's my duty now. And I don't know if this is the way forward. I hadn't anticipated so much struggle to decide.

I avoid everyone that night, counting the hours until darkness covers the camp in silence and I can think better. Facing Goliath didn't feel anything like this. The valley of Elah had been drenched in light, Yahweh's power bending the air around me. Here, I just feel used. Expendable.

I turn onto my stomach and shove my arms underneath my head. Perhaps not all battles feel the same. But what if Yahweh isn't calling this one? I might not die, but we could fail.

Uninterested in sleep, I leave my tent and head for the edge of camp.

The moment I step outside the ring of tents and torches, the night swallows me, and I feel the presence of God rushing in, like the first warm breath of summer chasing away winter's chill. The sense of home wraps me close, and I gasp in relief, recalling the first time I felt it. The night my mother died, I understood very little, except that I was alone, and no one wanted me. But I also knew Israel's stories. Our God takes men as His own. While everyone else was distracted, I wandered to the edge of Abba's fields, and without meaning to, without really knowing why, I'd said His Name.

Yahweh. That's all. And that was enough. I was never alone again.

This is where I belong. Not in Judah or Gibeah, but with Yahweh. His closeness has grown around me for years, doubling since my anointing. It's what Samuel promised without saying anything that day. But I still reel over how wonderful it is to feel Him breathing under my skin, all around me.

Everything is sharper and brighter in Yahweh's presence—the stars, the moon, the sweet scent of the forest. How many nights have I spent out here with Him, flinging His praises into the darkness? Now I know that He's actually come down to listen! To speak. To draw me close like a friend, even though He's my God. I drop to my knees, my arms outstretched.

"Yahweh..."

I whisper it, and chills race across my arms. He's here. But I can sense a change in the silence. In the pastures, it was a quiet brooding, a gentle covering that rested on me while I sang. Now, it's like the spark off a flint being coaxed into flame.

I picture the garrison, just half a mile away. It was deserted before Goliath fell. Now, it's a haven for the cowards who fled the battle, sealing off fields that have been sown by my people. Sheaves that will be offered to Yahweh first during the upcoming feast. The Philistines think their covert retaliation will go overlooked by the king's armies. But Yahweh sees.

Everything about Him rushes back into my mind—everything I've heard spoken and sung my entire life. And praises mount inside me, spilling over.

"O God, when you went out before your people, when you marched through the wilderness, the earth quaked, and the heavens poured down rain before you, the mighty One of Sinai, the God of Israel. You will drive them all away like wax melting before a fire."

Clarity scatters the clouds in my mind, and I have to smile. Yahweh is the giant-killer—just like He was the mover of seas in Israel's history. Our ancestor Moses had stretched out his arms, but it was Yahweh who'd made the waters crash down over the Egyptian army who'd pursued us. Yahweh had delivered me from Goliath. He's the only champion we need.

"I will sing to you, God. I will sing praises to your Name; I will lift up a song to the One who rides through the deserts. We will exult over you as you lead every prisoner to prosperity."

Something leaps inside me, and I gasp through it, breaking into a run back to the tents. I don't stop to understand the joyful power taking over, but I can't deny it. Our God won't stop with Goliath. He'll lead us in more victory as long as we're willing. As long as we're His.

The moment I say Jonathan's name into the prince's tent, he's awake, sword in hand.

I push his shoulder. "It's me, brother. Get the men ready, and lead them to the garrison."

"Now?" He stumbles as Ezra appears in the doorway.

"Trust me. Get them to come quietly around the south side where the weapons are stored. No shouting. Extinguish your torches before you get close."

Ezra scrambles for armor, and Jonathan throws his bow over his arm. "Their weapons stores will be heavily guarded, David. What are you—?"

I grab the medallion around his neck, forcing attention. "Yahweh's calling."

I barely wait to see the light enter his eyes before pulling away. Back in my own tent, I grab the bow and belt Jonathan gave me and drape a quiver of arrows over my back. On my way out of camp, I tighten my sling around my wrist, gratified by its familiar presence.

Yahweh is still my Shepherd, and the things He taught me in the pastures will never leave me. I settle easily into the darkness, allowing the stars to guide me across the path. What a relief to be filled with purpose, on the move again with Adonai.

It's not long before the cover of trees ends and the garrison walls rise in the landscape. We were closer to it than I'd thought. Torches illuminate the dark figures of midnight watchmen pacing the walls. At least two armed archers are ready to signal more from behind the massive wooden gate.

Careful not to get too much closer, I reach for an arrow, a wry smile teasing my face. Good thing Jonathan's pushed the bow into my hands as much as he has, when all I wanted was to swing a sword. He understands that some of our best attacks happen from a distance.

Fitting the arrow, I take aim, breathing steadiness over the zeal humming inside me. "God shall arise; let His enemies be scattered—" I release the arrow and watch the first guard fall from the tower with hardly a sound. "And those who hate Him shall flee before Him." In one fluid motion, I have another arrow notched and flying, and the second guard falls before he can alert more with his shouting.

I release the breath trapped between my ribs. Now I can get closer. Breaking into a careful run, keeping low to the ground, I stop within several feet of the walls and sling a stone at the man who peers over it.

"You—" A breathless guard comes around the corner on the ground, and I whip out my knife, sending it flying into him. This one makes far too much noise, and I pull my sword to finish him off.

Ignited by the rush of adrenaline, I don't wait to see if anyone heard the struggle. Grasping the keys at the man's belt, I unlock the gate, keeping behind it as it swings open. But the fortress yard is empty, only filled with the breathing of torches and the wavering shapes of iron weapons piled against the back wall. Weapons we need.

But first the guard tower has to go. The dark building houses the sleeping men who fled the battle at Elah. Probably a few commanders hiding out to avoid Achish's humiliated wrath and harass Judah while they're at it.

Slinking over to the south gate, I unlock it and swing it wide for Israel. Jonathan will have them here soon, and they'll pounce on the weapons while I handle the tower. The opposite of Abner's plan.

My back facing the cool, empty dark of Judah's wilderness, I pull a blunted arrow from my quiver and a flint from my belt. In seconds, the arrow's tip is flaming, pointed straight at the dry thatch of the tower's roof.

"Don't move," someone snarls.

The harshness of the voice claws my stomach, but I manage to keep my hands steady, shifting my aim toward the sound. The Philistine holds a sword, but I can shoot faster. "Put it down, boy," he commands, edging toward me, ready to strike if I don't.

Something in his face jumps out at me through the flames, and I know where I've seen him before. In the valley of Elah, behind Goliath's shield. I don't have to wonder if he knows me. The mixture of fear and hatred creates an inferno in his eyes. He glances at the tower. "Put it down, or I swear by the gods, you'll burn with it."

In seconds, I assess my options and pivot back into position.

My fingers free the arrow, and it sails in an arc up into the tower window. Flames catch almost instantly, leaping from the battlements, eating up the wood. In answer, I can hear Israel's shout, the roar of Saul's forces coming as one.

I barely have my sword out in time to block the armorbearer's vicious attack. Seething with rage, he leans hard into his blade, throwing everything he has against me. I stumble once, and the force of his arm nearly knocks my sword from my hand. I stagger backwards, grappling for balance while the Philistine's cold laughter crawls over me.

"Where's Goliath's sword? Too heavy for you?"

He slices the air inches from my neck, then stabs, cutting into the side of my arm. Only feet away, the tower is buckling under the weight of the flames, and panic is erupting within and around it, but the Philistine won't take his eyes from me.

"You think you saved anyone, Israelite? There are ten more giants where Goliath came from. For every chariot you burn, Achish will send a thousand more. Israel will bow."

Drawing myself up, I advance on him, torched inside by a very different fire. "Why do you look with hatred on what God has desired? The place He has chosen to dwell? The chariots of the Lord are twice ten thousand. Thousands upon thousands. And the Lord Himself is among them." I pin the man with my gaze and watch his arrogance wither.

"The Lord has summoned His power," I gasp. "And He wields it on our behalf."

For an instant, it looks like the Philistine might flee, but he yells instead, swinging his sword with greater ferocity. He's fighting desperately now, seeing Israel swarming the burning fortress, grabbing weapons, and turning on anyone escaping the tower.

A few Philistines jump into the fight instead of running, but Saul's men take them down easily. The fire and the fighting press closer every second, narrowing the perimeter around me and my assailant.

Cutting down a guard, only a foot away in the smoke, Abner whirls and looks at me once, long enough to distract me. Then iron explodes in my face. I barely had time to notice the metal greaves coating the armorbearer's fingers before he was swinging for me. My head jerks back, and I don't even feel the ground when I hit it.

I'm swallowed by an explosive rushing, muting the noise of battle. When sounds start to bleed back through, I'm being dragged by my collar into the dark. Grass pulls at my limbs on each side, and torches spark in my vision as I make out four other Philistines, besides the one who's holding me.

The armorbearer drops me in the middle of a field, and I see the flash of his sword before it enters my arm, slicing all the way through into the earth. I cry out and try to jerk forward, but the Philistine stabs through the chain mail on my left side with my own sword, pinning me to the ground. He shouts to the others. "Do it! Burn them!"

The Philistines fling their torches, and the fire sweeps into a full blaze in seconds. Defeated, they'll let the fields burn so that the farmers can't reclaim them.

Abner's face blinks in my mind, and I wonder if he saw them take me down. We'd killed more than enough to spare soldiers. Where is he?

I grasp at my sword with my left hand, but it's buried too deep in the ground. The harder I tug at it, the more the other blade tears through my right arm. And the flames are encroaching, gaining height every second. I force steady breaths as they dance closer.

"Yahweh, you always restored your inheritance as it languished. Grant me *chesed* now." The words are barely past my lips when something else starts to slash at my face besides embers and fingers of smoke. Something wet.

I choke in amazement, my gasps breaking into laughter as a heavy wall of rain sweeps over the fields, quenching the flames and soaking through everything. Blinding light rips open the night sky, and thunder tears after it, sounding in my chest like a drumbeat.

Ecstatic, I fling praises into the torrent. "Rain in abundance, O God, you shed abroad. In your goodness, you provide for your flock. Praise your Name forever, my Yeshu-hah. Praise your Name."

"David!"

The shouts are muffled, and I have to scream to be heard over the tempest. But no storm has ever been more welcome.

In seconds, I'm surrounded by Israel's warriors, and Jonathan is at my side.

"I'm fine," I assure him, but then his knee brushes the sword in my arm, and my head spins.

Jonathan's barely breathing through gasps of laughter. "You crazy lion of Judah! Here, hold onto me."

He frees my left side, and I brace against his shoulder while he pulls the sword from my right arm. Ezra's right beside him, working to bind up my wound while Jonathan holds onto me.

"It's ours, David! The garrison is no more. We cut down the commanders who fled the burning tower. Ishvi went after the ones that ran, but they won't get far."

I smile over the pain pushing through me. "And Yahweh has saved the fields."

Jonathan laughs, presses his forehead against mine. "The Lord is with you, brother. The Lord is with us!" he shouts, and the army roars with him.

"The Lord our God, the Lord is One!"

Adonai is with me. I still can't get over it. Our God's favor a greater reward than anything the king could bestow. Cheering, the princes surround us, lifting me into their arms. The commanders' exultation rivals the thunder on all sides.

But over Jonathan's shoulder, I see Abner at the edge of the group, watching. Just watching.

SEVENTEEN

Jonathan

———◆◆◆◆◆———

Three Years Later

Before I even look at the message my servant handed me, I know what it says. But my eyes consume the details anyway, fierce gratitude mounting in my chest. Another victory. Another massive assault averted and turned on its head. Several key commanders slain, including one of Achish's fiercest generals.

The message is likely several days old by now, but I'm feeling the news as though it just happened, my fervor every bit as strong as the day Goliath fell. David's writing covers the parchment with praise, his exuberance leaping off the page:

"I'm coming home, my brother. Within the week at least. Adonai's face shines on us, and our enemies flee from the brightness of His smile."

I almost laugh out loud, relishing David's ability to spin battle exultation into words. It's absurd to think that I ever doubted the idea of sending David into combat. I had questioned my father's motives at first, wondering why the king seemed intent on turning the brave youngster into a weapon of war so soon. But those first months with the army had only illuminated the truth that we'd all seen back in Elah. David was Yahweh's weapon first.

Ignoring the watching servants, I turn toward the window, spread my hands, and release my praises to our God in a single breath. *Once again, you've shown Your faithfulness to Israel through Your servant David. I'm in awe of You.*

In three short years, he's become the youngest commander of the king's forces, set over a thousand men after a victory that brought down a prince from Ekron. With every success, the people love him more, making songs that burn dangerously close to hero worship. But every note out of David's mouth makes his victories incense, a sacrifice of praise to the God he has a dozen names for—our Rock, our Fortress, our Deliverer. David won't let anyone forget the true Commander of our hosts, the One who goes before us.

I've had to place my brother back into God's hands over and over, forcing my mind back to the moment he'd prevailed against the giant with no weapons but a sling and Adonai's favor. We'd all seen it then. God was with him. He'd been thrown into the fire, as I'd predicted, but the flames had merely refined him. He's been burning for a long time.

Any hesitance on the part of the armies to take a city or run against a troop is met with David's calm pronouncement of Yahweh's faithfulness, "by many or by few." But his confidence doesn't carry the aftertaste of pride or arrogance. I've found him on his knees more times than I can count, begging for God's guidance, always pointing the army to the priests for inquiries before any major decision. And then to see him celebrate...

He doesn't just follow Yahweh. He loves Yahweh. And his submission and courage bring blessing to the armies he leads.

"Can you believe it, my lord?" a servant breathes, "Tyrian is dead at last."

Glancing back at the parchment, I notice another line beneath David's glowing summation, a piece of news I'd missed:

"Tell the king that I put an end to Tyrian in his fortress, as he commanded. I will bring what he required, as proof. The last thing the Philistine heard was the name of Saul."

I frown, concern overshadowing my enthusiasm. Tyrian has been on my father's personal kill list for decades. The Philistine general had wounded Saul years ago during a surprise attack on

Gibeah shortly after our Amalek battle. Shortly after his raiders had nearly killed me. My father had driven Tyrian back, but we'd lost over seventy men, and bitterness had festered along with Saul's infected leg wound.

He had always said he would kill Tyrian himself. Now, he sends David to slay the man in his own fortress? I've never been that deep into enemy territory myself. How many Philistines did David have to fight off just to get to that point?

I hand the message back to my servant. "Take this to the king. He should be on his way."

I know what my father will say, because it's his answer for everything. "He's my champion. He fights my battles."

But which battles are the ones we should be fighting? I fold my arms, considering how Saul will react to the latest news.

Over the years, my father has established a tenuous acceptance of David, embracing him heartily when he's home, shoving gifts his way, and then sending him back out to fight, usually without much warning, and more and more often, without me. Perhaps because he knows David won't refuse any mission. He can't, after all. But if he's trying to make the people forget him, he's failing.

Every battle David wins only increases his visibility. Everyone else can't get enough of him. The king can only take so much. It bothers me that so much of my father's heart lies beneath the surface.

Another servant walks in on my thoughts, announcing, "Your sister, my lord."

I straighten up as Michal walks in, followed by her servant. Naamah keeps her head down, and it occurs to me that it's been years since I've really seen her eyes. Not since that night Abba caught us in the garden. Just when I think I'm past all that, I see her again, and the wound is back open.

Shifting my focus, I watch Michal flounce across the room, her head tossed back. My sister's petulant manner is a welcome distraction from the broken memories Naamah carries with her.

"Sarrah," I bow playfully, teasing her with the princess title.

"Don't *Sarrah* me, old man." Michal's eyes are deeper than usual, and a heavy pulse beats in her throat. "You promised me you would talk to him."

"I've promised you a lot of things, usually without my knowledge. What are we talking about now?"

She folds her arms. "You know what we're talking about. You said you would speak to Abba about me and David, and I know you haven't."

This again. Ever since David's latest promotion, Michal has shown him special preference. But this past year, I've seen the most change in her. This is the second or third time she's insisted that I speak to the king about making David her husband, since Merab was given to someone else.

My father had hinted at a match between David and Merab for a while, only to marry her off suddenly, a move that caused considerable friction between us. I had to put some distance between that debacle before bringing up the subject again. Even now, I'm not convinced that the king will want to hear anything about this. He may call David his son, but that doesn't mean he wants him married into the family. Michal should be preparing for disappointment. Instead, she's more determined than ever.

Her bracelets jangle as she pushes a hand onto her hip. "Jonathan, I refuse to have Abba sell my position to some old warrior just because I'm the youngest daughter. And admit it, you wouldn't like to see that either."

I sigh. "No, I wouldn't. But it's not my decision." If I couldn't choose my own wife…

"You could influence him if you wanted to, though."

I roll my eyes. She knows too much. She's heard the advisors talk about how Abba does nothing without consulting me. And it's true. It's taken years, but I've earned my father's trust. I'm one of the few he really listens to. Most of the time. But I won't speak into subjects I'm uncertain about. Michal's preference is clear, but David has been much more discreet. As he would be.

"He's much younger than you, Michal."

"He's even younger than Merab, but at least I care for him sincerely. Merab couldn't care less." She steps forward, her hands clasped. "Jonathan, I love him."

I can't wrestle my smile back fast enough, and Michal takes instant offense.

"This isn't funny." She shoves my shoulder. "You don't understand. You've never been in love."

I don't dare look over at Naamah. "I have feelings, all right? Does that shock you?"

Michal smirks. "Somewhat. Abba gave his word."

"He offered Merab during a risky time. It's evident that he didn't mean it."

"Well, now she's in Meholah with Adriel, and I'm right here."

I lean back against the table, assessing her. I believe she knows her own heart, but I would rather not see David publicly rejected again. "Do you think David loves you?"

The annoyance in her face vanishes as she looks over my shoulder, sudden light jumping into her eyes. "Ask him yourself."

I whip around and come face-to-face with David climbing through my window.

Before I can react, David slides my knife from its sheath at my side, his eyes laughing. "First time I've ever been able to sneak up on you. Can we record that somewhere?"

Michal laughs out loud. "I'll remember. How did you know I'd be in here? Because I know you didn't climb all the way up that wall for Jonathan."

David shrugs, grinning, but a flush is creeping up his neck. Stepping around me, he goes down on one knee and places something in Michal's hand. "Sarrah."

Michal can barely tear her eyes from his face, but she gasps a little, holding up a thin golden chain with a blue stone at the end. It's likely something he stole off a Philistine, which makes the gift even more exciting.

"It's beautiful."

"Now she has something to look at when you're not here," I interject, enjoying the extra heat it pulls into David's face.

Undeterred, Michal looks me right in the eye. "Nothing in this kingdom is more beautiful than David."

I grimace. "You're sickening. Just go. Abba's coming, and I can't talk to him with you here."

Michal scrunches her face at me, but I don't miss the way she and David look at each other as she leaves, their eyes full of words.

After she's gone, I take advantage of David's distraction and grab his wrist, jerking the dagger out of his grasp. "This is why we don't allow women on the battlefield." I shake my head at him, feigning disgust. "I wondered who would end up taking her heart. Why don't I hate you?"

David shrugs me off confidently. "Because you have so few friends."

"Watch it. I'm armed."

I flip the dagger up and down in my hand, but it's still a bad joke. It should be unthinkable that anyone in this house would seek to harm David. It still bothers me that my father ever tried. I had still never officially confronted the king for his attempt on David's life, and David refuses to talk about it, insisting Saul wasn't in his right mind. I'll give him that. At least things have improved since then.

David glances toward the door. "I saw Naamah with Michal."

"Yes. She's her servant now."

"You don't talk to her?" David asks.

I shake my head, forcing a steady tone. "It would only jeopardize the position she has now. Serving in this house is her best chance for stability."

I've revealed Naamah's story to David in pieces over the years, and by now he has the whole picture. The sister of a palace servant, she's the only woman I've seriously considered marrying, but my father had forbidden it years ago.

Naamah lost her parents to Amalekite raiders, and my father resents any reminders of his failure to completely destroy that enemy as Yahweh had commanded him decades ago. As a token of our friendship, I've pulled enough strings to help Naamah and her brother, but that doesn't stop Ziba from deliberately turning away whenever I approach.

Pensive, David shakes his head. "I'm surprised the king doesn't try harder to get you married."

"Oh, I doubt I'll escape it. You won't either, come to think of it." I look sideways at him, glad to shift the subject. "That reminds me, I've been seeing Michal floating around with a piece of parchment, blushing like a rose. She walked into a wall yesterday because she wouldn't even look up."

"She's your sister," David shrugs.

"She didn't learn that behavior from me, if that's what you're saying." I lift my brows. "Did you write something for her?"

David's eyes dance. "Why would I tell you that?"

I step closer, letting him feel my extra height. "Because I'm your brother, and I can make you."

David sighs. "I was sure it would come to this."

I grin. "That's sweet. You're blushing! Come on. Sing me the song you wrote."

"No."

I poke him in the ribs, punctuating my words. "Sing me the song."

David's head comes up. "Go talk to Naamah."

I laugh shortly, spreading my hands. "Fine. You win."

David elbows me. "It's your own fault. You taught me everything."

"Not so that you could do all the fighting while I sit in court making plans for others to carry out." I lean against the table and flip my dagger across the room into the opposite wall. "Maybe my father doesn't trust my skills anymore."

David retrieves it. "You know that's not true. You're the crown prince. Saul needs you by his side. I'm expendable."

David says it in jest, but I can feel the familiar trepidation creeping between us.

The possibility of David's anointing still hangs in the background like a weapon on the table, waiting to be picked up and examined. I still haven't heard that he's Yahweh's chosen king—not in so many words. But everything I've seen only deepens my conviction.

I'll need to bring it up with David at some point. All I need is an excuse. But once it's out in the open, there's no going back. If it's true, any advice I give him could be interpreted as treason. I made a vow to protect him, not overthrow my father.

Yahweh, give us wisdom. Help me sharpen David for your service, not for rebellion.

I pull in a deep breath, hiding my thoughts. "Maybe I'll talk to the king myself. Tell him my aim is getting rusty. He might let me take on a few raiders."

David nods toward the corridor. "Here's your chance."

My father and Abner come through the door, followed by several guards.

David bows all the way to the ground, and I return my dagger to my belt, every sense alert. I never know what to expect, but it's my job to be prepared for anything.

Only last night, my father had complained that everyone was distracted by David's imminent return. But a week ago, he'd been ill, wishing for David to come play for him. He looks at me briefly before speaking over David's bowed head. "I see your priorities, Commander. My son, my daughter, and then me."

My defenses rise, but Saul says it through a chuckle, drawing a laugh from his guards. "Your success has gone ahead of you, as always." The king holds up the parchment David sent. "You have something for me?"

"Yes, my lord." David pulls out a heavy metal pendant, and I feel my muscles clench as I recognize the medallion Tyrian used to wear around his neck. I'm both impressed and disturbed by the reminder that David rubs shoulders with death on a regular basis.

My father takes the pendant and rubs his thumb over the Philistine carvings, his jaw tightening. Finally, his eyes return to normal, his face relaxing into a smile. "I never had a doubt that you would return in victory. Thanks to you, I am avenged of another enemy. God is surely with you." He spreads his arms. "Come to me, my son."

I breathe a little easier as Abba engulfs David in a hearty embrace, and Abner reaches out to clasp his hand. These are the moments I anticipate all year. The glow of pride coming off my father makes me wonder if all my concerns were unfounded.

Perhaps it was wise to allow David some space to prove himself over the years. Now my father can see beyond any doubt that the unpredictable youth he feared has become the most committed warrior he has. I pray Abba will finally be able to rest in that knowledge. He certainly seems grateful now. I can't remember the last time he put his arm around me like that.

"I have something for you as well." Saul walks David to the window and points across my courtyard to another building touching his fields. "Now that you have brought me what I asked, I have decided to give you a place of your own. Jonathan has inspected every inch to make sure it's acceptable even though you're far easier to please than he is. While you were gone, I had your belongings moved in and then doubled everything."

Startled, David looks over at me and then back at my father. Caught up in the defense of the kingdom, my friend still has little experience with wealth, and Saul's gifts never cease to astound him.

"My lord, I'm—I don't know what to say," he responds, staring out the window.

Saul claps him on the back, gratified. "Be valiant for me, and I will see that you want for nothing. We'll announce it over our meal tonight. Now, go and see it for yourself. Get some rest. My son has something to discuss with me."

I do? As soon as David leaves, my father turns to me. "Michal said you had something to say."

I almost laugh. She won't let me waste any time. "Well, it's actually about David, Abba."

"Of course it is," Abner chortles, folding his arms.

I ignore him, continuing, "Michal has been asking me to speak with you about making David her husband. Since Merab is married, and—"

My father's head comes up, defenses flaming. "I told you I didn't want to hear another word about that. Merab is my eldest daughter, and a Sarrah of Israel. It was in the kingdom's best interest to secure her alliance with—"

"I'm not criticizing you, my lord." I rush to talk over him. "This is about Michal. She told me she loves David."

"Really?" A thousand thoughts rush into my father's eyes in place of the anger that was building. He smirks. "Knowing your sister, I'm willing to bet she said more than that."

"At length." How he's missed this, I'm not sure. She's talked of nothing else but David for a year now, singing his praises and making extra efforts to follow him around when he's here.

"He's put her up to this, hasn't he?" Abner's tone is laced with suspicion.

I roll my eyes. "He's been on the battlefield for months, Abner. You know that."

"And you know for a fact he hasn't written to her?"

I have my suspicions, but they're none of Abner's business. "I don't. If anything, he thinks he's unworthy. All I know for certain is that Michal loves him."

Abner snorts, but my father interrupts, surprising us both. "You will speak to him, Abner. Tomorrow. Find out what he thinks about becoming my son-in-law, and report back to me."

Abner is aghast. "You're not considering this?"

Saul shrugs. "Why not? My daughter in love with the kingdom's favorite warrior? The people will be in a frenzy and praise my generosity. Besides, it will communicate to everyone that David is trusted here and under my constant supervision. Married to Michal, he won't be able to make decisions so lightly. He'll have a real tie to Gibeah, a wife from Benjamin. That will show the men of Judah where his loyalties lie."

Unconvinced, Abner talks over him. "What about the bride price? Other than spoils of war, which belong to you anyway, David has nothing to offer materially. I wouldn't throw away my last daughter so easily."

I'm standing close enough to see my father's eyes change. "Tell David I don't expect a bride price. But you're wrong if you think I have nothing to gain from this." He fingers the medallion, wrestling back a strange smile. "Tell him that I only require one hundred Philistine kills."

"A hundred? Are you sure, Abba?" The coldness is back in my chest, but Abner is still unimpressed.

"And how will you know if he succeeded?" the general persists. "If he's not in battle with the army, it will be difficult to know exactly how many he killed. You know how these young men are with their reports."

"I'm aware." My father doesn't even blink. "Tell David to cut their foreskins. That will be proof enough that they're uncircumcised Philistines. If he will bring me what I ask before the next new moon, he can have Michal." He arches his shoulders, enjoying our shock. "We'll see what the impetuous young warrior thinks of that."

Hopefully, he'll be as disgusted as I am. Carnage is one thing on the battlefield, defending our people. But there's a cost to it, a cost my father is completely discounting, making a game out of drowning David in blood.

"Abba, you didn't require any such thing of my brothers when they took wives." Or Adriel when he married Merab.

Saul's answer bites. "Your brothers are princes of Israel. David is a shepherd."

I lower my voice. "He hasn't been a shepherd for years, Abba. He's been risking his life fighting your battles..."

"As he wanted."

"Of course, my king. He wouldn't have it any other way. But if it's loyalty and skill you're after, he's already proven that."

My father's smile doesn't touch his eyes. "Why don't you let me worry about what he has and hasn't proven. Don't say anything to your sister until David responds." With one of his startling reverses of temper, he touches my arm. "He loves us all, Jonathan. He won't disappoint us."

I try to return his smile, but it feels like a wince on my face. As much as my father tries to hide it, I know David matters to him, and I've often heard him boast to the people about his Judean son. So, why is he so eager to risk losing him at every turn?

Frozen by my own misgivings, I stand in the middle of the room long after Saul has left, finally walking down to the antechamber balcony to clear my head. I've spent far too many hours in this room, deliberating over every enemy threat while David is out there putting our plans into action. Yahweh's plans. Eradicating the forces that would push us out of the land God gave to us.

Why would we put our most trusted weapon in harm's way? Then again, why not? Plenty of other kings do. The Amalekites sacrifice their own children to their gods before important battles, and Achish killed his own father and brothers in order to seize Philistia's throne. It's the way of the nations.

But Israel was meant to be different.

I wander out onto the terrace that overlooks the fortress gardens, my mind drawn back to the day my father had been crowned. I can hear Samuel's heavy voice carrying over the crowds that day in Gilgal, shaking me to my core. "Do not follow in the ways of other nations. Follow the Lord! Otherwise, you and your king will be swept away!"

The intensity of his mandate had made me wonder if the throne of Israel was too great for any man to have.

I shudder to think of how quickly my father tossed aside Yahweh's instructions, letting enemies live and desecrating priestly duties. Making hasty vows that threatened lives. God has another plan for Israel now, one that involves David. All the more reason he shouldn't be running off on fools' errands.

Arching my neck, I lean over the stone railing, letting my eyes wander through the foliage below. The garden has thickened over the years. The trees reach high enough for me to touch from above and vines trail freely over the lower wall. Squinting, I notice movement between them, and something jolts in my chest. A thick canopy of hanging branches almost completely conceals my sister. She's pressed up against the opposite wall, her hands combing through David's hair while he kisses her.

I pull back, assaulted by a dozen emotions. It's a riveting storm of delight, disgust, and incredible loneliness. My youth and my age confront me in the same instant, and I turn and head back inside, walking until my cheeks cool and my pulse slows. I had kissed Naamah in the same garden years ago, but I've muscled past the memory, disturbed by the way it ended. I'd like to believe things will be different for Michal, but I wasn't born yesterday.

I've always said I wouldn't let my sister go to anyone unworthy. But my father will still try to use her as a political tool. And she'll go along with it, as long as she can get what she wants. Hopefully, David will see through this, if it is some sort of trap. Though I can't imagine why it would be. Abba loves him. But certain scenarios can make love as dangerous as hate. And I know the motivation it stirs in a man.

Back in the armory, I stare at my collection of spears, remembering the one I'd found in Abba's chamber, in the wall.

My father is right. David won't disappoint us. He'll go to the ends of the earth proving himself to us, and that's what troubles me. I release a long breath, prayers wound up in it.

Yahweh, order his steps. Don't let my sister be a snare to him.

EIGHTEEN

David

———◆◆◆◆———

I draw my bow and breathe into my aim, all the way down the straight shaft of the arrow to the target beyond. The weapon's steadying presence in my hands still hasn't tamed the extra wings beating in my chest. But that's why I'm out here. To do something I'm good at, and try to forget what a foolish door I've opened. With a Sarrah, no less.

I've been so vigilant these past few years, refining my skills until they're sharp enough to send every enemy running. I've learned to think several steps ahead and anticipate every threat. But this one crept up on me, and it might be too late to avoid it.

I can tell by the way I release the arrow that it's going to hit crooked. Groaning, I walk to the target and remove it even though no one's watching. I came out here alone to clear my head. But I'm not going to stare at a bad shot the whole time. Just another reminder that I've ventured into dangerous territory.

Cloying images dance in my head, and I pull the memory of the last battle over them. I'd traced Tyrian to an outpost near Ekron where we'd discovered a harrowing collection of young Israelite captives who'd disappeared several years ago. Posing as slave dealers, my men had been able to infiltrate the fortress before the Philistines discovered I was there.

My sword had entered Tyrian's heart the same moment that Ishvi had taken out the archer who would have shot me from behind. It's taken me years to earn any respect from Saul's sons. The split-second glance of appreciation between us was a better reward than all the king's material gifts.

Throwing myself into the defense of Israel beside men I've admired my entire life has been more than enough to satisfy me. For years. But now it's all been overshadowed by the way Michal pulled me against her, kissing me until I couldn't breathe. Falling for her is the last thing I ever dreamed would happen.

I'd put marriage aside in general, planning to deal with it once I'd established myself in the king's army. As the youngest son of an older man, I just don't have what most men look for in future sons-in-law. If I'd stayed in Bethlehem, most of my prospects would have depended largely on Eliab, something that had never given me much confidence. I'd always known that any rank and wealth I might achieve would have to be earned, not inherited.

What I hadn't counted on was feeling this way. I'd never expected to fall so easily for a woman so different from me. For years, Abigail had been the only woman in my life, but she was different. Abigail had grown up alongside me and understood how I lived. I didn't have to impress her. She knew what I was feeling, so I didn't have to say it. Her friendship added pleasure and safety to my life. But I'd always known I couldn't give her what her parents would expect.

Michal is everything I'm not. She has the innate confidence of a person raised with wealth, and her beauty has been polished into a brightness most women don't achieve. She doesn't need me, which makes her preference all the more gratifying. Writing to her, I still had to make myself believe that she wanted me to. That she wasn't being promised to someone else like Merab had been. But now that I'm back by her side, I don't know how I stayed away.

"This still might not happen." In the garden, I had to remind her for my own sake, but she wouldn't hear it.

"Don't say that. Don't say anything. Just love me. That's enough." She'd pressed closer, her perfume unwinding my judgment.

"What about the king? He decides what's mine. I don't exactly have a history of getting what I want."

She'd simply wrapped her arms around my neck, smiling into me. "Don't worry. I do."

I wrestle my smile back, feeling foolish for entertaining the idea. Her persistence is flattering, and I've enjoyed the confidence of her dreams. But it's foolish to assume that the king has no better plans for his last daughter. I've learned that the hard way. And how smart is it for me to pursue Saul's daughter when the throne is meant to pass from his family to mine? I'm hesitant to doubt Yahweh's promise, but that doesn't mean I understand how it will be fulfilled.

Joab always laughs off my uncertainty, pointing to the country's overwhelming support as a sign of favor. In a few short years, my name, my songs, and the battles I've fought have become as well known as Jonathan's used to be when I was a child. But none of them know I've been anointed. Would they follow me if it meant breaking with Saul? I can't imagine endangering any of the men I fight beside.

And then there's Saul's family. They've become as close to me as blood relatives, especially in the years I've been kept from Bethlehem. The possibility of becoming someone they hate, someone they'd want dead, makes the breath constrict in my lungs.

I was almost relieved when Saul had sent me away initially. I had so much to learn, and it was a physical and mental struggle to keep up with men twice my age in combat. But I had gladly thrown myself into it, sweating and straining past the memory of the king's hand locked around my throat.

The years in battle have kept me in a constant state of turbulence, tugged between my desire to honor and impress Saul, and my resentment at the way he uses me. Usually, I'm able to convince myself that he only puts me forward because he knows I can handle it. He knows the skill I've developed and the desire that stirs within me to fight Yahweh's battles. He knows my God shields me.

But one conversation with Joab was enough to erode my confidence in Saul's motives.

"He's not blind, David. He sees Yahweh's favor all over you, and the more the people rejoice over it, the more he burns inside. Trust me, he hopes one of these battles will take you out."

My fingers ache, gripping my bow tighter than I need to. I refuse to believe that. Saul might fixate on the people's favor, but he knows me better than to treat me like a traitor. What bothers me more is how close I am to being one. I've been able to lose myself in the repetitions of war and worship, trying to forget I'm called to be anything more than Saul's commander. But how long will I be allowed to forget?

I shoot another arrow, remembering how it felt to have Jonathan place the bow in my hands. I'm certain this is all I'm meant to do for now. If there's something else, Adonai will reveal it. I hope.

The only thing that's become clearer over the years is my desperate need for Yahweh—a need that would overwhelm me if I hadn't spent my childhood obsessed with Him. The praises that have grown in me over the years push every fear behind my back, replacing them with the endless attributes of the God of Israel. He's the foundation under my feet and the only reason I'm able to walk steadily. I hold onto Him with shaking fingers, praying that I'll never let go.

Squinting at the target, I'm distracted by a slight movement beyond it. A familiar figure jogs along the path, coming from the other side of the stream. I lift my hand, and a birdcall trills back at me—something Joab taught his younger brothers from years of spying. And just hearing it unbridles powerful relief inside me.

The sight of Asahel's unruly hair and mismatched armor makes me feel instantly at home, pulled back into familiar territory. I lower my bow as he approaches, not even trying to control my smile.

Abner's always looked askance at my nephews even though they're some of our fiercest fighters. Even without showing off, Joab and Abishai are better at everything, and Asahel is such a fast runner that he's always appearing in places he wasn't expected. Most likely, Abner resents not being able to control them even though no one ever has. Their father might have been the only one who could have, but he died years ago fighting Amalek.

Asahel is the tamest of the three, but his energetic manner exudes a sense of freedom. He's calmly confident in his abilities and utterly unhindered by the restrictions that I'm forced to live by.

"Didn't want to have to bother with the guards at the main gate, Asa?" I tease him when he reaches me.

Asahel shrugs, grinning. "Now that you have your own house, I can come straight to you without having to deal with Saul's lackeys." Embracing me, he shields his eyes at the building in the distance. "That's the only thing that makes sense about it. What was the dear old king thinking?"

I glance back at the oversized structure. "Search me. I don't expect I'll be spending much time there."

"Have you been sent out again?" Asahel asks.

"Not officially. It's just become an instinct."

Asahel nods. "Your mother's getting tired of all the stories. We're always reminding her that by the time they reach Bethlehem, the tales are completely out of proportion."

A slight shiver darts through me. Living in Gibeah has made it easy to forget how isolated Bethlehem is. Until my brothers or cousins bring them news, my parents remain in the dark about most of my endeavors. I'm often too busy for regret, but the king could have allowed me more access to my family. That wouldn't have affected my loyalty to him.

"How is Eema? Besides worried," I ask.

Asahel's smile is reassuring. "She's not as worried as you'd think. She knows Yahweh's favor follows you."

"Doesn't mean I can't get wounded."

Last year, a Philistine had tried to rip my shield from my arm, dislocating my shoulder with a sudden snap that had taken my breath. Dispatching the threat, Jonathan had simply knelt beside me, locked his arm around mine, and popped it back into place. I'm more indebted to that man than I could ever repay.

"Your mother wants you to come home if you get hurt." Asahel laughs, but something heavier lurks behind it. I watch his gaze shift from my eyes to my bow.

"Is she well?" I press him cautiously.

Asahel pulls one of my arrows and taps it against one hand. "That cough is back. The sickness from last winter. It's like your father. She has moments where she struggles to breathe, especially if she walks too far. One night—well, she frightened everyone. I was about to send for you, but she woke up. Jesse has sent for the local healers, but there's not much to be done except keep her from working too hard."

I'm close to trembling, concern eating through my exterior like frost. How could they let her get so bad without telling me?

"Here. Take this." I reach for the leather purse at my waist. I've started carrying small amounts of money with me, the way Jonathan does. You never know when you'll come across a needy countryman or need to bribe your way across enemy lines. I hand it over without a thought, but Asa's eyes widen at the weight.

"Tell my father to send for a healer from Jebus. Someone more experienced. Whatever he has to do. Tell him I will send more if he needs it."

Not that he'll take it. My father has more than most people in Bethlehem, but I've tried to let my position benefit him as much as possible, knowing he'll help others.

I tap Asa's shoulder. "If she gets bad again, I want you to let me know. No matter where I am, I will find a way to come down. Saul doesn't have to know."

Asahel nods, pensive. "As you wish…my king."

He barely whispers them, but the words slice through me. "I'm not your king, Asa."

"But you will be."

I glance sideways at him from behind my bow. He's as straight as an arrow, exuding calm assurance.

I sigh, looking away. "How many people has Joab told?"

"Our mother. Some of the influential men of Judah. A few from the resistance—Korah and his clan. Remember him? The man everyone says has the face of a lion? He tried to rob Jesse's pastures one year."

Wonderful. The man had tried to slit my throat in my own father's fields before Joab came, and now he knows my darkest secret. "I remember. What has your brother been telling them?"

"Only to watch and see what Yahweh will do."

I'll have to be satisfied with that, though I'm not willing to believe those were his only words. I arch a brow at my nephew. "Anything else you need to tell me?"

Asa's face tightens. "Watch out for Saul's new chief herdsman. He's definitely a spy."

The warning makes my skin crawl. The Edomite named Doeg has been in Saul's service for only two weeks, but I already don't trust him. I'd written the suspicion off though, believing it had more to do with the predatory way he talks to Michal.

Asa's expression changes, his attention shifting behind me. "Abner's coming."

"You'd better leave then. Unless you want to answer a million questions."

"I'm going." He prances like a deer about to flee from a hunter. "Just remember. You're still the king of the land. That's what we call you. Blame Joab." Grinning, he disappears.

Now I have to shove my own smile deep enough that Abner can't find it, even in my eyes. I keep my face against the bowstring, my eyes locked on the target.

When the general reaches me, I can tell he's looking off toward the edge of the fields. "Commander," he mutters.

"General." I release the arrow, hitting dead center. I've always done better under pressure.

"What did your nephew want?" Abner demands.

"My mother is sick." I hate saying it.

"He can bring that information to the king." Abner's tone bites, and I can't help a stiff response.

"We wouldn't want to bother the king with such trivial matters."

Abner grimaces, narrowing his eyes. We deal with each other so much better on the battlefield. When we're in Gibeah, I swear he still sees me as a shepherd boy.

He clears his throat, pulling a diplomatic tolerance over his dislike. "I've come on behalf of the king."

I try not to react, but my pulse hums, anticipating some kind of accusation. Instead, Abner murmurs, "You must know that the king views you as a son. You cannot deny that he has been a father to you."

"I don't deny it."

"And all the people love you; that's clear." He stiffens, his voice flat. "Therefore, the king has sent me to ask you to become his son-in-law."

Utterly caught off guard, I let the arrow escape me, and it spears the target on an awkward angle. Flustered, I fit another one into the bow, trying to decide how serious Abner is.

We've had this conversation before—about Saul's older daughter, the one he'd offered to the killer of Goliath. Over a year ago, the king had acted like he was going to keep that promise, only to marry Merab off to someone else. Someone rich. I had understood the decision at the time, but it was still humiliating to have the offer snatched away from me to make a point. Now he wants to do it again?

Abner's brows lift. "Are you aware of what an undeserved honor that would be?"

A heavy pulse beats in my throat, but I talk through it. "That's exactly what it is. Undeserved."

A trace of mockery slides into Abner's tone. "I thought you cared for each other. It's obvious that she prefers you."

She does. Which makes it even worse that Saul is trying to taunt us with something he doesn't intend to give. I can see the glimmer of disdain in Abner's eyes, waiting for me to admit that I could never afford the bridal price of a king's daughter. I knew I shouldn't have kissed her. I set the bow aside, giving my face a chance to cool before I look up.

"I'm a common man, Abner. Everything I have is from the king."

Abner smirks. "Yes. Jonathan has thrown enough finery at you to distract the people, but we all know what you are." He leans over, contempt staining his tone. "I know something else too. Something the king will have to work very hard to keep hidden if he lets you have Michal. All of Bethlehem seems to know about it."

The general's gaze digs deep and finds the shame that has lurked inside me since my birth. I can feel it waking up, stirring into defensiveness.

"What does he want?" I say stiffly.

Abner's eyes light up, pleased that he hit the right mark. "The foreskins of one hundred dead Philistines."

A dare. That's rich. The king is using his own daughter as bait and possibly trying to get me killed. Or at least see how far

I'm willing to go for Michal. I stare at Abner, letting him see the steel enter my eyes. I'm not afraid. But I'm also not my own.

As much as Saul has tried to make me his weapon, I'm Yahweh's first. It's His direction that wins me victory in battle. Rash vows only breed trouble. I retrieve my bow and fit another arrow, blocking out Abner's judgment so I can listen to the silence.

Should I go, Yahweh? Will you be with me?

Zeal jumps around inside me, and I hide a smile.

"Tell the king I'll do it." I send my arrow flying and split the first one.

Abner stares at the target, refusing to allow any approval to surface. "I'll tell him. The Sarrah will be pleased."

Will she? She probably won't even find out about this until it's all arranged. I manage to stay silent, my gaze turned away until Abner leaves.

It's certainly not how I planned to find a wife. It's dangerous and excessive. But that's been my life ever since I killed Goliath, and I'd known it would be. The fighting has become so common that Jonathan has stopped telling me to be careful. He knows that my life doesn't leave much room for caution. And that Yahweh is a faithful deliverer.

I stare at the splintered arrow across the field, waiting for my thoughts to settle.

I'll have to move the target again. The contest is always changing on me.

* * * * *

"You must be joking."

Joab's reaction is everything I expected. He stares openly, waiting for me to admit I was teasing him. When I don't, he scoffs, rubbing the hilt of his sword. "He really does want you dead."

Hearing him say that is starting to anger me. "He wants me for a son-in-law. That's the opposite of wanting me dead."

"Is it?" Studying the weapons on my wall, Joab pulls a curved Philistine sword from its sheath. "You know, when I wanted to marry Deborah, I asked her father, and he said yes. That's how it usually works."

I take the sword from his hands, smirking. "Yes, but you're you. Her father was probably terrified to say no. And she was probably terrified to say yes."

"This isn't a game, David. You could end up with Saul's daughter for a wife!"

The possibility is making my heart jump, and I'm relieved Joab can't tell. "So, you're certain I'll succeed? Because I will."

The mockery drops from Joab's eyes. "That's an easy bet. But it's not what I meant. Is Michal as unsuspecting as I think she is?"

"I haven't told her about the anointing." I turn my back, returning the sword to the wall.

"Wonderful way to begin a marriage," Joab infers caustically.

"You're saying Deborah knows everything about you?"

"I'm saying that Saul will have a perfect excuse to snatch Michal away when he finds out who you are. Is she worth all this if you're just going to lose her?"

"She's worth it." I answer through a throat that's shut tight. As much as I resent it, I can't ignore my own misgivings. There's so much Michal doesn't know about me. But I'm convinced it would be unwise to risk telling her. I love her, and she loves me. That will have to be enough to carry us through whatever comes.

I point at Joab. "You're coming with me. You and your brothers. The king said I could bring whatever soldiers I need."

Joab shrugs, but I know his resolve is tougher than iron. "We'll follow you anywhere. You know that. Even Eliab would too, at this point." He folds his arms. "Do you have a plan, or are you going to show up in Gath and explain your errand to Achish?"

Anticipation grips my veins. "Funny you should mention him. Thanks to Asa, I know that Achish has summoned a new contingent of warriors from his eastern training camps. They're traveling through Judah on their way to meet him in Ekron." And they're known to take Israelite heads on their way as trophies for Achish. Except they won't reach him this time.

Joab's brows lift. "Let me guess. A hundred?"

"Two hundred. We'll get every last one."

I've done it. I can see the battle gleam overshadowing the doubt in Joab's eyes. Unfortunately, that doesn't stop his mouth.

"If anyone had told me three years ago that we'd be hunting down Philistines for a Benjaminite Sarrah, I would have laughed in their face."

* * * * *

My mission is complete long before the next new moon. Every Philistine on his way to serve Achish is now dead, and I have proof. On my way back to Gibeah, I send word ahead to

Saul that I want Michal there when I see him. I want to make it clear that I did this for her, not him.

In preparation, I ride ahead of my nephews and guards, and go before the Lord to purify myself. A man never appears before his bride while his hands are stained with blood. Even the blood of his enemies. I watch it wash off in the stream, wondering if I'll ever really be rid of it. I still remember the first man I cut down, for Jonathan. Now I've killed two hundred. For his sister.

"Make me worthy of her, Yahweh."

Strangely, I feel more trepidation now than when I'd left. Becoming Saul's son is the strongest commitment I could make to him. And I would do it without reservations if it weren't for the anointing I'm hiding. If he knew who I am, he'd spear me right there in his throne room when I return. I splash my face, trying to drown the wild scenarios doing battle in my head.

Most of them vanish when I go before the king. His daughter is on his left, his son on his right. Jonathan's smile has never been bigger, but my eyes are riveted on Michal. She looks at me as though no one else exists. Encouraged, I force myself to meet Saul's gaze before lowering myself to the ground.

I've sent the bloody evidence ahead to the king, giving him plenty of time to verify my success and practice his response. But a sliver of annoyance traces the curve of his smile, giving me an answer to all the doubt I've carried around where he's concerned. He's not pleased with me. Not anymore. He didn't expect me to return. Joab was right.

I bow my head, letting that sink in before Saul says what everyone is expecting to hear. "My son."

Standing, I allow myself a brief glance at Abner before addressing the king. "My father."

Saul swallows, but he doesn't dare stay silent. He lifts his chin. "No one in Israel is more worthy of my daughter than you." His voice sounds hoarse.

When he nods, Michal comes to me. The moment her hands slide into mine, she catches her breath, pressing our foreheads together. Two tears slide down her face, and I pull her close as her arms come up around me.

I whisper into the curve of her neck. "It's all right. I'm here. We're safe."

"I know," she whimpers, her voice barely audible. "I just—I was upset when I found out." She lifts her eyes to mine. "Why would Abba do that?"

"He loves you." And hates me. I lean my cheek into hers so that she can hear me as the room erupts with applause. "But I love you more."

* * * * *

Michal and I are only married three months before Saul sends me out to fight. My attack on Achish's prized unit had prompted the Philistine king to send out his finest commanders, the princes of his territories, to threaten Judah. Two towns precariously close to Bethlehem were the first to be raided, leaving me extremely torn. The Law of Moses mandates a full year of peace for a newly-married man, but I was a fool to hope for that.

Jonathan argued against me leaving, but I'm hesitant to anger Saul. I send Michal to stay with her sister in Meholah until I'm able to return, hopefully for a longer respite.

When the Philistine princes have been scattered, their army decimated, I return to my house and find Joab waiting in my armory, wearing a storm cloud on his brow. Exhausted, I barely make an effort to cover my annoyance.

"Whatever this is, I don't have time. I have to make my report to the king." I untie my cloak and fling it aside. "Four of the Philistine governors have been killed, which means their territories will be weakened for a time. This is a prime opportunity to capture as many blacksmiths as we can, try to keep our weapon stores built up."

Which will likely mean more battle errands and less time at home. Will my wife have the fortitude to be married to a commander? "I have to send word to Michal that I'm back."

"I didn't come here to discuss pleasantries," Joab snaps. "Aaron came to me a few days ago."

"Aaron, my father's hired man?" It's been years since I've seen my old mentor.

"Yes," Joab grits his teeth around the words. "The man who apparently knows things about you that no one else does."

"I never told him about the anointing, Joab." My nephew's agitation is seething into me, and I muscle past it, praying my old friend is safe. I hadn't considered what Saul might be up to in my absence. "What happened?"

"He met Doeg; that's what happened." Joab's eyes are ablaze. "I told you that son of Edom was trouble."

The spy's name is like a fist in my stomach. Why does he feel the need to cause dissension? "We've done nothing wrong, Joab. What does Doeg think he'll find out?"

"You know what he's trying to find out!" Joab unfolds his arms, barely restraining himself. "Be smart, David. Saul has been trying to figure you out for years, and Doeg desperately wants favor with him. If he can prove that Samuel anointed you, then Saul will have what he needs to openly destroy you instead of sneaking around, hoping the Philistines will do it. You have to protect yourself and those who are loyal to you."

"I told you, Aaron doesn't know anything."

"But others do," Joab insists. "All he has to do is ask around."

"Thanks to you."

Veins explode in Joab's neck. "I am not the enemy, David! I'm simply an opportunist. Back in Bethlehem, there are plenty of people who would love to see you crowned. But we might not have time to wait as long as you want to. Doeg threatened Aaron, and the old man told him everything he knew."

"And what is that?" My mind rushes back to those days in the pastures, trying to isolate something.

Joab sighs sharply. "Nothing definitive. But he said you somehow knew about the battle with Goliath. You'd been having dreams about it."

I fold my arms over the tumult in my chest. "I knew something was coming, and I was meant to be part of it. That's all."

Joab's eyes lock onto mine. "He said that when you were fourteen, you jumped into a battle at Aijalon, and saved Jonathan's life, but never told the king."

"It wasn't my place—"

"And he said you took something from Jonathan's body that day, some kind of message from the arrow that struck him."

The message that's addressed to Melek Israel. That could be bad.

Anyone else would have assumed that Achish had been threatening Saul with that message. But how would I explain why I'd kept it? The inner witness that it was meant for me? Good thing I keep it on me and not in my house somewhere. The Edomite has likely been through my belongings looking for it.

I don't have to tell Joab that it's all true. I can feel the alarm in my eyes.

He nods, assessing me. "You're an idiot, you know that?"

I turn away. "I didn't know what was happening back then, Joab; I only knew that I had to keep my eyes open. There's no proof of rebellion in any of that."

"That's not the point." Joab shoves a chair out of his way. "Doeg can twist all that and use it to prove that you were working behind the king's back, hiding things. Saul will jump at the chance to make the people believe you are dangerous. *His* people, anyway."

Offense beats inside my fear. "They're all our people, Joab. Whatever tribe, we're all sons of Israel."

"Sons of Israel have tried to murder each other before. I'd suggest you leave while you can."

"Leave Gibeah?" I'm affronted by the suggestion, but what angers me more is that it might actually be necessary. "Joab, I'm married! I'm under the command of the king. I can't just leave."

"You said Michal is in Meholah with her sister. You can send a message to her explaining…"

"You're insane!" I shove away from him. I've been married for three months, and already he's suggesting I leave Michal!

I stand at the window, feeling Joab's gaze digging into my back. "You like them too much," he purrs. "You think you can lie low and pretend to be one of them. But you can't. Sooner or later, they'll figure out who you are, and then you'll see how little they actually care."

I refuse to turn around and let him see how much that hurts. "You don't know them like I do."

Joab's voice pulls tight. "Fine. Then tell Jonathan. I dare you to tell him who you are and see what happens." He walks away, leaving a trail of warnings behind him. "Mark my words, David. If you don't take charge, this is going to end very badly."

* * * * *

After a sleepless night, I send for Jonathan, only to be told that he's been pulled into a sudden council meeting. Bad sign. If the Hassar has been called in, it's possible there was some attack. But why not include the commanders then?

Everything feels covered by a dark cloud since Joab's visit. I go out to the fields and pace the hours away, meandering through the paths that I've walked and ridden with Jonathan. Any other prince would have let me drown in the expectations that were hurled at me after Goliath. Not Jonathan. He's never left my side since that day in Elah. His consistent instruction helped me keep my head above the current and grow stronger.

Joab can't be right about him. We made a promise before God. He won't harm me. But that doesn't mean he won't be angry. Everything I've kept from him tosses inside me until I feel sick over it. I'm going to let down the one man who's been there for me every time I've needed him. And now I'm married to his sister! What am I going to tell Michal?

I pace, begging Yahweh to ease my mind's torrent.

It seems like years before I see the prince approaching from the fortress. Jonathan looks like he's aged overnight, carrying a heaviness that wasn't there before. I go to meet him, wondering which of our enemies is taunting us now. If I'm being called out to fight again, our discussion will have to wait.

Jonathan doesn't waste time. "I just came from my father's council." He shoves the words out like it's an effort to draw breath.

"Another attack?" I ask him, my defenses rising.

"I wish." Jonathan grinds his jaw, looks at the ground, then lifts his eyes. "He commanded me to have you killed."

NINETEEN

Jonathan

———◆◆◆◆◆———

David's mouth forms one word, but no sound follows it. "What?"

All the color pulls from his face, and I can almost feel the ground shudder under our feet. "He told all his councilmen to put you to death."

My own words feel like a betrayal. They're spearing me from the inside, and all I want to do is dispatch them like enemy threats. But this kind of attack won't be so easily countered. The hot breath of treachery still hangs around my shoulders like smoke clinging to a garment. My father's courtroom had never felt so oppressive. I'm amazed I was able to get out of there without losing my temper.

The accusations still sting like embers on my skin. How could the king be so quick to believe such evil reports? From an Edomite, no less! The half-brothers of Israel have proven untrustworthy one too many times. Yet Doeg's report had stirred my father's wrath. Violence had seethed from the king as though he'd been holding it back for years.

"I want David dead!" He'd gripped his head the way he used to in the old days of torment, handling his fear with desperate anger. "That backstabbing pretender wants to steal the throne from us, and we will have to strike first before he gets any closer to it."

Restraining my own horror, I had tried to placate him, wondering if the evil spirit was returning. "Abba, are you ill? Do you want me to get—"

"No!" My father had recoiled as though I'd struck him. "Don't bring that misbegotten shepherd here unless it's with his head under your arm!"

The darkness closing in over us had made my head swim. I've learned how to fight every physical enemy that threatens my father, but this evil trying to separate him from David is a much more sinister foe.

With the king's rage still hammering in my head, I can barely look at David. He reacts much like I did, the shock on his face disintegrating into anguish. "What have I done?"

"Nothing. You've done nothing." Livid flames sear my throat. "It's just Doeg's lies." I'd never dreamed the Edomite would make it his personal mission to go after David. He'll regret ever speaking a word to the king. He doesn't know my brother like I do.

We've fought in battle together, David and I. I've seen him remain faithful to Israel and to God, continually willing to lay his life on the line to defeat the Philistines. I had finally begun to believe that things were improving—that the king was no longer insane. But now fresh jealousy is stirring the fires of his rage, and the unfairness is choking us both.

Turning away, David holds his fists up to his head, his words mangled in a near- sob. "Why is he doing this? I've done nothing but serve him faithfully. I married his daughter. Why does he hate me?"

Simple. I release the truth in one breath. "Because God chose you over him." I lift my eyes, pinning them to David's so he can see my certainty. "You're the man after God's heart, the one anointed to replace him. Aren't you?"

I've never said it, but I've known it for a long time. It's a relief to admit it aloud, to have no more secrets between us.

The terror darkening David's eyes seals my certainty. "Who told you?" he whispers.

My laugh comes out in pieces. "You did. By accident. That first morning you were in the fortress, when we came out here. But I could already see it."

I pause, my chest constricting. "It was obvious from the beginning that there was a different spirit about you. I had never met anyone who always had Yahweh's praises ready on his tongue. You continually set yourself to do His will, even if you didn't understand it. And after Goliath—it was just confirmed over and over. God's favor follows you wherever you go. You will be the next king of Israel."

The moment the words leave my mouth, they feel like a pronouncement. Finality settles into my heart. No more waiting, wondering whom to watch out for. My father's frantic scheming will come to nothing.

David will be king. As he should be.

"Don't...don't say that..." David's anxiety pushes back.

"But it's true, isn't it? Samuel anointed you all those years ago, before you even came to play for the king. Didn't he?" I search his face.

David turns away from me, a tight gasp escaping him. "Jonathan, I haven't plotted anything against your father. I don't want to take the throne from you."

When I grab his shoulder, I can feel him trembling. "It isn't mine. Yahweh is King of Israel. We fight for His glory. He chose you because you remember that."

David looks sick. "Does your father know?"

"If he hasn't guessed by now, I'd say he has his eyes closed." Even so, it's not something I plan on revealing. Not yet. He'll see in time. And hopefully repent before then, for all our sakes.

David shakes his head. "He's tried to kill me before, Jonathan. And then all those times in battle, trying to get rid of me. I didn't want to believe it, but he wants me dead."

I dig my fingers into his arm. "Stop saying that, David. You know he loves you, as I do. It's just the evil spirit trying to come back."

David rolls his eyes. "Jonathan, no one loves me as you do."

I chuckle, desperate to shake off the weight that's dropped onto us. I do love David. Even before I adopted him, he was like a brother. "Relax. I'm going to talk to him."

"Talk to him? He's already said—"

"Hold on." I lift a hand to stop him. "I know what's happening. His spies are playing with his head, exploiting his jealousy. It's only a misunderstanding." Hearing myself say it aloud clears my head. I can fix this.

David's eyes burn with unshed tears. "What about this?"

He pulls a scrap of stained parchment from his cloak. The words are faded but chilling. *And so it begins, Melek Israel.*

"From Achish?" I ask.

David lowers his head. "I can't explain why I kept it." His eyes lift enough for me to see the pain streaking his face. "Still think I'm innocent?"

I bury the paper in my fist and place both my hands back on his shoulders. "Listen to me. You took this from the arrow that almost ended my life. That's enough for me."

Will it be enough for Saul? The question screams behind the relief in David's face.

I push the paper back into his hands. "Go to the south field today and hide there. I'll bring my father around and talk to him about you, help him see the truth. Then I'll come find you, and tell you everything."

"You would risk his anger after he already commanded you?"

"He won't be angry for long. The accusations they brought against you have nothing to do with insurrection. He just doesn't see it yet."

In the meantime, I'll do what I've always done where my father is concerned. Shift the attention. Talk over my own fears. Help him see.

"I'm certain he doesn't want to kill you any more than he wants to kill me. He just had one of his insecure moments, seeing enemies where there are none. He wouldn't back down in front of the officials, but I'm sure he will listen to me in private. We'll have you back at his side in no time."

David winces, unconvinced. "What about you?"

"Me?"

"You're not angry? Knowing what you know?"

I consider for half a second, but I'm really not. Fighting God is a futile mission, something I want no part of. I would much rather work with Yahweh, as I'd done at Michmash. The possibility of a new king is something I've known about for years, and if someone else has to rule Israel, I can't think of anyone I'd rather serve under than my best friend.

I shake my head, sincerity softening my face.

"I wanted it to be you."

* * * * *

Back in the fortress, impatience claws at me while I wait for my father to be left alone, free of his councilmen and the prying eyes of guards. The news of his pronouncement is filling the fortress like smoke, dragging the oppressive weight of fear with it. I see the sickened question in every servant's eyes. If David isn't safe, is anyone?

Abner lingers as though bound to my father's side.

"General!" My voice claps in the empty antechamber, startling both men. "Why are you here?"

Abner stammers, "Well, I—"

"When the king gives commands, I expect to find you carrying them out." I don't stop until I'm inches from him. "Does Israel's general expect his men to make his arrests for him?"

Abner's expression snaps shut, and he steps around me, leaving the room.

My father eyes me from his throne, a wine glass dangling from his hand, and I feel a shiver of pity. These bouts of rage always drain him. If only he would stop alienating the one who's brought nothing but peace, he might find some.

"Where have you been?" he slurs. "Looking for David?"

"Actually, yes."

Saul sets his wineglass down and rubs a hand over his eyes. "He'll turn up. He can't hide from Abner. I can't find anyone today. Doeg was supposed to return, but he hasn't. Summon him, will you? I should reward him for uncovering this—"

"My lord, I must speak with you," I interrupt him.

My father blinks, startled. "Now?"

"Preferably. Will you come out to the fields with me?"

He sighs, wincing. "Jonathan, I'm exhausted."

"Please, my king. This matter is urgent, but it must stay between us. We cannot be too careful."

Alarm glimmers through the weariness in Saul's eyes. Urgency is one thing he understands. "Very well."

It seems to take ages to get through the fortress, with every guard and servant asking if we need assistance. Finally, my father snaps, "Is my son Jonathan not assistance enough? He could fight better than any of you when he was a *child!*"

His words settle into me, and by the time we clear the outer gates, I'm aching with the magnitude of everything that's changed since my youth. When my father had been chosen by Yahweh to lead Israel, I'd never been prouder of anyone. Any fear of what we might face had been melted down in the furnace of my fervor. All that mattered was that I became strong enough to defend my father and my country. I had poured myself into doing that, dragging any weakness into the open so I could grow past it.

I had never dreamed that things would unravel so quickly. The noble, stalwart father I'd loved had disintegrated into a suspicious egomaniac willing to threaten his own children to preserve a throne that wasn't his anymore.

Now, it's all being threatened—everything we've built over the years with David fighting God's battles and helping to ensure Israel's power in the region. Everything he is to me and to my sister. The stability he's brought my father. Surely, we're not about to lose it all. We can't expect Yahweh's blessing if we destroy David.

I lift my eyes, watching the sun bleeding into the edge of the fields as it sets. *Please, Yahweh. Help him see the truth.*

"How much solitude do you need in order to speak your mind?" My father leans against the tamarisk tree. "We haven't walked this far alone since you were a boy."

I didn't expect to feel bereft, remembering. My father and I had been close before Michmash. After that, he'd started to look at me the way he looks at David now.

Folding his arms, Saul closes his eyes, his head against the tree. "I'm surprised you didn't resist me earlier today with my order to have David killed. I know how much you like him."

I suck in my breath, trying to see through the burn filling my eyes, my head.

My father blinks, studying me. "He used to remind me of you. Except that your ambition knew its place. You used it to serve me, not steal from me."

I twist my seal ring around my finger, resisting anger. I wonder if he regrets those years when he'd leave me bruised and bloodied after a bout of rage. Or if he thinks he did right, beating me into submission. Either way, I've earned every bit of respect and position I have with him. And I'll need every bit of it now. In addition to *chesed* straight from Yahweh.

"Do you trust me, Abba?"

His face pulls into a half-smile. "You are one of the few I still can."

"Do you trust that the counsel I give you is because I seek to honor you, and Yahweh?"

"Yes." He frowns, impatient. But he has no idea how much I love him. And David.

My breath frozen in my throat, I lower myself to one knee.

"My lord and king, I beseech you not to sin against your servant David. I have looked into the reports Doeg brought before you, and I have found nothing worthy of death."

I lift my head, my voice twisting. "He took his life into his hands that day to kill Goliath and rescue Israel. Achish was mocking us, trying to undo years of work, but David lifted our armies back to the place that you paved for them with your battles. You saw it and rejoiced! Everyone knew that you were wise to elevate him and make use of his skills."

My father stiffens, darkness trying to push back into his face. "I was wise to honor him when he was a shepherd boy, full of humble courage. But the favor of the people has changed him. I would be foolish not to answer these threats."

"My lord, Doeg's accusations have to do with the past, before Goliath." I lower my head briefly, praying that any wrath might fall on me, and not my brother.

I breathe deeply. "I was the reason you never heard about what David did at Aijalon. I didn't want you to know what danger I was in. Not with your health the way it was back then. And I didn't think it would be fitting for so much attention to go to David at that time. But he saved my life that day, Abba. He used my own spear against the Philistine who shot me."

My father shoves off the tree, his attention fixed on me. I can see my words working through his mind. "And what about what he took from you?"

"David ben Jesse hasn't taken anything from me." Nothing that wasn't already his.

"He has given me much more than I've given him," I continue. "I call him my brother, but he's more like a son. He loves Michal; he risked his life for her. And he's risked his life for you more times than I could count. Should we be so quick to believe a foreign servant who seeks favor from you by accusing your own son-in-law?"

My father stares, unblinking.

I clasp my hands. "Believe me, Abba, I have done much more against your orders than David has. And yet you've spared my life."

"You're my son."

"So is he."

My father's eye twitches. Chewing the inside of his mouth, he turns aside once, then looks back. "He saved you? Truly?"

"And he didn't leave my side until he knew I would be all right. Someone bent on rebellion would have let me die. He's had so many chances to turn against us, and yet he always chooses honor. He doesn't want any more rewards. Only your faith that he's no traitor. Your favor means the world to him, Abba." As it does to me.

I've never been more relieved to see my father's eyes full of tears. When he unfolds his arms, I can see how he's trembling. I go to his side, and he clasps my shoulders.

"Where is he, Jonathan?"

"I'll find him." I set my jaw against the relief sweeping through me. Abba's face is softer without the darkness.

He touches my face, his lips quivering. "Yes. Bring him back, Jonathan. I will not take his life."

* * * * *

I let a day go by without summoning David, waiting to see how my father will react to the delay. But Saul is nearly frantic by the second sunrise, no doubt worried that David will disappear into Judah's territory and reveal how he was treated.

"Are you sure he'll come back, Jonathan?" Abba's shadow-rimmed eyes are bloodshot from lack of sleep. "It could take me a lifetime to find another like him. I'm furious at myself for not verifying those reports."

"You believed Doeg could be trusted, Abba. You had no way of knowing he would deceive you. But you're right. It's much wiser to trust someone who has proven himself over the years." He's fortunate this happened while Michal was still in Meholah. I hadn't figured out how I would have explained this to her. "You will see David tonight. He never planned on leaving you, my lord. He was just afraid."

My father touches my shoulder, gratitude spreading through his face. "You are a wise man, my son. You will make a much better king than I."

I dismiss the comment with a smile, but anxiety lights a warning signal inside me. This isn't over.

Leaving Ezra to make sure no one follows me, I head out to the fields and follow the southern path until it forks beyond the tamarisk tree. "David."

My friend emerges from behind the boulders but doesn't come to me.

"My father has relented," I tell him.

David's eyes are huge and dark. It's evident that he hasn't slept either. "What did you say to him?"

"I told him that you aren't a threat. Reminded him that he doesn't want to harm you."

"Doesn't he?" David exhales sharply, looking away.

I step closer and lean against the giant boulder Ezel that faces the south.

"He's worried now. He's sick that he believed Doeg over you. I convinced him those reports were hearsay, slander even. That Edomite won't be returning to court for some time." I nudge David's shoulder. "The king asked me to make sure you came back tonight. Everything will be fine." I say it over a shudder that's buried so deep I don't want to touch it.

His arms folded, David watches the long grasses bowing in the wind. "How can I walk back in there and face Abner and the council after he accused me to them?"

"They've all watched him accuse others. They know you've done nothing wrong." I sigh deeply, trying to unwind the tightness in my chest. "Many of them were there when my father tried to kill me."

David looks up, pain opening wider in his eyes.

"It was after Michmash, and he was about to kill me for breaking a vow I didn't know he'd made. But Abner and several of the officers stopped him. They knew he would have regretted it."

"He does anyway." David's whisper is ragged.

I nod, my jaw twitching. "So, you see, they all know he has a tendency to get caught up in suspicion and mistrust. Even the best king needs counselors to remind him to open his eyes and stop seeing threats in his head."

"But I am a threat. And he knows it." David drags a deep breath over the words, resisting the emotion shaking in them.

I lift my chin. "But you will never harm him. That's all he needs to know right now." I wait, but David doesn't speak, doesn't look up. I push his shoulder, trying to shake off the cloud that has settled. He needs sunlight. "Come on, giant-killer. Trust the brother Yahweh gave you."

A smile touches David's eyes, but stops there. I study him, something unruly dancing around inside me. I'm tired of all this suspicion weighing us down. Both of us have lost plenty of youth to war and politics, and it's a slow death. But our lives are not over. Why should we act like they are?

Glancing down the path, I get an idea. "Come on." I grab David's arm, dragging him along.

He looks around, confused. "Where? What are you doing?"

"Just come on."

I lead David down the barely-used path that winds around to some cliffs at the edge of the fields. The shady section of trees used to conceal my brothers and me in our youth when we wanted to escape for a few hours, reclaim some freedom. Within a mile, the ground slopes away from us, dropping down to the rushing chatter of the stream below. The water's breath is already traveling up the hillside, cooling the sweat on my forehead. Swollen with all the recent rains, the pool beneath is plenty deep enough.

I turn around, unbuckling my sword, and tossing it under a tree. Then I do the same with David's.

"What are you doing?"

"I want you to stop looking at me like you've been condemned. It's a new day. Your wife is returning tomorrow. The future Yahweh has for Israel is brighter than that sun over our heads. That's what I want to see on your face from now on." I grin at him, feeling like I've shed five years. "Now jump."

David blinks, looking over the ledge. "Jump? Why?"

Anticipation dances inside me. "Suddenly you have a problem with heights? Jump, or I'll push you in."

"Jonathan—"

"Fair enough." I grab his shoulders and yank, pulling him off the edge with me. There's barely enough time for him to react before we plunge into the water.

The coldness swallowing us is deeper than I remember, pulling us down several feet before our heads break the surface. Filling my lungs, I yell as though I've won a war, while David chokes through angry laughter.

"You're dead—" He lunges at me in the current, but I shove water in his face. Swiping hair from his eyes, he ducks under for a moment.

"You think you're safe down there?" I taunt him. I'm barely touching ground, but I don't think David can. Wrapping my arms around his waist, I toss him further into the current.

Struggling to breathe, David kicks back at me, his real smile emerging. "You're crazy! How did you become so wild?"

"I'm of Benjamin." I wink at him, gratitude lifting inside me. I've missed this. The old days of David's early training when we'd hunt and explore together, sharpening battle skills, comparing Benjamin's reckless tendencies with Judah's fierce nationalism. Being brothers.

Swimming toward the rocks, David coughs, forcing water from his lungs. I climb the bank behind him, and he glares at me. "Watch your back from now on. I have plenty of cousins who would love to throw you off a cliff."

"And I have a dangerous younger brother who won't let that happen." I grin, swiping water from my eyes. It's such a mystery, what's happened between us, but it's real. David is bound to me in a way that even my blood relatives haven't been. We're brothers. The threat to his safety made me realize we always will be.

Thank God I didn't lose him.

TWENTY

David

———◆◆◆◆◆———

Israel's army camp hums with activity. Only a few miles outside of Gibeah, the mood is as golden as the harvest sunshine, and I breathe it in from the door of my tent, waiting for it to reach the coldness lodged in the center of my chest.

With the way the Philistines seek my life, I should be thankful to be coming home. After weeks of fighting our neighboring enemy, the Geshurites, it's gratifying to return and see Israel's fields brimming with abundance. A bountiful year is always cause for celebration, and the city will be in a frenzy with it by the time we return, anticipating the autumn festivals at the advent of the new moon.

The more ground we take from our enemies, the more we're assured of continued fruitful seasons. Our returning armies allow the people to see their security on display, and their appreciation grows with each year. Crowds of exultant families followed us north from the borders of Geshur, singing and throwing floral garlands.

Everywhere I go, men point me out to their sons, and women dance around me, letting their shawls touch my face and shoulders. In the training camp just outside Aijalon, Saul's commanders and special forces spar with each other, sorting through the spoils and making the most of the comradeship that only exists out here.

Their shouts reach me through the walls of my tent, and my heart turns wistful. My position with Saul's finest has been hard-won, but it warms me. It's filled my life to such an extent that to imagine losing it makes me feel like the earth is moving under me.

In battle, I understand my enemies and how to outwit them. But the closer I get to Gibeah, the more I feel the pull of darkness. An uneasy tide tugging me down paths I have no answers and little skill for.

No one in the army had believed Saul's accusations. Or at least, they haven't talked about them. Most people brushed the whole thing off, hearing Jonathan's account blaming Doeg for his slander. But then there's the men who really know Saul—Abner, his kinsmen, and cousins. They know there's more to the story. They know that if I hadn't run, I would've been arrested and killed. They know I had to hide and wait for Jonathan to speak for me. And they probably know I haven't recovered.

Since Saul accused me, I've been flinching through each day, muscles locked in anticipation of another blow, one more devastating than before. Even buried in battle, I have to steel myself, unable to erase the fear that one of these days, he just might march into camp and bury his sword in my chest regardless of anyone. Though it's more likely that he would keep himself out of it, maybe assign paid mercenaries to follow me.

Whatever form his next attack will take, it's clear that in spite of everything Jonathan has done, Saul's heart hasn't softened.

Every time I straighten out of a bow, I search his face again, hoping I'll find the fatherly appreciation that was there before. The coldness in his eyes might be overlooked by anyone else, but I can see the difference, and whether or not they realize it, everyone feels it. Everyone, it seems, except Jonathan.

I shove more items into my pack, hit by another fist of agitation. Our friendship is just one more thing that Saul's hatred is trying to poison, though Jonathan will fight tooth and nail to prevent that. I still see him shoving me in the river, his laughing eyes daring me to hope that Yahweh will hold things steady.

It's true, of course, but I still felt relieved when the Hassar wasn't included on this mission. Saul kept him back, coming up with a litany of things for him to do in court. It's easier when circumstances separate us, and I don't have to avoid Jonathan.

He's still with me though. Everything I've learned from the king's son runs through my mind as I fight. I can't get through war council meetings without feeling his absence. The gold pendant etched with the face of a lion hasn't left my neck since he put it there. It thumps against my chest, reminding me. I'm in Yahweh's keeping. And my brother's.

I miss Jonathan. I hate avoiding him in private settings, keeping our interactions in the open so that I don't have to say anything meaningful. But I can't risk it. He's far too adept at reading my mind, and he won't agree with what's there. How can I prove it, after all? How can I explain to him that when I look at Saul, I absolutely know that he's still hoping to remove me somehow?

Discouraged, I crumple up several parchments, unfinished letters I've tried to write to my wife. Michal won't understand, but Jonathan should. I've heard the stories about Saul's attempt on his life. And Abner had hinted once that Saul used to beat Jonathan. Even without that information, I know the prince has borne the worst of the king's anger. So, you'd think he would notice it being directed at me.

Just the opposite.

I know what the past several months have meant to my friend. Since his father listened to his counsel and sent Doeg away, Saul has kept his son closer, drawing out his diplomatic skills in court and lifting him up publicly in a way he hasn't in years.

"I have more pride in my son than I have in myself," Saul had said recently at his table, before I'd left for Geshur. And it was like a curtain dropped from Jonathan's face, revealing the purest shock and pleasure. He's been starved for this kind of surety, and he wants to believe it's real. My ribs ache remembering it. I know what it's like to yearn for your father.

In spite of his love for me, Jonathan will go to his grave believing that Saul still has a grasp on integrity, even if it's barely noticeable. Something in him has to believe it. He's willing to set aside Saul's order to kill me, blaming it on the evil spirit he's struggled with. But I remember those days when I was first brought to Gibeah.

Saul's torment would start with rumbling hints of anger, like clouds rolling in. Then the uneasiness would begin to pull him apart, following him into his dreams, draining him of strength like a disease would. While I played, Saul would cower and tremble, pleading for help until my music calmed him.

It's different now. Since the day I married Michal, I know he's been looking for another chance to get rid of me. More and more of my missions are isolated and dangerous, no doubt by design. And when I play for the king, he watches me.

I remember plenty of starless nights on the hills of Bethlehem, encamped with my father's sheep, when I would see wolves just beyond the circle of my fire. Their eyes gleaming through the flames. Their husky forms pacing just out of reach, waiting for the light to disappear. It never did. And my music always steadied me, coaxing my courage out of the shadows until I could stare any danger in the face.

But that's how it is when I play for Saul now.

There's a reason it's so easy for him to appear normal with Jonathan. His anger has a target now, and he's fixated on it. His suspicion is no longer aimless, wandering from person to person, occasionally stopping to wonder about me. Now, he knows who the threat is. And he knows what backs have to be turned in order for him to do something about it.

His anger tumbles out in mutters I can't understand. But I know he's cursing me under his breath. Threatening me. Aloud, he's made remarks that are too pointed to be mistaken. And he makes sure Jonathan isn't around for most of them. Saul has been shifting much of the kingdom's governance to the Hassar, allowing him sway over matters that don't require his direct supervision. Making it clearer than ever what his intentions are.

Whatever struggles they've had in the past, Saul intends for his son to rule. Another reason why he has to get rid of me. And that's something Jonathan will never participate in. I adjust my armor vest, my hands sweating. Clearly, the king believes it's better to ask forgiveness than permission where I'm concerned, but he's the one person in the kingdom who isn't afraid of Jonathan.

One day, Saul will realize that he's underestimated his firstborn. But for now, Jonathan's kept ignorant. And busy.

Michal, on the other hand, senses far too much. To this day, she knows nothing about Saul's attempts on my life, but she keeps count of every time I'm sent out to battle, and she's starting to take her father's treatment of me personally. She's stopped sending messages to me while I'm out here, but I can hear her as clearly as though she's in the tent with me.

"Why does he use you like some sort of good luck charm? Doesn't he realize you could be killed? He doesn't ask Malchi or Ishvi to go out so much! And he let them stay home with their wives for a year! You would think the champion of Israel would mean more to him—if not his own daughter. But I'm the youngest, I suppose. He doesn't care."

She complains that I'm on edge and distant, though I try not to be. My bland excuses only make her angrier. Sooner or later, I'll have to tell her what troubles me. But I can't do that without revealing how her father accused me of treason. And then she'll go to Jonathan, who will say everything's fine. And I'll seem like a paranoid soldier who's seen too much combat. Michal thinks that's the reason I don't sleep well anymore.

"Sing for us, David!" The commanders' high spirits begged for songs last night, but I could barely play through the strange shaking taking over my fingers. While everyone else slept, I stayed awake for hours, anxiety stroking unruly strings inside me. I couldn't drift off until I started focusing on the rustling of the trees and the distant call of night birds.

It's been years since I wanted to run from something, and I resent the sensation. Even in the pastures, grappling with my father's silence and my own unrealized dreams, I'd trusted that Yahweh would open the right paths before me when the time was right. I never used to be like this.

I touch the weathered curve of my lyre, edging through its frayed wool covering, wishing I could believe that everything in my life isn't going to unravel.

"My lord…"

I tense when my servant pushes into the tent. I'm still not used to being called anything other than David.

On the edge of people's respect, I still hear Eliab's mockery sometimes. And then I have to remember that I wasn't anointed to be Saul's commander, but Israel's king. How many of these men would try to kill me if they knew that?

It feels shocking and yet completely appropriate that the next words from my servant are, "Saul is here."

"Why?" I ask. My bored tone is meant to cover the way the news bites through my nerves. It doesn't. My servant looks just as unwound as I feel.

"I don't know, my lord. He knew we would reach Gibeah by the end of the day."

I lift my bow and force myself into the sunlight without giving myself a chance to think. Facing Saul with a weapon steadies me slightly, even if I would never use it on him.

The commanders are scattered among half-packed tents, animals, and a few targets they'd set up the night before. One glance, and I can tell Saul's presence has unnerved everyone, in spite of their efforts to hide it.

Though he's gone out to fight plenty of times throughout the years, Saul rarely shows up unannounced. It's even stranger to see him here without Jonathan. But I've learned to expect the unexpected with Saul. My appearance ends the men's startled silence, and several unsteady greetings lift toward the king.

Against my instincts to blend in, I step forward and bend into a bow, grateful for the chance to collect my nerve.

Striding back and forth in front of us, Saul studies each warrior, his hawk-like assessment not revealing any clues about his reasons for coming. "You're not pleased to see me." It's not a question. And not particularly directed at me, so I don't answer.

"Why would we be anything else, Abba?" Ishvi laughs, lifting some of the tension. "It's like old times, seeing you here after a battle."

The men mumble agreement, their responses slowly building into the overdone enthusiasm everyone uses in the court to cover anxiety.

One of Saul's commanders, Beriah, takes a half step forward. "If you've come to see if we've been victorious, my lord, you will not be disappointed."

Saul moves through the lines of soldiers. "Why would I have to come here to find that out? The songs are already beginning back in the streets of *my* capital."

This time, the words are aimed at me. I can feel their points darting through, sinking every bit of enthusiasm I've been riding on these past few days. Those ridiculous songs. I wonder why the youths of Gibeah don't realize their mistake in throwing someone else's triumphs in their king's face.

The commanders chuckle, and Malchi tries to cover my silence. "The people do love to recount the victories of their leaders. Have you not heard how they sing about you in the streets, about the thousands you've slain?"

"But not tens of thousands. Like David." Saul's voice is like iron, weighing everyone down. Not a single soldier is looking him in the eye.

Only Beriah attempts to lighten the mood with a jovial shrug. "We all knew that when you handed him over to Jonathan, you'd create a monster."

"And who do you think trained Jonathan?" The king's statement quenches the nervous laughter that emerges.

Beriah adjusts his grip on his spear, trying to salvage what's going to pieces around him. "My king, every Philistine from here to the sea hopes you won't come out against them. Still, it's good to know that there are strong young warriors at our side, ready to defend us in our old age."

"You speak as though that day were already here." Saul stares him down, his eyes like daggers. His deafening silence allows for three painful heartbeats. Then, he calls without moving his head. "David!"

I move around in front of him and bend at the waist. As calmly as I can with everything clenching.

Saul angles his chin to the edge of camp. "Stand in front of the target."

Sharpness enters my chest while the men whisper amongst themselves.

Beriah stammers, "My lord…"

"You've said enough." Saul's gaze commands mine, forcing me to look into the dark resentment that burns inside it. "David trusts my skill. Don't you…son?"

I cringe at the way he bites through that last word. Even before I was his son, I wasn't safe. I don't trust him anymore. Not with my life. But I can't refuse him in front of his army. He's not requesting this. He's commanding it. Still, he wouldn't dare do either if Jonathan were here.

Barely feeling the ground under me, I go to the chosen target, staked in the ground at least seventy paces off. Anxiety hums through my limbs, drifting down to my feet. But when I face Saul, the tension turns, stiffening into a flinty resolve that's taken hold of me many times in battle. It's a wild sensation, forcing me to lift my gaze above whatever chaos spins on the surface. But it's a familiar defense, one that has shielded me from every attack.

I adjust my shoulders and open my fists, relaxing into the sense of covering that follows me. I don't trust Saul. But I trust Yahweh. He's saved me before, and I have no reason to assume He'll stop now. I release a slow breath with prayers tangled up inside it and feel peace flash through me in response.

My expression clearing, I level my gaze at Saul's face. Let him use me to show off. Yahweh is my Shield. The God who saved me from Goliath and countless Philistines won't let me be harmed by a jealous king.

Saul's first shot goes over my head. Barely. I can feel the wind around the shaft, pushing at my hair as it enters the target. A few men murmur, but most are deathly quiet, the air sucked out of the moment. I don't breathe either, managing not to flinch when the next arrow slams into place just above my left shoulder. The last one strikes just shy of my neck, taking some skin. Icy sweat prickles my face.

Saul's shout feels like a blow, even from a distance. "Satisfied now? Numbers mean little. But knowing where to strike is everything. Remember that as you return."

Murmuring strained approval, the men disperse to collect their weapons and prepare for travel. I can see the storm clouds on every brow. Even with all my success, none of them would trade places with me. They're hesitant to appear too loyal to me even though I've led them in battle for so long. Saul has eroded our bond in a matter of months with his accusations.

I wait for Saul to mount his mule before approaching. I need time to shove down the battle fury sweeping over me, pumping my veins with tumult that's designed to eliminate threats. This one won't be fixed that way. I'm not in combat, but I'm in danger.

There isn't even much relief waiting for me in Gibeah. I'll have to deal with Jonathan and Michal, figure out how to avoid talking about what Saul did, and why he might have. My life is becoming a whirlwind of erratic storms and unsteady calm, and I just can't explain it anymore, even to my best friend.

Saul knows this. He's tried to isolate me for years, counting on my obedience and abusing my discretion. Because he can.

He doesn't speak either. Because we both understand what just happened. He yanks his mule's head around and rides away, followed by his guards. The same ones I'd seen prowling Gibeah in search of me while I'd hidden in the south field.

"That was…strange. Even for him," Malchi acknowledges. More words wait in his silence, but they don't surface.

"He's been away from your music too long," Beriah suggests, slapping my shoulder on his way past. But the cloud Saul left behind is undisturbed, shrouding the camp while everyone gets ready to leave.

My servant brings my mule, and the reins are barely in my hands before the man mutters, "I wouldn't be his son for all the riches in the world."

I lift my head, staying quiet. What can I say when they already know so much? Saul might know where to strike, but did it ever occur to him that sometimes choosing not to strike is the stronger option? Of course, I've rarely had that luxury. And neither has he. The last man he spared point-blank was Jonathan. Then me. I don't want to look deep enough to see if he has it in him to do it again.

I ride ahead of the others so that they don't see the pain pushing to the surface. Even the frenetic pace of a life in battle is better than this plague of covert hatred. What hurts the most is that it comes from a fellow Israelite, someone I've sought to serve all these years! And to think as a boy, I'd imagined Achish would be my biggest problem. I stare at the countryside opening up before me, not seeing much of it.

Maybe it's time to take decisive action. Nothing against the king, of course. But I need guidance. Perhaps if I went to see Samuel, I'd have some sort of direction. At least enough to take a few steps out of this fog.

The idea relieves my mind, but insecurity nags just behind it. I'm shocked that I haven't sought Samuel's counsel until now, and I'd like to believe it's because I was confident that Yahweh would show me the way forward. Now, my nagging inner voice whispers that I can't seek the prophet after so long.

Hardly riding, I slow my mule almost to a stop, gripped by the anxiety I've uncovered. I'm afraid to face Samuel now. After all this time, he might take one look and tell me I'm failing. That I've missed something I'm supposed to do because I've been so busy trying to please the king. He'll chide me for being foolish enough to believe that marrying Michal would earn me Saul's respect. If anything, it's pulled me closer to the king's volatility.

Sharpness stings behind my eyes. It kills me that they were right—all those men who'd tried to warn me in my youth, mocking my idealism, telling me Saul would eat me alive.

I'd been so convinced they were wrong. I had grown up on battle stories, yearning to fight for Israel, believing Saul would be the way he was when Samuel had anointed him. Even with the news of his decline, I'd marched into the fortress with my harp, believing that he would thank me for my help. Only three short years have shown me otherwise.

I feel suffocated when I'm around him, always sensing a fire building. I'm brutally careful with my words, hoping he won't misinterpret anything. I can't lose myself in worship anymore when I play for him. I have to keep vigilant. Between the chaos of military missions and false accusations, it's been a long time since I openly led the people in worship. The priests love my songs, using many of them for weekly *shabbat* services and feasts. But Saul has sought to control even that, demanding to be present whenever I speak with any priest or seer.

How long will he wait before he gets tired of this game of control and decides to eliminate me?

Enough. Determined to outrun my apprehension, I shove the mule into a full gallop, relishing the feeling of the honeyed summer air hitting my face. I refuse to stay where I can't breathe. Saul can't force his torment on me. Whatever point he was trying to make today, his arrows only prophesied one thing. He shot at me, but he won't hit me.

Yahweh is the strength of my life, and the path He has placed before me cannot be thwarted by one king's jealousy. Our God has given us victory after victory against our enemies, and the only proper response is open gratitude.

Glorious rebellion tugs my faith to the surface. Welcome sparks of excitement dance through me until I want to shout, sensing the words ready to release in song. Before I was Saul's commander, I was the singer of Israel, and Yahweh's praises should always be on my lips. I don't need to wait for the king. I stretch my voice, flinging joyous declarations toward the pristine skies.

"Adonai, you are my God. I have no good apart from you.

"You make known to me the path of life.

"You fill me with joy in your presence!"

My heart expands to let the light in, and I urge the mule faster, letting the wind tug my hair and scatter my heaviness. My mind dances through every memory of God's presence rushing through my veins. At the altar with the anointing oil. In the fields of Judah, being speared with rain that quenched the enemy's fires. Facing Goliath and knowing he would fall, not before me, but before the real Lion of Judah.

The pleasures at Yahweh's side are greater than any earthly trouble. His presence is the relief that makes my whole being exult. Something unruly dances in my heart, and I allow a laugh to break open my smile. I'll overtake the king and worship in Gibeah's streets, the way I used to when I was a boy.

Because Yahweh is still worthy.

If Saul is going to watch the people dance and sing around me, he's going to remember why.

* * * * *

As soon as my feet hit Saul's stone porch, I fling myself over it to the ground. Sweat claws my body while I push through the garden gate and run, thankful that no guards follow me. I sprint all the way back to my house before the attack overtakes me, commanding my full attention. As soon as I slow my pace, the protective cloud of adrenaline lifts, leaving me feeling exposed.

I bend over, hands on my knees, and spit blood from the cut Saul's hand opened in my mouth. Seeing it in the dust sends dark fear rushing back in, filling me like a cistern drowned in rain. It's over. Saul doesn't care anymore. He doesn't care about his daughter or his son or any vows he might have made. He just wants me dead.

I swipe the blood from my mouth, breathing in hard around the knife-edged cramps in my ribs.

Only a few hours ago, I'd been soaring on the praises of my God, accompanying the priests in worship and dancing with the people until my lungs gave out. I had ignored Saul for most of the celebration, refusing to pay attention to the way his anger was mounting like a thunderhead.

After what happened at the camp, he'd expected a show of submission—a restive, browbeaten soldier whose king had used him for target practice. Instead, I returned as myself. The wild, worshipful shepherd boy he can't control.

But it was worth it to see my wife laugh and my friends abandon themselves in worship before the God who has given us everything. The exultation had scattered my anxiety like rain clouds driven by wind. It's been too long since I danced like that.

I was still trying to regather my breath when the king ordered me into his private chambers to play for him. Alarm rakes through my veins as his words tumble back over me.

"You think the people look at you and see a shepherd? Brandishing a Philistine sword. Dancing in the streets. Warbling about Yahweh's victory." Fingers clamped around the spear, Saul had leaned forward, commanding me, "You will never behave like that again."

His tone was laden with ice, but my response was so gentle that the room didn't even pick up the sound. "My king, I was a worshipper long before I was a soldier. But honoring Yahweh doesn't make me any less your servant."

That was when Saul hit me, his roar exploding into echoes that hurled rage back over my head. "You're no servant! You're a conniving manipulator who wants to yank everything out from under me. You've taken my daughter, deceived my heir. You have Judah. What's next, son of Jesse?"

His violence would have paralyzed me as a boy, but after years in battle, I was able to see past it to the way his hand was gripping his spear, his arm muscles surging, ready to throw.

I'd been able to jerk away fast enough to let the spear smash into the door. The tree trunk nearly split the wood in a deafening crack that the whole house probably heard. But I was already jumping out the window onto the upper terrace, scrambling to the ground before Saul could send anyone after me.

"You can't hide behind my son forever!" he'd screamed through the window. "And Michal will thank me for destroying you when she finds out what you are!"

Michal. I can't believe I've dragged her into this. Unaware that I'm in my own courtyard, I drop to my knees and bring my fists up to my head.

"My lord?" One of my servants peers through my door, confused. I straighten up, rubbing the blood from my face. Tears stab my eyes when I hear Michal's voice through the window above us. I stand up, raising my hand to her.

"I'm coming."

It feels like years before I get upstairs and order the servants out of our room, closing the door behind me. My wife's questions are not even making it to my ears, bouncing off me as I try to think through the fog thickening around us.

"David! What's wrong?" She grabs my hands, and something about her touch helps me get the words out.

"Your father tried to kill me."

"He tried to what?"

The raw fear in her voice makes me want to drive a fist through the wall. How can Saul do this to us?

I open my hands, letting her see the blood in them. "He tried to kill me, Michal. It's hard to explain, but this isn't the first time, and—"

"Wait—this has happened before?" She nearly screeches, and I grab her shoulders.

"Shhh. He hates me, Michal. He's hated me for a long time. He hates—what I am."

"What does that mean? Why would he hate you?" Michal has gone gray, and her eyes are expanding, trying to take it all in. Feeling her starting to shake, I pull her close.

"I'm sorry. I'm so sorry, but I don't have time to explain. I need to get out of his way for a while. I need to talk to Samuel."

She pushes back from me, confusion joining the fear on her face. "Samuel? Why?"

The dread of telling her is still buried between my ribs, not budging. Why didn't it feel like this telling Jonathan?

Because you didn't. He told you.

I lock eyes with the woman I love, praying that there's something in her that can handle this. "This is going to sound crazy, but there's something I have to tell you…"

But I never finish. Midsentence, her expression changes, shifting over my shoulder, and I follow it out the window. Ten of Saul's guards are approaching the gate and fanning out, surrounding the house. Gripped by shock, I don't even hear myself speak. "They followed me."

Michal steps back, gripping the bedpost. "Oh God."

My mind floods, and I'm caught in the current, trying to grasp for solutions. "Maybe I can...talk to them. Or send for Jonathan."

"No! Stay right where you are!" Michal slaps me in the chest, tears appearing.

Resisting her panic, I keep trying. "Michal, they know me. They wouldn't just..."

But she's shaking her head, her breath coming short. "You don't understand. When my father intends to harm someone, no one can talk to him. He tried to kill you, and now he's sent men to watch the house." The look in her eyes freezes me. "Nothing can stop him when he's like this. You'll be dead by morning." A huge tear rolls down her face.

My stomach turns over. "Yahweh..."

I force the name of God through the panic and anger ripping my certainty to shreds. *You're my Shepherd. You won't let this pack of dogs attack me. Not when I'm trapped like this.*

Michal jumps, and suddenly she's moving with purpose, tearing at the tapestry hanging on the wall. "Help me; hurry! We can cut these cords and use them to let you down the back wall. The guards won't check that side since it opens over the garden." She smirks, and my spirits lift. She knows that garden gates don't bother me.

Moving as one, we pull the tapestry down and use my knife to slice through the ropes of thick fabric. It's almost too soon before I'm leaning out the back window, ready to throw my weight against the cords that will lower me halfway to the ground. I still have to figure out how to reach the stables without being seen. I'll need a horse if I'm going to make it to Ramah before Saul gets wind of where I've gone.

I stop halfway over the ledge and face Michal. "What about you?"

She's gripping the windowsill as though she's the one who's about to be lowered down. "I'll send for Jonathan. He'll die before he'll let anything happen to me."

I wince. Only Saul's guards at my gate could have forced me to leave both Jonathan and Michal behind. *Shield them, Yahweh.*

This still feels like a twisted nightmare I can't break out of. Only Michal's fingers biting into my arms tell me it's real. And the saffron sunset spearing the edges of my vision.

"Will you come back?" Michal is trying not to whimper.

I open my mouth to say yes, but then remember how I'd never returned to Bethlehem. Dread grips my stomach.

In the absence of my answer, Michal's face twists. "I'll pray you come back. If my father asks where you are, I'll say you're ill or something. Just send word as soon as you can."

"I will." I pull her forehead to mine and kiss her before slipping into the dark. "I don't deserve you."

TWENTY-ONE

Jonathan

———◆———

I should be sleeping. It's nearly midnight, and the celebration to welcome the army back left me drained. But I've been sitting at the table in my armory since returning home, conflicting images swimming behind my eyes. I wish all I could see was a joyous occasion with nothing under the surface.

Israel has plenty of reason to rejoice. It's been another strong military season, and the harvests have been plentiful. Michal and David have been strained lately, but tonight, I watched them dance and sing the hours away, and felt my own youth returning a little. Only to crash back down when I noticed my father, hanging back, watching the festivities like a hawk.

Am I imagining that look in his eyes now, the way he always keeps David in his sights? I'd run back through our last conversation in the fields a hundred times, at the way his eyes had welled up when I'd told him David saved my life. At the way his voice shook when he'd made me promise to bring him home.

Why should I doubt his sincerity, even if he's thrown spears in the past?

I glare across the room at the torchlight magnifying the shape of my weapons against the wall. That was over three months ago. Abba brought David back, and everything was the same. Except that it isn't.

David is still Israel's most successful warrior, but he's aging before my eyes, with Michal complaining that he's different. I've put her off, but tonight was the first time I've seen him laugh and sing in weeks. And my father went personally to meet the officers at the camp today. Something he hasn't done in years. Every single one came back edgy and nervous, refusing eye contact.

I rub at the nagging ache in my temples. Why can't I get away from this? If Saul no longer sees David as a traitor, why did he spend the feast watching his every move? What is he looking for?

Then, when I'd finally begun to relax in the course of the evening, my father had leaned over my shoulder. "See that girl over with Merab?" I'd barely had time to follow his gesture before he'd announced, "I've spoken to her father about making her your wife."

Just like that. Not even a name. I'd barely heard any of what followed…how Joram's people are of Benjamin, and how they've been supportive of all our decisions from the beginning. Abba acted as though I had to talk to the girl before he finished his next breath.

"You should speak to Joram before the night is over. Make certain he knows your intentions align with mine."

I just stood there, amazed that he hadn't said a word until now. "Does she have a name?"

My father had looked at me as though I was being purposely stubborn. "Jehosheva."

At least it's a name I've heard before. She's several years younger but still someone I'm used to seeing around Gibeah. I vaguely remember interacting with Joram's sons before Abba became king. When his daughter was only a child. But apparently, she's been in love with me for years. Or something like that. I'm willing to bet Abba fabricated that part of his discussion with Joram.

Either way, I can't sleep now.

Agitated, I pick at the fletching of an arrow. I'm not the dreamer I was when I'd imagined I could have Naamah. But I had allowed myself to hope that the decision might still be mine.

Now I feel foolish for hoping. Of course, my father would make my marriage a political move. I'm his heir. My brothers had been content enough with the wives he'd chosen for them. But I'd waited too long, disheartened by the prospect of admitting defeat where my first choice was concerned.

Maybe I should speak to my mother. She might have more insight into this matter. Perhaps she can help me understand why I feel so ill-prepared. But she's been aloof from my father lately, not appearing at his side in public as often.

Ezra lightly taps the half-opened door before edging inside. "Someone to see you, my lord."

Jarred out of the silence, I lift one hand. "Now?" It's hardly a normal hour for visitors. And Ezra's smile is far too playful for this time of night. "Who is it?"

"Someone you said I should always let in without asking questions."

I frown, but then Naamah appears beside him, and heat shoves its way through the confusion on my face. I'm halfway to my feet before realizing there's no reason to jump out of my chair. But it's too late to sit back down. I struggle for a moment with my mouth open before finding coherence. Ezra is gone already, leaving me alone. With her.

It's so normal, even after all these years, that I have to remind myself it's not.

"Sarrah Michal sent me, my lord." She says it quickly, but her eyes aren't jumping around like they usually do. They're firmly fixed on my face, full of urgency. The small change is enough to command my attention.

"What is it? What's wrong?"

She inhales, her fingers mangling the cords on her cloak. "I don't know. I think—she may be in trouble."

"Michal?" I take a step toward her, refusing to jump to conclusions. More than likely, she's had an argument with David, and she wants to vent to someone. Almost disappointed, I don't try to hide a tired smirk. "Did she think of asking her husband for help?"

I'm startled by the instant offense that stiffens Naamah. She arches her neck, all traces of humility gone. "I heard her crying. After my master returned from the fortress, they spent an hour in their chamber with the doors locked. When your sister came downstairs, she wouldn't speak to anyone, wouldn't go to bed. There were soldiers in the yard, surrounding the house, but she told me not to look outside."

Alarmed annoyance hammers in my chest. "Soldiers? Outside David's house? Why?"

You tell me, her eyes seem to say. Aloud, she continues, her voice almost accusatory. "Soldiers paced around the yard for hours. Your father's men. When they finally came to the door, they insisted on searching the house. That's when my lady sent me to you. She was afraid they'd take her to the king. She wants you to talk to your father tomorrow, see what you can do to diffuse the situation."

I rub my forehead. This makes no sense. "What situation? Where's David?"

"Gone. He said something about Ramah and needing to talk to Samuel. My lady let him down through the back window. I think she thought the king's men were looking for him."

The words shove through my gut before I've decided whether I believe them. My father wouldn't send men to hurt David at night in order to hide it from everyone else! He wouldn't kill his own son-in-law in front of his daughter! The thought makes the room tilt.

When I can see clearly again, Naamah's come closer. "Something's changed, hasn't it? There's a whole world inside your eyes that I have no idea about, isn't there?"

My answer sounds distant. "It's not as complicated as you'd think. At least, it doesn't have to be."

A hint of disdain colors her tone. "It's the king we're speaking of."

"It's also my father."

"I know," she purrs, keeping steady.

As much as I love it, I also hate the look in her eyes. She's reimagining the way my father exploded when he'd caught us kissing in the garden. How he'd struck my face and slammed me into the wall. But that was years ago. And Amalek was still fresh in his mind.

"He's changed," I insist.

"He's worse," she rejoins.

Bitterness stabs my throat. "Did you come here to tell me how to handle him or just to repeat what Michal said?"

And just like that, I hate myself. I half-turn away, rubbing my neck. I'm so tired of making excuses for Saul. I start to apologize. "I'm s…"

"Don't. You owe me nothing." She barely blinks. "I only came because I know you'll fight for your sister."

Even if I couldn't fight for others. I stand there for a moment, waiting for the pain in my stomach to subside.

Naamah laces her fingers together. "It's David, isn't it?"

"What do you mean?"

Naamah inhales again, her expression holding me at arm's length. "There's something about him that the king doesn't trust. Some connection with Samuel. And of course, you've chosen to put yourself in the way."

Her choice of words leaves me grasping for my own. "He carries the Spirit of God. After he killed Goliath, I—I can't explain what happened. Yahweh bound us together."

Something sharp darts through her face, and she winces, looking down. I don't understand it until she whispers, "So… he'll take you down with him."

I stiffen, realizing her motives. She doesn't know David or care about him. But she knows my father's temper. She's worried about me. But my father wouldn't hurt me. Not now.

I step back, my hand against the table. "I will speak to the king. But I can guarantee you, he's not thinking about David tonight."

Naamah's mouth twists. "You mean, he's too busy getting your marriage arranged?"

I throw up my hands, both amazed and offended. "How is it that you knew before I did?"

A sheen of tears enters her eyes. "Oh, Jonathan. You still think you're the first person to hear of your father's plans. You're the last."

TWENTY-TWO

David

———— ◆◆ ◆ ◆◆ ————

I'm crouched in the corner of Samuel's upper room, wrapped in fresh fear that keeps my head lowered and my wrists clasped around my knees. I've been in the Roeh's private outpost for seven days now, awaiting the inevitable. Saul has sent two contingents of soldiers to Ramah since I left, but they're detained by the same arms that conceal me.

The prophet had anticipated my coming and welcomed me into his home without questions, listening patiently while I tried to tell him everything. The tumult of leaving Michal and escaping Gibeah without being seen had shaken my core, and in the Roeh's courtyard, surrounded by the feeling of sanctuary, I could feel all the pent-up emotion unfurling in my words. I'd kept my head bent, certain that Samuel would chastise me for my weakness.

But he'd merely opened his arms and embraced me like a grandfather. His robe smelled like spices, and I'd let myself sink to my knees at his feet while he held my head, murmuring close to my ear, "You're safe. Yahweh reigns here, and He is your hiding place. He surrounds you with songs of deliverance when you are afraid."

With those words, any questions I had, any fears wandering around inside me had fled, leaving my chest lighter than it's been in years. It didn't matter whether Saul came after me. I would find sanctuary in my God.

I understand now why the Roeh told me not to bother hiding. Yahweh's protective presence hovers in the room where I sleep, wrapping me in a thick cloud of safety that I'm sure nothing can penetrate. The flames of the oil lamps routinely leap to attention when He breathes, the distinct whisper I heard at Elah filling the air around me.

My Refuge, my Fortress. My Strength, my Deliverer. Never have I felt the declarations of my songs draw so near to my flesh. His closeness makes me tremble, like the presence of a lion, magnified a million times. And yet, this is the best I've slept in months. Utterly rested, even in the middle of the night, I sit up and bow my head over my knees, wishing I didn't ever have to leave His arms.

The door opens, and Samuel enters the room. One glance at the Roeh's face tells me everything I need to know.

I sit up. "Saul is here?"

Samuel doesn't bother to move, his hands calmly folded. "Yes. He's here."

I try to swallow, but my throat is closed. "Will he look for me? Or will he leave?"

Samuel's eyes spark. "He won't find you. But he won't be leaving for a while."

When I try to get up, he holds out his hand. "No, stay where you are. He's not fit to be seen. He's been apart from Yahweh's presence for so long, he doesn't know what to do with it. I doubt he'll even remember this night."

Samuel closes the door, his expression twisting with something like grief.

Amid the disturbance outside, the strange lilting sound of Saul's voice in the courtyard goes into me like a blade. The king of Israel, the man I've served and loved like a father has come to the house of Israel's prophet to seek my life. The nightmare I've dreaded since my anointing is unfolding before my eyes, and I can feel the shaking beginning. Every foundation under my feet, every support that has held me up is threatening to fail me.

All but One.

I bow my head again, ashamed that I'm still able to doubt in Yahweh's presence. I try to reason that it's not really my God that I doubt. It's Saul. And myself.

I look across the room. It's been years since I've seen the stalwart prophet of Yahweh who'd marched into my father's house to anoint me in front of my brothers. I have no way of knowing if he'll be angry to hear this, but I can't hide the truth any longer.

"Roeh, I...I can't do this."

I can only hope he knows my meaning. I can't kill Saul. I can't take the throne, destroy his family, drag the country into war.

Samuel sits on a bench across from me, the sadness in his face shifting. "Yahweh anointed you to lead His people of Israel, not murder Saul."

Even as relief dawns, I have to face the rest. "But he wants to murder me. He knows I've been anointed to replace him, and he wants me dead. If he goes much further fighting this, Judah will revolt to protect me, and I can't let that happen. Please, Roeh, just tell me what I'm supposed to do!"

Samuel's expression quiets, his attention shifting into something I can't see. "Saul was willing to wait for the Word of the Lord once. When he turned from Adonai, I grieved for years—until Yahweh stopped me with the news that He had chosen another. When you walked out onto that porch in your shepherd's rags, I felt the grief leave me. Because I heard Yahweh's voice telling me to anoint you."

"You told me I had to believe." The memory is thick around me.

Samuel continues, "Every man must choose whether to believe the Word of the Lord or to reject Him. Saul has made his choice. What will you choose?"

Tears stinging my eyes, I bow myself to the ground, speaking directly to the powerful presence wrapping me in peace. How can I do anything other than choose the One who chose me? "God of Israel, I have made you my refuge. You're my Shepherd. Don't leave me."

The hands that grip my head are stronger than Samuel's should be at his age. The Roeh lifts my face, holding it like he did the day he'd poured oil over me. A tear trickles into his beard, catching the lamplight.

"He will not leave you, David. If you remain faithful to Him, He will accomplish all He has promised to you. By Him, you can run against any troop. By your God, you can leap over any wall. He has trained your hands for war and your fingers for battle, weaving Himself into you with every song you've written. His strength will cover you and save you from your enemies."

I exhale, awed and relieved. Adonai has always been faithful. He will not leave me now, when my need for Him is so great.

The prophet smiles, something else appearing in his face. "He set someone else to the task of training you as well, didn't He?"

For a moment, I don't understand. When I do, fresh sorrow grips me. "Jonathan."

Samuel nods serenely. "When you leave here, go to your brother. He will tell you what you are to do next."

* * * * *

Seven days after fleeing Gibeah, I follow the rumors back to the fortress. Some men whisper that Saul has turned back to Adonai, while others worry he's sinking further into madness. By the time I reach the city, I'm grateful I didn't see whatever Saul did in Yahweh's presence.

Approaching my house from the back, I swing myself over the garden gate and kneel in the dirt a few moments, trying to feel some relief amid everything else crashing over me. After a few seconds, I decide it's no use. This isn't home, no matter how much I want it to be. I still have to speak to Jonathan, but it might take longer this time to deal with the king's anger. I can't just disappear again without seeing Michal.

Hoisting myself up the back wall, I do battle with every doubt that's plagued me since I left. I might live to regret fleeing so quickly, without my wife. Leaving her to face the king alone. Surely, he wouldn't have—

When I swing my leg over the windowsill and see Michal walk into the room, relief rips my chest in half. The king didn't harm her. I embrace her quickly, burying her half-scream into my chest. "It's all right. Michal! It's just me."

Instead of clinging to me though, she pushes back.

"Crazy man, climbing in here like a raider..." She presses her hands against her chest, trying to recollect her breathing. But nothing about her looks relieved to see me. Her voice is harsh, and she's looking at me like a stranger, keeping her distance.

"When were you planning on telling me?" she demands.

"What?"

She drags the words out as though they hurt. "That you're planning on being king. You're the one we've been afraid of all these years."

Coldness tightens my chest as something heavy steps between us. It's the last thing I planned on discussing with her now, but I also hate myself for not doing it sooner.

Michal laughs harshly, covering a sob. "You know, when Abba asked me why I let you go, I lied to him. I told him you had threatened to kill me. I suppose my little falsehood was closer to the truth than I realized."

"How can you think I would ever hurt you?" I feel sick just imagining it.

Her expression bends into something I've never seen before. "Because you've been lying all this time! Is anything about you real?"

I clench my fists at my sides, forcing a calmness I don't feel into my tone. "Michal, how could I tell you when I don't understand it myself? I couldn't tell anyone."

Anger burns through the tears in her eyes. "Except Jonathan. Because you made him promise not to betray you. So, you've made my closest brother a traitor while you bide your time. Waiting for a chance to murder my father."

"Never! Michal, I gave an oath before God that I would never harm Saul or Jonathan." I'm aching to get closer, to make her understand, but she's staring me down like an archer taking aim.

"But you might have to hurt me. Or my brothers. Or Abner." She's breathing fast, anger building. "Because that's what it will come to eventually. Did you expect Abba to place the crown on your head without a fight?"

"No—I mean, I don't expect anything." I try to touch her shoulders. "Yahweh will determine how things will work out. In the meantime, I'm content to fight for Saul. I've done nothing but serve him, and I won't change."

"How can you say that?" She slaps at my chest, horror gaping from her face. "How can you claim to fight for my father when you've been conspiring against him? Against all of us?" She shakes her head, her eyes flooding. "After everything we've done for you, you're going to betray us all."

"No!" I reach for her hands, but she jerks back.

"Don't touch me!" She's trembling, feeling behind her for something to lean on.

"Michal—"

"Don't!" She claps a hand over her mouth, choking on a sob. "You're a traitor!"

I flinch, wishing she would hit me rather than say that. "I'm not, Michal. I'm no king either. I'm nothing by myself. Yahweh chose me."

Michal is shaking, twisted inside out by pain, and I can see the moment hatred burns through the tears on her face. "He was wrong."

TWENTY-THREE

Jonathan

———◆◆◆◆◆———

As soon as I can break away, I go to see my mother. She's living in extended quarters, a new wing that stretches to the far side of the fortress. Abba has piled wealth around her, filling her chambers with every conceivable luxury, but Eema's face is empty. When I look at her, I realize how many days I've been sleepwalking, obsessed with avoiding this tempest I've been dragged into. Actually, it hasn't been days. It's been years.

Eema locks eyes with me and then turns away for a moment, gathering strength. Pain eats through the silence, making me wonder if I should have come. My mother is the first person I ever tried to protect, and the only one I never can. She's one of the few who's actually seen evidence of what my father used to do to me, and she reads me so well.

"You can leave us alone," she tells her servants. When they're gone, she crosses the room and touches my face. "It's been a while." Her brave smile is enough to make me want to break down. But I don't have time for that. I need answers.

Eema's brows lift, and she moves to a cushioned chair across the room. "If you're here to talk about your father, you'll find I don't have much to say." She sits down and lifts her face to mine, waiting.

I shrug, helpless. "What's happening, Eema? I don't understand him anymore." If I ever did. "I talk to him, and I get nowhere. He dismissed my questions about David and Michal and then followed his soldiers to Ramah, refusing to see anyone when he returned. I want to help him, but I can't if he won't be honest with me."

Eema's eyes drop. "He hasn't been honest with you since Michmash. That's just the way it is." She lets that hang in the air a few seconds before continuing. "And Michal has always expected you to stand in her abba's place."

I wince. Of course. My little sister has always preferred to come to me rather than deal with our father. I dig my fingers into my temples, trying to relieve the pressure.

"She refuses to see me. She thinks I've betrayed her..." I don't finish, remembering that my mother doesn't know about David's anointing.

Eema sighs. "I tried to tell Michal that marrying David wasn't the best option."

My shoulders drop. "That's not—" I shake my head, trying to uncover my real questions. "Why haven't you been in court? I haven't seen you for weeks." I'll start there.

An unrecognizable cold enters my mother's face. "He's taken a concubine."

My stomach turns. "I see." It's a common move for kings, but it was something I'd never expected of my father.

Eema fidgets slightly. "Her name is Rizpah. Since she came, I haven't been summoned. I'm not sure I would come if he called."

I watch her, hating the hardness in her expression. Finally, it drops, shifting into sadness. "He's trying to get rid of David again, isn't he?"

Dizziness shoves over me, and my mind swims with every threat and rumor I've been fighting the past seven days. "Again..." I murmur, crestfallen. How many times has he tried behind my back? How long has the wool been over my eyes?

Eema blinks. "Didn't you talk to your sister about what happened?"

"I did. That is, Naamah came to my house and told me." Breathless, I sit next to my mother, braced for her honest opinion. "I was hoping you'd say she was wrong."

"She's not wrong. But I can only hope she's misunderstood one thing."

"What?"

My mother stares at her lap for a long moment before lifting her eyes to mine. "Michal is saying that David intends to be king." I can tell by Eema's tone what she thinks of that. "Until now, I thought that was all in your father's head. You know how suspicious he's been of that upstart from the beginning. But, if David is a traitor..."

I push off the couch, clenching my fists. "He's not, Eema! He's—"

"I know!" She pivots on the couch to face me. "He's like your brother, and you love him. But is it worth losing your father's support over this? One thing happens, and David runs to Samuel? What are we supposed to think?" She leans forward. "Are you absolutely certain David wouldn't turn against you if it meant he could have the throne?"

I drag in a long breath, forcing myself to stay calm. Why does it feel like I'm losing control of everything? "Eema, if I'm certain of one thing, it's David's integrity. My friendship with him should not make me Abba's enemy. We're both his sons."

She stares at me, tears gathering. "He doesn't deserve either of you."

I leave with more questions than before, struggling to withstand the pain of what's been uncovered. My father ignores my concerns, focusing on his new concubine and Joram's daughter, while Eema, Naamah, and my sister all look at me like I've been blind. They all think Abba means David harm. And none of them think I'll be able to stop him.

Will I?

Ezra meets me at the gate of my house, shifting the storm of my thoughts. "My lord, one of your servants brought word; someone's waiting for you in the stables."

His face wears a secrecy I can easily interpret. My heart immediately shoves into a full gallop again.

Ezra's expression changes. "Do you want me to go with you?"

"No." Not if it's who I think it is. "Just make sure no one follows me."

When I enter my stables, the first thing I notice is my sword propped up against the doorframe. My old sword, draped with the cloak and belt I'd given David after the Elah battle.

Then, for no reason at all, I see him.

David is crouched in the shadows of a stall, out of reach of the light from the door.

Immensely relieved, I cross the room, grasp his shoulders, and heave him up into my arms. "Are you all right?" When he doesn't answer, I tighten my grip. "I didn't know you were back."

There's a new layer of age in David's face, resignation covering over the depths of hurt. "I slipped inside to see Michal. Probably for the last time."

"Don't say that. She loves you." Still, my head hurts around the image of her screaming at me, slamming the door in my face.

David shrugs. "She did. Maybe. I don't know anymore. Maybe what she loved was just in her imagination. Either way, she hates me now. She's convinced I'm a traitor."

I wince. I'd predicted David would make enemies, but I'd never dreamed so many would be from my own house. I fold my arms. "I found Abba's spear in the door of his throne room a week ago. What happened?"

The memory enters David's face, and I can see him bracing against it.

"The king tried to kill me. He was angry the whole day of the celebration, and when we were alone, he just exploded. He sent men to follow me home, but Michal let me down through the window." David folds his arms tight. "I went to Ramah, and the king sent two contingents of soldiers after me before coming down himself."

I breathe out slowly through my nose. "I heard. Yahweh's presence was intoxicating after having been away from it for so long. He wasn't sure what to do." My father won't speak of the encounter, and I'm not sure what to do with the rumors of him lying naked all day and night, trapped under the presence that wouldn't let him leave until David escaped. "Did you speak to Samuel?"

David sighs. "Yes. He said your father won't kill me."

Finally, some sense. "Do you believe him?"

David looks everywhere but my eyes, forcing breaths in and out. "I don't know. Every time I hope he'll change, he—"

Doesn't. Pain digs into my chest, but I'm encouraged by Samuel's words. "He's a sick man, David. Sick with shame over losing Yahweh's favor. And that comes out in rage against those who have it. But you're not going to die."

"Jonathan—"

"No! Listen to me!" My voice matches the anger building in my chest. My father's jealous temper has made David's life a torment, and that has to stop. But he can't be plotting murder. Not again. "My father doesn't do anything without consulting me, whether little or great. Why should he hide this from me? It just doesn't make sense."

David drops his head to one side, a look of pity joining the grief on his face. "It makes perfect sense. Your father knows the favor I have with you. He knows how it would grieve you if anything—if he—" His jaw bunches. "He knows you won't support him in taking my life, but I swear to you, Jonathan, there is only a step between me and death."

I stare at him in silence, my inner raging crowding out words. I can feel my survival instincts rushing in to protect my mind and heart. The inner armor has shielded me for years, insisting I keep believing in my father. I had to believe he still loved me even when he threatened my life. Just like I have to believe it now.

In all my life, I've never felt such a conflict. It's as though I can see my father and David locked in combat, each battling for mastery, and I want to save them both.

I'm so caught up in the struggle, I barely hear David's inquiry.

"But we're friends...aren't we?" he ventures, shakily. "Our covenant still stands in your mind? Nothing's changed?"

I blink, waiting too long to respond.

His face gray, David heaves a few unsteady breaths, then picks up my old sword and holds the handle out to me. "If I'm guilty...if you can't go against the king, just kill me yourself. Right here." He exhales tightly. "I'd rather you do it. But don't bring me to your father."

And add the sin of betrayal to my litany of burdens? Not in a hundred years. I take the sword and toss it aside. "You would have me break a vow I made before Yahweh? Look at me."

When he doesn't, I take his face in my hand, forcing it up. "I don't know if my father means you harm, but may God strike me if I don't find out. Now, what do you want me to do for you? Think. You're a commander."

A soft laugh escapes David. He's still breathing fast, but his mind is at work, resisting panic.

"Tomorrow is the New Moon festival," he begins hoarsely. "I'm supposed to eat with the king every night this week, but... what if I don't show up? I'll go hide in the fields, where that path breaks off to the stream by Ezel, and if your father asks about me, you can tell him I've gone to Bethlehem for some urgent family gathering. If he's all right with that, we're safe. But if he loses his temper, you'll know he intends to harm me."

Yahweh, have mercy.

"Agreed." It's the head of the year; a trip to see his family will be a reasonable cover for David's absence.

"How are you going to get the message to me?" David asks.

I can see the fear struggling to overpower any hope in his eyes. Suddenly, I feel closed in.

"Let's get out of here." I grab his arm. "We can walk in the fields. Come on."

The fields outside Gibeah have always been a haven for me, but never more than today. It was here that I came to grieve the loss of my father's love, sending my pain through my bow and into targets. And it was here that I'd discovered the Lord's new anointed king and decided not to betray him. It's fitting that these same fields will conceal David until we can figure out what comes next.

I point ahead. "You wait here by the boulders. As soon as I have an answer, I'll come out here to practice with my bow, and I'll shoot past the target. If I tell my servant that the arrows are off to the side, then you'll know all is well. But if I say that the arrow is beyond him, then you will know that my father means you harm."

David squints into the setting sun. "Then what?"

My throat tightens. "Then, you can go in peace, wherever Yahweh leads, knowing that we've sworn a covenant before Him."

Dizziness bends my vision as I allow myself to picture Gibeah with David gone. If my friend has to flee, then all of Israel will know something is wrong. When news of David's anointing gets out, the people will draw their own conclusions and have to choose sides.

The unrest could pull us into war against ourselves in less than five years, giving our enemies dangerous leverage. I don't need a prophet to tell me which side will prevail. God has been with David for years.

I stare at my friend, grasping for certainty. "Look, whatever happens, I know this. God will cut off every enemy that tries to come against you. That's why I need you to promise me that you won't destroy my household. That any family I might have would be able to find a place with you. Even if I'm not...even if things are different."

Suddenly, I have to know this for sure. We'd sworn the brother-covenant years ago, with little idea of what it might come to mean. My father will choose his own path. But once I'm married, I know I want my wife and our children to come under the covering of my pledge with Yahweh's anointed.

David doesn't move a muscle. "I promise. You have my word, before God." A half-smile darts through his eyes. "Where else am I going to find someone desperate enough to adopt me?"

Surprised by his attempt at humor, I elbow him gently. "I have a feeling Joab would be capable of shoving you into a stream if you got stubborn enough."

David grimaces. "Joab once threatened to break my wrist."

"Really?" I smirk. "That's ironic. I actually broke Malchi's wrist once."

A brief lightness enters David's face before dismay chokes it back out. Forcing my smile to remain, I grip my friend's shoulders. "You'll always be my brother. That won't change. May the Lord be with you, as He used to be with my father. Now, go and find a place out of sight, but don't go far. I promise I'll get word to you by tonight. Tomorrow at the latest."

David squeezes my arms and ducks behind the boulders, heading down the streambed path. I walk backwards, raising my hand once. "There's still hope," I call after him.

As little as I believe it, I repeat it with every step back to the fortress. Still hope.

* * * * *

The appearance of the next new moon signals the Feast of Trumpets, the start of our new year. The priests blow the ram's horn in succession over several additional sacrifices, reciting words of repentance that resound in my gut. My fists are clenched through the whole ceremony, my own prayers tangled up behind my fixed expression. We will not go against Yahweh. We will not break with David. I refuse to believe it.

When I appear before my father for the first evening meal of the feast, I begin to doubt my own plan. His smile is as close to normal as I've ever seen it, and he embraces me without hesitation, as if the previous week never happened. Once again, he points out Jehosheva sitting amongst the women of her family in a place of honor near our tribal leaders. By now, everyone knows she's been singled out for me, and most of the room's attention is on her.

But once we're sitting down, everything changes. My father's eyes lock onto David's empty place beside me and stay there for a good portion of the evening.

I've never felt tension like this night. With every second that passes, my defenses rise higher, building an invisible wall around me. My smile feels incredibly forced, doing little to hide the tempest raging beneath the surface.

"What's your problem?" Malchi elbows me halfway through the meal. "You haven't eaten a thing."

"I'm not hungry." I allow myself to glance over at Jehosheva, hoping to deflect my brothers' attention. It doesn't work.

"David's not here, so everything's not right," Ishvi rambles under his breath. "Look at Abba's face. It's not enough that all his sons are here—"

"Be quiet!" I silence him through my teeth and spend the rest of the evening pretending to eat. How can they all sit here and act like nothing has happened?

My sister is traumatized, refusing to leave her house. My mother is secluded. The city is abuzz with news of Saul's visit to Samuel and his brush with the *Ruach*. David is missing. And yet here we sit, laughing and talking through the motions of a feast as though none of that exists.

No one asks any questions. The men of Benjamin watch the king and imitate his demeanor. The evening manages to appear so normal that my father makes no mention of David.

I arrive at the feast the next night barely concealing my agitation as the same motions proceed around me. Indifference isn't what we're looking for. I need a definitive answer, one way or another. I'm so focused on praying for it that my father's sudden question makes me choke.

"Is David unclean?" he demands.

Nothing is funny, but I laugh anyway, trying to bury my apprehension. "No, of course not," I ramble. "He's been with the prophets, not in battle. Why would he be unclean?" I fold my hidden hand into a fist under the table. Saul knew I would answer.

My father sets his wine glass down. "Will you look at me, Jonathan?"

I lift my head, hoping he can't sense my unrest.

"Where is David?" He raises his voice, and instant silence steals the chatter from the room. "Why has he not come to eat at my table either tonight or yesterday?"

Saul's offended look touches Abner and each of my brothers before coming back to me. He drums his fingers on the table. "Last night, I thought he might have been unfit to appear, but this is getting insulting. Suddenly, he's too busy for his king?"

"Not at all," I answer quickly, my pulse biting my throat. *Here we go.*

I look straight into my father's eyes. "He earnestly asked my permission to go to Bethlehem. He received an urgent message from his brothers requiring him to be home for some family gathering. It's been a while since he's seen his relatives, so I said he could go."

I'm as casual as possible, but I can already feel the rage seething toward me. My stomach twists. *Don't, Abba.*

Before I can move, Saul's arm jerks violently, knocking his wine glass across the table. Planting one fist, he points at me, rearing over like a lion about to pounce. "You ungrateful, disloyal son of a perverse, rebellious woman!"

"Abba!" Ishvi protests while I sit like a stone, my heart racing faster and faster.

"You think I don't know what's happening here?" Saul rails at me. "That you've chosen the son of Jesse to your own shame, and the shame of your mother?"

"Leave her out of this!" I shout, my voice cracking.

"Don't you understand that as long as that traitor lives, your own kingdom will never be established?" Saul's nearly spitting with rage, wildness twisting his face.

I shove back from the table. "David is no traitor! He has laid his life down for you countless times in battle while you sit here scheming how to remove him from your presence. Why, Abba? Tell me why!"

"Shut up, you fool! You have no right to contradict me!"

My head is spinning, battle fury pumping through my senses, but I push past it, taking a half step toward the king. "This isn't you, Abba. He's your son. You don't want him dead!"

Discounting my appeal, Saul's anger twists through his neck, lifting his voice to a near-scream. "I don't care who or what he is. Go and get him, and bring him to me. That traitor must die!"

I step forward, pushing a chair out of my way. *"But why? What has he done?"*

Saul pivots, grabs his spear from the wall, and flings it across the room, directly at me. I barely avoid it, throwing myself to the side. But I still feel its weight, slamming into the wall just inches from my head.

Everyone screams, several leaping from their seats. A few plates and glasses clatter to the ground. I'm senseless for a moment, drowned in the shock of adrenaline. Then, I feel the floor under my hands. I see the spear. And a fist reaches deep inside me and wrenches.

It's like Michmash all over again, where I felt my life suspended over a cliff, threatened by someone who should've stood with me. Except this time, he's shoved me over the edge, and walked away. And the pain is infuriating.

Barely coherent, I shove off the ground. Dragging air through my chest is like breathing through a blade. Saul is still watching me. The lack of remorse in his face mocks my lifelong loyalty, my obsession with his favor. It makes me sick.

"Maybe—" I pause to breathe, "maybe it's not only David you hate."

It's all I can manage before storming from the room, leaving him behind.

My wild heartbeat gallops ahead of my footsteps as I cross the outer courtyard, enter my house, and head for my armory. I feel the quake through my entire body, waves of outrage and disgust pulsing in my veins as though I'm heading for war. Or coming from it.

Ezra's the only one who accompanies me, quietly ordering servants out of my way. They all watch me grab my weapons, but no one will follow. I'm sure of that. I often go shooting to clear my head of chaos. And this has been the most chaotic night of my life.

My mind still refuses to make sense of what just happened. He commanded me to kill David, as staunchly as though it had been a reasonable request, and then went pale with rage when I questioned him. As though he didn't know either of us. As though all our years together meant nothing. My head echoes all the protests I leveled at my father while I was still determined to hope.

He's your son! He's my brother! I made a covenant of peace with him. We all did.

I say it out loud to my empty chamber. "He's done nothing wrong."

But my father's spitting insults and the spear he'd launched at my chest roar louder than the voice of reason. The king wants my best friend dead. And he wants me to kill him.

Suddenly exhausted, I slump against the wall. I'd feared this day would come. No—I never really did. I'd seen the ice enter my father's gaze when the streets first erupted with songs of praise to David, crediting him with more kills than Saul. And I'd stood there shocked with the rest of his advisors when he first gave the order for David's death.

But I'd persuaded him out of it. His anger had cooled, and David had been welcomed as before. He is married to my sister, inextricably bound to our family. It's no light thing to get rid of a son. Or a brother.

I sit there in the dark, incredibly drained. No one bothers me, and as the hours count down to dawn, I can feel my anger shifting into sorrow. Whether or not anyone expected it, here we are. My father wants to kill David, the Lord's anointed, and he'll kill me if I stand in his way. I don't know who to trust or believe anymore, but once again, it's clear what I must do. Yahweh's given me that, at least.

As soon as the sky turns pale with morning, I shoulder my bow and swing a quiver onto my back, clenching my teeth against rising emotion. Selecting a young servant who doesn't usually attend me, I head for the fields, pretending to wander aimlessly toward the very specific outcropping of rocks where I'd left David.

I didn't think I would need to remember the instructions I'd given him. I made the arrangement mostly to appease him, to assure him of my loyalty as a friend, but now they will save his life. I stop, sensing movement a few yards off. I'm in the right place. I fit an arrow and then struggle to aim through clouded vision.

David is the Lord's anointed, chosen of God. And he's my friend. I have to save him. Then what?

I finally let the arrow fly—too high over the distant boulders. The boy who runs after it won't find it for a few minutes at least. Enough time.

"Keep going!" I shout after him, but my voice shudders. "Isn't the arrow still beyond you?"

My chest feels as tight as a bowstring as I wait to see if David heard my hidden message. He cannot stay. The king can no longer be trusted to do what's right. Can I? What will I have to do in the days to come as my father fights for what he can no longer keep?

It's times like this I remember the vow I'd made years ago as a youth, when I'd first faced the disparity between man's way and God's. Seeing that my father couldn't be trusted with my life, I'd given my future into Yahweh's hands. But I'd never foreseen this.

I close my eyes briefly, breathing promises from the depth of my being. "I will be faithful, Yahweh. Keep me faithful."

There's momentary peace, like a hand on my shoulder. Then David appears from around the rocks, and everything implodes inside me.

David won't look up. He takes one step and then flattens himself on the ground, bowing two more times before he even reaches me.

Taking his shoulders, I lift him up, as I've done so many times before. David inhales hard, his breath broken by sobs.

I try twice before I can speak. "So, it has come to this. My father, the king, has turned against you." My voice bends and twists, unruly with emotion. "He threw a spear at me, David. I was so sure—"

But I was wrong. Tears roll down my face. "I don't know why he's choosing this. All I know is you have to leave, quickly. Get as far away from here as you can." I glance behind me to see if I've been followed. I don't want to watch my brother die.

David clings to me like he's dying already. Even that day he was pinned to the ground under a Philistine sword, I didn't feel him shake like this.

His pain breaks something deep inside me, something that hasn't been touched since the night I'd wept over Samuel's final message. That same night, I'd met a shepherd boy with a heart so full of faith it spilled out his mouth in healing praise. Now, he's broken and sobbing, his head in my chest.

I grip his arms. "Is there anything I can do?"

David lifts his head. His eyes are bloodshot pools of pain. "Will you get my family out of Bethlehem? Send word to them that they have to leave. Joab will know what to do."

I frown, affronted by the idea that Saul might go after them. "David, I don't think the king…"

"Please." David's face jerks. "I don't know the king's intentions, and I can't risk—" Pausing, he gasps as though a sword has entered his body. "Oh, God! Michal!" He moans, holding his head.

I grab him, holding his face in my hands. "David, she'll be fine. She's my sister. I've been watching out for her for years." I shove a halfhearted laugh over the pain. Michal has nothing good to say about either of us anymore. But that's a battle for another day. "If the time comes for her to join you, I will make the arrangements."

I pull him close, tightening my grip as sobs tear him open again. "Steady. Yahweh has made you strong." Even as I say it, my heart revolts. We're both strong enough to fight enemies. But family? "May Adonai strengthen us both."

I kiss his forehead and embrace him one last time. My courageous brother. His heart seeks God the way a trailing vine climbs toward the sun. Why must he suffer like this?

"I wish I could do more," I murmur, hating that I can't even return to get provisions. There's no time.

"You've—" David's voice shudders. His fingers dig into my vest. "I'll never be able to repay you."

"It's not like that with us, and you know it."

I squeeze his shoulders. We've waited out here too long. "Go in peace, for God is with you. Don't forget our covenant. Remember that Yahweh can save His people…"

"…by many or by few," David barely whispers it, touching his lips.

"Go." I shove him, and he breaks into a run, taking half of me with him.

Once he's gone, I spot my servant running back through the brush with my arrow in his hand. "I've got it, my lord," he puffs, but I don't wait for him to reach me. Lifting my weapons, I hand them over and point back toward Gibeah.

"Carry them back to my house. Hurry. Don't wait."

I watch until I'm sure the boy is heading for the city gates. Then I drop on all fours and let the armor I've encased myself with for twenty-seven years go to pieces.

JONATHAN

My gut twists, winding tighter than it ever does in battle. I straighten my shoulders under my breastplate, silently fighting back. Abner is the last of my father's men to leave the tent, the only one who's not browbeaten. Abba's done berating them, but there's a reason he hasn't told me to go.

My lungs constrict, tired of breathing through this fog. The dark cloud on my father is becoming commonplace, stealing closer every day, eroding our bond. This is the second battle he's fought that Samuel has refused his messages. Refused to send priests to inquire of the Lord for him.

"He still won't speak to me!" Saul seethes as soon as we're alone. "What kind of prophet doesn't respond to his king?"

There's a dangerous slant to his voice. In the tents of war, he's more my king than my father. But I'm still closer to him than anyone, sharing his thoughts before they leave his mind. And I've felt the presence of Yahweh helping me fight my own battles. I can make him understand.

"Give him time, Abba," I advise him quietly.

He whirls, eyes blazing. "Time for what? For us to suffer another defeat? Who does he think I am?" He digs his thumb into his chest. "I am king of Israel, and I deserve loyalty from my prophets."

"He's Yahweh's prophet, Abba." And I've never seen Samuel look more grieved than he did after we fought Amalek.

My father paces, snarling, "I should send soldiers to Ramah. See how quickly he responds then."

Ice grips my arms. "Attacking the Roeh would hardly command anyone's respect."

"You're no better." My father grinds out the words, crushing parchments and tossing weapons into corners. "You don't think I'm worthy of this crown. Even though I'm the one who made you a prince! I'm the reason you are what you are!" He spins around, his anger spitting at me.

"Abba…"

"Shut up! You wish Samuel would toss my crown into the dust. That way you could go back to following no orders and serving no king, prowling the countryside after Philistines yourself." He kicks a helmet across the tent, then freezes, his voice changing. "Or maybe…you want it."

"What?" Emptiness gapes in my chest as my father turns around.

"Maybe you're the replacement the prophet spoke of," he muses coldly, his eyes glittering.

I can't move, but panic pushes my chest up and down. There's nowhere to run.

I try to back away, but Saul's hands grasp my breastplate instead, shaking me. The darkness pulses through him, feeding the terror in my veins.

"So, Adonai will sweep me aside and choose my son? Is that what's happening? Samuel's using me to get to you!"

"No! Abba, no!"

The words scream in my head, but under my father's grip, they're nothing more than a rasping cry. The king shoves me aside and grabs his staff, saliva dripping from his chin.

"They all stood against me to protect you. I spared you at Michmash, and now they all despise me. I saw how they looked at you when you brought Agag in. They'll defy me at a moment's notice to elevate you!"

His staff slams into my body, and I bend over on my knees, taking the blows to my side and my back where my clothes will hide them. His frenzied anger has to burn itself out. And I'm just in the way. I've answered this accusation before, but he doesn't remember. He doesn't ever remember what happens in these fits of rage.

"What has Samuel plotted with you? Answer me!"

Tossing his staff, he grabs my collar, whipping me around, but Abner's voice drifts through the door. "My king? The spies have brought back their reports."

He knows better than to come inside.

My father takes two breaths before flinging his command at the door. "Gather the commanders. We will follow."

Abner doesn't respond. After a moment, I hear his footsteps leaving. I wonder if the spies are really back or if he just wanted to help me. He knows more than he reveals. Everyone does.

My father releases me and faces the door while I pull myself to the side. His breathing is labored, and he digs his fingers into his temples, groaning softly. When he looks at me again, I can't help flinching. The sharp movement chews through my middle.

"Get up. You're not hurt." He looks dazed as though he's waking up from a dream.

I force myself to stand. I always do. Straightening helps the tremors to subside. The aches will deepen into bruises, but I don't think anything is broken. He's always careful not to do any permanent damage. Not physically, anyway.

When I try to step past him, he grabs my shoulder, and I bite down hard.

"Don't say anything. They can't be trusted." Torment eats through the familiar lines on his face. The ones that used to smile. "No one can."

The burn inside me is worse than the aches under my armor. I'm not a traitor. But he won't see it. I've already wasted my breath saying it. He knows I'm not anyone to fear. But I'm the closest target—until he finds another one.

The blinding sunlight outside the tent is maddening, mocking the darkness eating me alive. I'm tempted to run far and fast, maybe go to Samuel, and demand to know why he won't come back, why my father is losing his peace and his nerve with each day that passes.

Instead, I run into Abner. His grip on my wrist angers me, and I jerk away. "Let go!"

He steps in front of me, his face bent with concern. "Are you hurt?"

"Don't speak. Just walk."

Abner grinds his teeth, falling into step beside me. "If that prophet knew what trouble he's causing by refusing to come back…"

"It's not his fault, Abner. Whatever Samuel said, it shouldn't be enough to put my father over the edge." My armor shudders, concealing what hurts underneath.

Abner keeps pace with me. "We all know he's wrong. About you."

"Of course he's wrong!" I snap, my voice breaking. "You think I want to divide the kingdom and grab glory for myself at a time like this?"

"I didn't think you did." Abner slows. "What do you want, Jonathan?"

I keep walking, desperate to hide what's pushing into my vision. "Nothing you can give me."

I charge up the nearest hill and out of Abner's sight. There's only one thing I want. My insides are screaming with it. Samuel's the one person who might be able to tell me what's happened to it, but he won't come back. With no one watching, I dig my hands and knees into the ground and cry without making a sound.

I want my father back!

TWENTY-FOUR

David

———◆◆◆◆◆———

I'm fatigued, but I'm too afraid to rest. In the last two days, I've run nonstop, drawing on the strength I've built up in battle, barely pausing to drink from the finger-thin river I'm following. I've slept only a few hours in total, and only when I can be completely concealed in a ditch or a tree.

I'm balancing on the edge of my strength, my energy depleted by the strain. I'm obsessed with every step I've taken, measuring how easy it will be for Saul to overtake me now that I'm on foot. And unarmed. How could I not think to have Jonathan bring me a weapon? Or food?

I'm finally far enough from Gibeah that I can feel the cramps of hunger through my urgency to escape. Fortunately, the first city in my path is another Ramah—a peaceful city of sanctuary populated by the priesthood. Ahimelech lives here, with his sons and their families.

The last time I saw the elderly priest was during the celebration where I'd worshipped in the streets before Saul threw the spear at me. Ahimelech won't turn me away. Though the city of Nob is still too close to Gibeah to provide me with shelter for long.

Dread bites into my hope, reminding me that Ahimelech doesn't know what happened. No one does. Yet.

Pulling my hood down over my face, I slip through Nob's side gate without speaking to anyone. I've stopped at the priest's house a dozen times bringing spoils of war as gifts for the temple. Several holy articles are temporarily situated here, since the destruction of the temple Samuel served in at Shiloh.

Ahimelech's house is modest but pristine, and I try to shake some of the dust from my clothes before approaching. I don't have the time or the means to wash or do anything to make it look like I haven't slept on the road. Ahimelech will have to draw his own conclusions.

The elderly priest comes to his door as soon as his servant opens it.

"Son of Jesse!" He looks beyond me, up and down the street, then studies me with concern. "What's happened? Has Gibeah been attacked?"

"No." I shake my head, trying to settle my breathing. I can only imagine how strange this appears to him. "The king sent me on an urgent mission, and I've been traveling as fast as I can to meet up with my men. They're waiting for me in...Hebron." I blurt out the name of a southern city, then curse myself for lying. He's a priest!

Yahweh, have mercy.

Ahimelech nods, his mouth still open. "I see. I assume this is a covert mission then."

"Yes," I rasp, my breathing still too fast. "The king strictly charged me not to say anything to anyone, which is why I had to leave so quickly. I didn't even have time to pack provisions." I swallow, dazed by the thought of food. It won't be safe for me to stop in many more cities after this. "Do you have any bread on hand that I could take with me?"

Ahimelech looks at his servants. "Not enough for an army, but we have a few loaves of the holy bread in the temple. We were just about to change it out for some fresh bread. You can have that, I suppose, as long as the men haven't been...you know... with any women."

I try to laugh over the panic turning me inside out. Saul's men could arrive at any moment. "No, of course not. Our missions for the Lord are sacred. We don't sleep with women during a time of battle."

A smile tweaks Ahimelech's mouth, and suddenly I want to tell him everything. Why not? Saul will tell the whole country his own version soon enough; it would be a relief to have one man know the truth.

I open my mouth, but my eyes catch a serpent's gaze over the priest's shoulder. Through the back door, in the outer courtyard, the king's Edomite spy Doeg is sprawled on the ground as if drunk.

My face must be as frozen as my heartbeat, because Ahimelech follows my gaze and explains, "Oh. Doeg. He showed up here a few days ago, looking for you. We told him we didn't know you had planned to come here, but he was welcome to wait. He's been here awhile."

I stare at Doeg, noting the way he's flattened on the ground, as if trapped under a mighty hand. Like Saul's men at Ramah. "The *Ruach* won't let him leave," I mumble, amazed.

Ahimelech shrugs, smiling. "You've felt Yahweh's hand yourself a few times, haven't you? He always conceals you from your enemies."

I nod, tears burning my eyes. I can't say anything with that spy so close. The truth will only endanger the priests. I tense when Ahimelech's hand pushes onto my shoulder.

"Are you all right, son? You know I can inquire of the Lord for you, if you need."

If I need? I exhale, almost breaking down. "Please..." Before the priest walks away, I catch his wrist. "Also...I don't know if you have any weapons on hand, but I didn't bring any."

Ahimelech's fatherly smile widens, letting me in. "We only keep one weapon here, beside the *ephod*. Come with me."

He leads me across the courtyard and into a back room thick with incense. Retrieving the linen cloth and gemstones from a golden platform, he struggles to lift a heavy sword wrapped in leather.

I gasp when the covering drops away. "Goliath's sword!"

Ahimelech nods. "You struck him down with it. No one else should have it but you."

I grasp the handle, the memory of Elah filling me with fresh hope that softens the sting in my eyes. "I'll take it. There's none like it."

"Indeed." Ahimelech folds his hands over his white robe, his matching beard lifting in a comforting smile. "Your courage rallied all Israel that day. Whatever you face now, Yahweh's strength in you is sufficient."

I blink, looking up. "Is that the Word of the Lord?"

Ahimelech smooths the *ephod.* "Sometimes, He has the answer ready before we ask." He places his gnarled hand on the side of my head. "He's with you, David. You have nothing to fear."

I nod a few times, wishing I was really heading to Hebron to meet Saul's men on a mission. Instead, I'm thinking I need to get as far away from Israel as possible. After leaving Jonathan, I'd run south out of instinct, but Judah is the first place Saul will look. I have to get out of his reach, at least until his anger subsides.

The stones on the edge of Goliath's sword glower at me, giving me an idea. It makes me sick, but it's a heading that won't endanger anyone. Except me.

I pat the priest's hand, wondering how long it'll be before I can get this close to the temple again. "Thank you for everything. I should go."

Something shivers in Ahimelech's face, and for a moment, I wonder if he knows more than I've revealed. Ducking my head, I move away to retrieve the bread from the servants. I can't afford to waste another moment here, not if I'm going to get to the edge of Judah's territory before Saul sends men to cut me off.

At the border of Nob, I head south until I'm out of sight of the watchmen on the walls. Then, I turn west, hugging the streambed that cuts the land all the way into Philistine territory.

Yahweh's with you.

The priest's words follow me, and I repeat them feverishly, trying to believe they'll still be true in Gath.

* * * * *

Two months later

This is a mistake. The thought lifts in my mind for the hundredth time as I study the coiled hilt of the sword in my hands. Dagon's serpentine image curls around the weapon's gold-tipped handle, sneering at me. *Why are you here, giant-killer?*

I rub harder at the sword with my oiled cloth, as if I can polish away the pagan image, and find an Israelite weapon underneath. I've been in Gath for weeks, and the icy breath of fear still tickles the back of my neck. It should be second nature by now, but it still catches me off guard, usually taking the form of some aggressor. Like the seven-foot Philistine standing over me, poking my scarred shoulder with the edge of his knife.

"Pretty bad wound," he snarls, knowing full well he put it there.

I don't look up, but I can feel the others gathering from the edges of the barracks. Gath's mercenaries are drawn to mockery like vultures to a kill.

Without speaking, I pull the makeshift bandage back down over the burn on my arm. I have nothing to treat it with, and it still stings deeply.

The taunting Philistine angles his blade close to my face, flicking a clump of hair out of my eyes. He'd heated that same knife in the fire three days ago, and six of his men had held me down while he'd burned me with it. It's something I've often seen done to their soldiers as a punishment. But so far, I'm only guilty of being an Israelite.

"Why didn't you fight back?" the man presses me. "I thought you Hebrews had a powerful god."

"Back to your business!" The commander's growl is barely enough to dissuade them.

I barely glance up as the men disperse, back to the piles of stolen weapons they've been cleaning. The commander's stare feels like another burn, scorching me from across the barracks.

No one questions Ittai. He's heavily muscled, with a deep scar trailing his face, and all the mercenaries fear and resent him. From the barracks at night, we can hear the screams of anyone sent to him for punishment. But from my arrival here, he's tried to steer me clear of trouble. I can't tell if his pity originates from an appreciation of my skill or something else. Either way, his gruff protection has been the only good thing I've found in this place.

I wait until the room has cleared before I get up. I've been in this dark, cramped space for hours, bent over the Geshurite weapons we plundered in the most recent raid. Sweat scalds my body from the furnace several feet away where scrap metal is being melted down. I head over to it, carrying a crooked sword that won't be any good for fighting.

As I move past him, Ittai blocks my way, speaking through his teeth. "There's a feast tonight. They'll be drinking heavily." He lifts his eyes to the upper battlements several feet over the barracks. "Go up to my quarters and hide there until dawn. Then come down."

He toughens his voice as though he's scolding me, and I nod and slip away, not daring to linger. There are too many watching.

Some of the men under Ittai's command are of Ammon or Amalek or Geshur, not directly of Philistine descent. But they all want to sink their claws into me. I've held back in the practice bouts the captain makes us fight, not wanting to reveal too much of my skill. But with each mock battle I win, they hate me more.

I've been preyed on before, but three nights ago, I was dragged awake by six Philistines who were after blood. Unable to see them in the dark, I was beaten and kicked until the commander broke up the attack. He'd stitched up the torn side of my face, but the incident has kept me from sleeping since. There are no laws here to prevent the death of an Israelite, no one obligated to protect me.

Fear is my new companion, adding extra weight to my shoulders, reminding me I'm surrounded. I flex my fingers, wishing I could use my sword against it. But this enemy is not flesh. In Israel, fighting for Saul, any anxiety would dissolve, spun into praise the night before and then burnt alive by zeal as I'd fling myself into combat again and again. I had worn Yahweh's protection like a garment, the best armor I had. Now, where is it?

A raucous shout from below sends dread slicing through me again. I'm hidden by shadows several feet above them, but the ribald laughter building in the streets signals danger. Every other day, it seems a new god is being celebrated with revelry and blood sacrifices under every terebinth tree. The soldiers will be drunk soon, but it will be hours before it's safe for me to show myself.

I rub my face, agitated by my own stupidity. Why am I here? Gath is Goliath's hometown, and the oppression that chokes the air makes it hard to breathe. I yearn for Israel, dreaming every night that I'm in Saul's fortress or in the war camp beside Jonathan, only to wake up here, usually with a Philistine foot in my side.

From the moment I arrived, I knew I wouldn't have it easy. The guard's iron stare had pierced me through when I'd dodged his question about my heritage.

"You're an Israelite. One of Saul's castoffs."

"I have no country," I'd told him, reasoning that it was true.

I'd been desperate enough to feel relieved when Ittai had told me I could join the king's mercenaries. I had barely eaten since visiting the priests in Nob. I'd somehow kept Goliath's sword hidden, wrapped in a leather sheath. Its familiar presence is a constant reminder that I was Yahweh's warrior once. And that this is a mistake.

Another explosion of laughter makes me shudder. Other than the giants, the mercenaries are the worst Philistia has to offer—criminals and former captives hardened by killing or torture. Among them, I'm little more than a slave, polishing and sharpening weapons to be used against my people in exchange for a little food and a place outside Israel. They've despised me from the beginning, forcing me to hide out separately to avoid their predations. My patience is wearing thin, but I can't openly fight them, not without incurring trouble.

I trace the gilded handle, my heart twisting. I can't even sing. My harp is back in Gibeah, along with everything else I left behind. The verses that wander around inside me are little more than desperate, disjointed pleas for protection. I whisper some now, barely allowing the notes to reach my vocal cords.

"Break the teeth in their mouths, God—let their arrows be blunted as they aim. Only you have kept count of my tossings, my restless complaint because of my enemies."

Could anything in that become a song? What kind of melody would accompany such writhing? Is it even acceptable to Yahweh? Ahimelech had said I have nothing to fear. So, why do I feel like I'm drowning? Like a powerful current is about to take me under?

I'd never considered how the men of the resistance lived, wandering in exile, but is this how they feel? Oppressed? Trampled on?

I close my eyes. "Be gracious to me, Yahweh. Keep my path secure."

A deep, familiar voice breaks into my prayer. "Why did you come here?"

My fingers close around my sword. It's the first time Ittai's seen me with it. "Saul cast me out," I say without turning around.

Ittai folds his arms, his muscles tight under his shoulder greaves. "He cast out his famous champion who's slain tens of thousands?"

I look at him, my stomach clenching. Calm certainty stands out from every hard line in his face, demanding that I answer it.

"How long have you known?" I whisper.

Scorn darkens his face. "How long did you think you could hide it? The others are too drunk and stupid to notice how you walk like royalty and fight like a man possessed by a god. But if they saw the sword of Goliath, they might stop to think about it." His voice grows heavy. "It was a mistake to come here. There's not a man in this city that doesn't dream of killing you."

Somehow that doesn't hurt the way Saul's hatred does. "Saul threw a spear at his favorite son for helping me. He wants me dead. I'm not going back." I tighten my grip on my sword. "Why are *you* here?"

Ittai's face closes. "I'm a Gittite. Gath is my home."

"But those aren't battle wounds." My eyes skirt his shoulders where deep scars wind around his arms like ropes.

A subtle shiver eats through his masked expression. "Achish's father took me for a slave when I was twelve. I thought he would send me out to fight when I was older, but instead, he set me over the war captives. And men who have nothing to live for."

My muscles clench. For years, he's been Achish's personal instrument of torture. And I can see every inch of it in his eyes. Something shifts inside me, and compassion moves in, covering my fear for the moment. "There are men who live in the hills of Israel. They would give anything to have someone who could offer real fighting skills, leadership…"

"I wasn't trained to lead men. I was trained to break them," he scoffs harshly. "If you're suggesting I go to Israel, you're even more of a fool than I thought. You think a Philistine would be more welcome there than you are?"

I shrug. "My great-grandmother was from Moab. My other ancestors were refugees from Jericho. Yahweh is merciful. He receives those who keep His Word." Saying it aloud makes me want to weep.

A muscle jerks near the commander's eye. "Return to Him, then. This is no place for you." He stalks away.

Once he's gone, I go to the wall and press a fist into it. I should return. But I've been over this before. Saul will search Bethlehem and Ramah first, confronting my family and the men of Judah. Better that they know nothing about where I've gone. It's probably the first time in my life I've prayed for Joab to take action. But he's my family's only hope of escaping Saul. I press my forehead into my fist.

"Yahweh, shield them."

As certain as I've been of Yahweh's protection and favor, can I really count on it now? I'm unclean just by being here.

I force my mind back to the memory of Samuel's upper room and the presence that had embraced me there. "Almighty God, you're still my Fortress. Preserve me, for I take refuge in you." I open my eyes, sensing movement.

As quickly as I notice the second shadow joining mine, a sharp blow cracks into my back, and my hands and knees touch ground. I whip around, reaching for my sword, but I can't grab it. Eight Philistines are standing over me, crowding close like jackals.

"What are you doing up here, Israelite? Too good to eat with the rest of us?" The man's eyes are dull with intoxication, but I've seen the glow of bloodlust enough times on the battlefield to recognize it.

"More likely planning to murder the commander," another sneers. "Talk, Israelite!"

They're all armed, however unsteady on their feet. One lumbers closer, seething wine-soaked hatred. "We know how to help you find your voice."

While my eyes are on him, another jabs his sword up my leg, opening a deep cut in my thigh. I barely make a sound before my sword is in my hand and over my head, the hilt slamming into the man's temple. The others chortle as he staggers to the ground, knocked out. I'm giving them exactly what they want.

"Who'd you steal that from?" the Philistine slurs, his eyes grazing my blade.

Ignoring the blood dripping down my leg, I keep my eyes trained on him, grappling with the battle flames crackling inside me. I'm not here to kill Philistines. But if I don't, I could end up dead. No one will care.

When the Philistine's blade darts up toward my throat, I bring my sword down, slicing through his wrist. Shouting, he drops his weapon, holding back the blood while I cut through two more assailants, sending both to the ground with surface wounds. One grasps at my neck from behind, trying to yank me over the edge of the battlement, but my elbow in his jaw sends him tumbling to the street below instead.

Fierceness ignited, I lean into the fight, cutting right and left until the shouts and taunts become moans around me. Once they're all stretched out on the ground at my feet, everything lifts off of me like a cloud, the fist of fear dropping back into my stomach. I never should have come. There's no way I can keep my head down and be mistaken for a mercenary. I can feel the last shreds of my courage withering under the reality.

"You—" The single word cuts me like a whip.

Three Philistines draped in rich embroidered robes darken the doorway, watching me. The setting sun catches their rings, one on each finger. They step closer, and I can see earrings, armbands, heavy medallions. But they have the eyes of wolves. They must be Achish's councilmen, returning from the high places.

"That's a Philistine weapon," one observes. "Where did you get it?"

My fingers ache around Goliath's sword. Ice encases my body, sealing off movement.

The man snaps his fingers, advancing closer. "I'm talking to you, Israelite. Where'd you get it?"

My heart races, dragging terror through every limb. I've drawn the attention of the whole barracks now. If I kill these three, the rest will attack. I want Jonathan more than anything right now.

"Only the giants carry blades like that." He drags his gaze down the length of the sword. "Like the champion Goliath. Does it surprise you that we know of him?"

I'm sweating, the evening air breathing cold against my skin.

The nobles spread out, circling around me. "If I recall correctly, he was killed by a Hebrew shepherd boy. David." The way he spits my name sends lightning bolts of panic through me. "Sound familiar?" He pivots to face me.

"I was...just a servant of Saul." My voice sounds empty, distant.

He sneers. "I'm sure it's a complicated story."

"It's not complicated. It's just none of your business." Losing composure, I let my voice lash out. Foolishly.

The Philistine strikes my face, every jagged ring digging deep. Once I'm bent over, his men drag me backwards and shove me up against the wall, holding me there with a staff across my chest.

"I'll ask again. Where did you get the sword?"

Someone picks up my weapon from the ground while panic pulls through my lungs.

"This *is* the sword of Goliath!" I can hear the anger igniting the man's voice, catching fire among the others. "You are David, aren't you?"

The man in front of me nods, his brows lifting in a smile that stops my heart. He shoves the staff deeper into my throat. "Everyone, behold the king of the land! This is the shepherd they sing about in their dances—their sickening, overblown celebrations of blood shed on Philistine lands. By this one."

He shakes his head at me. "Achish will have to thank Saul. He never expected such a gift."

Dizzy from not breathing, I try not to look at Goliath's blade angling against my face.

"Bring him," is the last thing I hear before I'm knocked out.

I have no idea how much time has passed before a sharp blow to the small of my back rouses me. I move one muscle, and iron digs into my neck. The chain leashing me to a Philistine guard is spiked, slicing into my skin with every movement. I'm face down on a stone floor, my hands bound behind me. Every mocking sound echoes in the vaulted ceiling. When I lift my head, torchlight glimmers off the grotesque faces of a dozen Philistine gods, carved into the walls around a golden platform. They've brought me to the throne room, to turn me over to Achish.

The fear is so intense, it screams inside me, mangling the priest's words in my mind. *What can flesh do to you, David?*

Plenty. Why should Yahweh protect me now, when I've wandered foolishly into a trap without consulting Him? What kind of king is that? I'm no wiser than the sheep who follow their wayward companions right over a cliff.

A deep inner witness reminds me I still went after them, but the brief breath of peace is short lived, and I'm left grasping for it, feeling like I'm in a nightmare, tossing toward the surface. Except there is none. This pit I've wandered into is reality.

Adonai, what should I do?

Anxiety grips my mind until it feels like it will burst with the pressure. Amid the thousands of thoughts weighing heavier with every breath, only one stands out that will get me out of here alive. Convince them I'm not David.

It helps that Achish has never seen me up close. And I've changed significantly since killing Goliath. But if I can't convince the king that I'm not who they think, I could be stuck here a very long time, tortured in order to extract something from Saul and Jonathan.

I sense the change that comes over the guards and councilmen as a shadow fills the doorway. Every man straightens, their attention tightening.

"What's this?" The Philistine from my nightmares appears only seconds after his voice enters the room, riding the echoes through my mind. This is the man who sat mocking for a month while Israel trembled before Goliath. The man who sent raiders to kill Jonathan. I still carry his message with me. Another thing he can't find.

Jonathan had said the king of Philistia was a coward, content to hide behind giants, a man we didn't need to be afraid of. But looking into his narrow eyes, I know I am.

Achish spreads his hands sharply at his guards. "Well?"

"We've brought you Goliath's killer, my king." Achish's breathless councilman rushes to explain while his guard yanks me up by my hair. "And here is the giant's sword. See for yourself. There's none like it."

"I see it." Achish stares at Goliath's weapon, then flicks his fingers at his guard, who hands it to him. As soon as the blade is in his hands, the king's eyes shift to me, and I stop breathing again. The perverse pleasure pouring into his face is chilling. "Bring him to me."

I barely resist crying out when they yank me across the floor by the chain, opening cuts under the iron collar. With my hands bound, I can't do anything to alleviate the sharp pull. The chain keeps me right where they want me.

Achish holds the sword against his palm, assessing me. "So… this is the one they make so much of. Saul's shepherd-singer."

The Philistine councilman is glowing with satisfaction. "How much do you think Saul will pay to get his war trophy back?"

"That depends," Achish purrs. "There are so many… options."

The king's tone makes sweat break out on my forehead. He can't find out who I am.

My own bold declarations in worship dance around in my mind, mocking me.

Many are arrayed against me, but He redeems my soul in safety from the battle that I wage.

How do I get out of this one?

As many times as I've faced death on the battlefield, it's never breathed down my neck the way it is here. Except for those times in Saul's chambers.

Suddenly, an idea burns through the tumult, one that's as desperate as I am. It's absurd, but I've seen enough of Saul's erratic behavior to know what to do. Plus a few town drunks in Bethlehem. It helps that panic is pushing into my vision, clouding the edges.

When Achish grabs the chain and yanks it, I let myself scream. Too loud. Startled, the king steps back but doesn't let go. "What are you doing so far from your master?" he questions me. "Where are all the men of Judah who were so eager to crown you in Saul's place?"

"Saul?" I open my voice and let all the terror I'm feeling bleed into it. I say it over and over, then cry out again, trembling as though terribly cold. I jerk away from Achish, dragging myself back across the floor.

A guard grabs the end of my chain, resisting my efforts, and I can smell the blood escaping down my neck, but I keep up the act, throwing myself onto the floor and stringing words together incoherently, letting saliva drip down my chin into my beard.

"Saul has no power here," I hiss. "This is Dagon's realm." I force myself to laugh, silently begging Yahweh to forgive what I'm saying.

The guards' baffled laughter crawls the stone walls, but it's working. The councilmen are gaping at me, and Achish is cutting them open with his gaze. "You two, come here," he orders them.

They both look as though they'd rather not, but they obey. Achish stares them down for a few moments and then drags his gaze back to me. "Do you think I don't have enough madmen in my court that you have to drag another one in here? An *Israelite?*" Affronted, he lets them think for a minute and then shouts loud enough to make them shake. *"Well?"*

His councilmen fumble, bending into nervous bows. "My lord king—David is your greatest enemy. If there was any chance it was him, we had to be certain."

"What about Goliath's sword, your majesty?" they persist. "Where would he have gotten that?"

"You've never heard of stealing before, imbecile?" Achish screeches, his pride hurt. "You think I can't tell the difference between a madman and Israel's champion?"

Both men stammer reluctant agreement, shaking in place.

The king rotates the sword, aiming it. "Now, I will give you one last chance to use your heads before I remove them. What do I want done with him?"

The nobleman wrings his hands. "We can get rid of him here and now, my king."

Achish laughs. "So that I can be haunted by whatever god has possessed him? No thank you. Just get him out of here!"

"You mean, let him go, my lord?" The men gape, incredulous.

"Yes! Let him go. Get him out of my sight!" Achish snaps.

"He's an Israelite. A servant of Saul—" the men continue, glaring at me.

Achish pops his eyebrows at them. "Do I look like I care? While we're wasting time over this one, Saul has probably sent his good luck charm ahead of us to Keilah. Just get back to work, and don't worry about this…thing. There's nothing from here to Adullam. Starvation will take him if Saul doesn't. Now, get out!"

The men grab hold of me and drag me away before Achish can even turn his back.

I keep up my act as long as I can, scratching at the gate and fighting their grasp until we're outside the gates by the fringe of wilderness that becomes Judea in miles. I cringe when they tear the chain from my neck. Blood drips into my collar, but I force a smile.

The Philistine guard grimaces, kicking me out of his way. "Haunt these gates again, madman, and we'll kill you, all the gods notwithstanding."

As soon as they leave me, I find the closest thing to a puddle and lean my torn neck into it, letting the wounds sting in the water and dragging my thigh through it. Then I work on freeing my hands. Jonathan has bound me before, training me to get out of several different knots in as little time as possible. Finally loose, I lean against a tree and let myself shake.

I still can't believe I came so close to Achish and escaped. It's certainly not the way I would have imagined meeting the Philistine king, who's lurked in the back of my mind for years. He'll burn with anger if he ever finds out he really did have me in his power today.

His self-satisfied grin shreds my nerves. What is he planning to do at Keilah? And what can I do about it with no weapons?

I'm already missing the weight of Goliath's sword. Yahweh put that weapon in my hands, and it's already gone. I was barely able to lift it that day in Elah, and yet I still brought it down on the giant's head, the hands of God supporting mine. Tears enter my eyes. He's supported me my whole life. He's the reason people sing about me and eagerly follow me, even though I'm the youngest commander in Israel's army. Or was.

The lion. The bear. Saul's spears and arrows. Goliath and the Philistines. Yahweh rescued me from them all. And yet I sat there trembling on the end of a chain, acting like I'd been forsaken.

Even now, when everything's been stripped away, I couldn't trust that my Shepherd would still be with me? What does it matter who injures my cause, who plots against me if the God of Israel's armies is at my side?

I drop to my knees, deeply shaken. "Forgive me, Yahweh."

Facing the east, I wait there in silence, letting the truth ease its way back into me.

"I trust you, God Almighty. Your Word is my praise. You have kept count of all my tossings. You've recorded all my wanderings." I lift my head. "I will not be afraid. What can man do to me?"

The words flow like tears as I stumble through the next several days while the temperature drops and winter rains battle Israel's southern countryside.

"I will bless the Lord...at all times. His praise will...always be in my mouth."

I repeat as many verses as I can, as many as I've written, and dozens more phrases flooding my mind. The praises I've committed to speak battle with the rest of me that's suffering and unsure where to go.

"My soul makes its boast in the Lord." I declare it defiantly while hiding in ditches, waiting for unknown men on horseback to pass.

Every day has become a fight to keep warm. But the land is taking a beating under the torrential rain, and I'm soaked all the way to my bones. Too wet and cold to sleep. The murmured praise keeps me moving.

"I sought the Lord, and He answered me, and delivered me from all my fears. Those who look to Him are radiant, and their faces will never know shame."

At the edge of a field, I spot a handful of farmers and their servants—the first men of Israel I've seen in weeks. Either way, their first instinct is to grab stones. They don't even notice that I'm unarmed. And injured.

"Those who fear the Lord have no lack. The young lions suffer want and hunger; but those who seek the Lord lack no good thing."

I'm starving. The roadside plants and roots aren't enough to hold me together, and I can feel the edges of my thoughts starting to drift. Weakness drags at my limbs, and every morning it gets harder to lift my head. It terrifies me to feel my own strength draining away.

"This poor man cried, and the Lord heard him and saved him out of all his troubles. The angel of the Lord encamps around those who fear him, and delivers them."

I'm in trouble. The pounding rain won't stop, and now I'm feeling sharpness in it, pieces of ice slashing my skin. I'm too exposed, with no weapons. I have to be near the southern slopes of Adullam by now, but I've lost all interest in direction. This rocky region is scarred with caves and dugouts used by shepherds and travelers during the shearing season. I need to get into one and get warm.

Thunder breaks the clouds open, shuddering through my chest. I pull my way up past the rocks to the first opening I find, the first cave carved into the landscape. The moment the roof stops the rain, exhaustion hits me, and I collapse.

Thank you. The words don't even make it past my lips.

The floor is rough, and jagged walls of rock slope over my head, but at least I'm not being pelted by rain. A pile of brushy kindling fills one corner, alongside some dry, stacked wood. Some traveler has been here, and not too long ago. I need to build a fire. I need to get warm. I should be feeling the urgency more sharply. But everything is dull, fading in and out. I try to remove Jonathan's robe, but it's clinging to me like a second skin, and my fingers aren't working.

I need to rest. But I can't sleep like this. I'll die.

Somehow, it doesn't seem like such a bad thing. My eyes drift, and the cold drags me down. When I collapse against the dirt, time vanishes, and I don't know if I'll get up again. Something pounds outside the cave. Into the cave. But I don't look up.

"God of Abraham!" The familiar gruff voice is harsh with fear, and the image standing over me is blurred. Joab.

I can't tell if I'm saying his name or just thinking it. My mouth won't move. Everything entering my mind stops there, dropping off. All my body can do is shiver.

"What is wrong with you, David? Are you trying to die?" Yanking me upright, my nephew is thanking God and cursing at the same time. "Asa! Asa, get in here!"

I can't see anything with my head flopped against Joab's shoulder, but I can feel his voice deep in his chest, ordering his brother to help him.

"Get a flint to that wood, now! We have to get him warm."

Joab is already tearing my wet clothes, wrapping me in what feels like a heavy animal skin. "Go tell the others we found him. Hurry!"

Asahel disappears before I even see him. In a few moments, I hear the hiss of sparks catching wood. Joab drags me as close to the fire as he dares, holding me up against him. His hands work the warmth into me, rubbing feeling back into my limbs, growling Saul's name like a curse. "He can't get rid of you that easily."

I feel a smile at the back of my mind, but I can't move. I'm so exhausted, I can't even feel gratitude that Joab's here. For now, it's enough that he is. At the end of my strength, my Shepherd went after me on the hills and gave me shelter. I don't even try to think past that.

TWENTY-FIVE

Jonathan

———◆◆———

At my father's door, I struggle to regain the composure that fled the night of the New Moon feast and never returned. It's been over a month since the king threw the spear at me, but it's still a battle to face him.

The day after David had fled, I'd expected to feel the red-hot stirrings of temper facing Saul. But the moment I'd walked into the antechamber, I was gripped with a weary pain that's taken up permanent residence in my bones. My grief is heavier for my double loss. Not only is my best friend gone, but there's a bloodthirsty stranger in place of the man I've called Abba.

He'd turned on me the moment I arrived that first day.

"He's gone, isn't he? We waited too long, and he's escaped. How did I end up with a son like you?"

My response had dripped venom. "Perhaps I'm more like my mother, the perverse, rebellious woman you raged about last night."

I could sense the slap coming before it connected with my face. I had to grip the edge of the table, summoning every ounce of self-control to avoid striking back. I'm not his enemy, no matter how often he acts like I am. And David's not his enemy either. But how can I make him see that? His hatred has been unyielding since that morning.

"I rage for your own good! Without me, you would not be half the warrior you are. And without me, you would never become king. You would remain ignorant of these Judean threats until they overwhelmed you. Now, what has David told you about himself? What is his connection with Samuel? Does he plan a revolution with his nephews? I know you know!"

I still wouldn't look at him, absorbing his outburst until silence stretched between us. Some of his anger had finally evaporated, escaping in a slow exhale. Still, everything in me cringed when he touched me.

"When I threw the spear..." His jaw flexed. "I couldn't fathom that you were planning to leave me defenseless, with no information about my enemy."

I turned to look at him, easing my shoulder out of his grasp. "What information do you want? Have you considered that the sons of Judah are no match for our God?"

He'd nodded, misunderstanding. "Yes, and if Yahweh gave me the crown, we cannot expect men like that to…"

"That's not what I meant. You've asked me about Samuel and the men of Judah, but David's connection with Adonai is the only one that matters. Yahweh is the only One who could put the crown on David's head."

"What are you saying?"

I'd managed to keep my gaze level. "Yahweh said He would choose a man after His own heart to rule. If David has been anointed by God, as you were, why would we want to stand in the way?"

I had taken another slap after that, but since that day, he hasn't touched me again. He's hardly spoken to me, summoning only Abner and his councilmen, as well as some spies whom he grills behind closed doors.

One of them is waiting outside the antechamber door now. Dislike prods the pain in my eyes when I see who it is. "Doeg."

David's old accuser doesn't straighten up or address me, lounging against the wall with a crooked grin that makes me want to throw him out the nearest window.

"Are you summoned to the king?" I demand.

Doeg's brows lift, disrespect staining his smile. "Are you?"

"Watch how you speak to me, Edomite. You think you can stay here for long if I don't allow it?"

He shrugs, immediately seeing through my threat. I had sent him packing last time, only to have Saul bring him back. It's clear who my father wants to believe.

I enter the antechamber, slamming the door in Doeg's face. It's not much of a comfort, but it's something. Without waiting for a command, I march up to the king, facing him across his table. "Are we to speak in private, my lord, or is Doeg supposed to hear this?"

Saul responds with his eyes, looking too pleased with himself to get angry. Bad sign. "What I have to say to you does not concern an Edomite spy."

"Then why is he here?" I demand.

Again, Saul dodges the question, folding a map in half and angling his head out the window. "You're taking a dozen Philistine horses to Aijalon as a gift for Joram, along with a few talents of fine gold." He lifts his eyes. "I was serious about his daughter. Your life has been unfairly consumed with war. You've been denied the natural pleasures common men take for granted."

I almost smile, completely baffled. He really picks his moments.

Saul continues, "She comes at a steep price, but her father is overjoyed at the offer, and it will secure a valuable ally. Joram's sons have influence among many Judeans, but they have not been tainted by distractions."

Meaning they have no connection with David.

"I've spoken to your mother and she also approves," he finishes.

I stiffen. "So, you've seen my mother?"

Saul's eyes stab my forehead. "Don't criticize me. We're discussing you. Our situation is precarious, and you are the first hope for our dynasty. You must take a wife and produce an heir." Finished looking at me, he returns to staring at the map. "We will marry you quickly. Given the circumstances, her father was willing to forgo the traditional engagement."

My heart stumbles over itself. "So, we're abandoning the Law…"

Saul's tone hardens. "*In our present circumstances*, we cannot do otherwise. The Law was written when Israel had no king. I'm giving you six months to give her a child, and then you will come back to court. You will have plenty of funds to make her comfortable."

"Six months?" I nearly choke.

He waves his hand. "I know the usual time is a year, but I need you. You will go to Aijalon now and speak to Joram. I sent word to him, so he should be expecting you. If you give him assurance that you will be back for his daughter, all will be well. Now go."

I stand there for a few pointless seconds, considering. He's not giving me a choice, as I knew he wouldn't. This is the moment I've been avoiding since he'd refused me Naamah. Today, I will meet the woman who will become my wife. Hastily, because my father wants to secure the throne against David.

"You can send Doeg in now," Saul orders.

I grind any response between my teeth, shoving past the Edomite outside without saying a word. Doesn't the king know that if he chooses to align himself with slander and hatred, that's what will come back on his own head?

The miles to Aijalon open a welcome refuge for my thoughts, and I surrender to the pull of uncertainty that's plagued me for weeks. *Is it right for me to do this, Adonai? Marry a girl who thinks she'll be queen when our house is not meant to stand? Should I have gone with David and left all this behind?*

No answer enters my mind except a firm resolve that's been at my side like armor ever since my father was crowned. No, I won't abandon him. He'll need me to keep the voice of truth and reason alive in his ear. And perhaps one day, it'll reach his heart. If I left him now, he'd never forgive me, never stop hating David. But maybe I can change his mind as I did before. *Adonai, strengthen me.*

I'm grateful for the cover of darkness that conceals my arrival in Aijalon. Joram and his sons rejoice as though they're welcoming a blood relative, and it's almost an hour before he presents his daughter to me.

Jehosheva bows gracefully before looking up, but I'm impressed that her gaze doesn't move after that. I wait several moments in silence, but the quickening only grows, the sense that the woman behind those brown eyes can be trusted. There's something there, if only hope.

My brothers know very little about their wives, and the Sarrahs are mostly ignored when it comes to matters of state. But

I'm the Hassar. My wife will be a prime target for the danger and manipulation that my position attracts, and her responsibility will be greater as well, undergirding the kingdom with the children she raises.

I study the beautiful young woman with the gentle eyes, and my heart races when I remember she was there when my father threw the spear at me. Does she think that's what awaits her in Gibeah?

Sudden panic strokes my nerves, and I turn to Joram. "May I speak with your daughter alone?"

Her father hastily agrees, but the moment he disappears, my stomach drops and my cheeks bloom. I take a short walk around the room, trying to pull myself together. I've done this before; it's just been a long time since I've had to start fresh with someone new.

"My father..." I start, and then pause to breathe. "My father, the king, said your family has desired this match for years. Is that true?" I smirk a little, remembering Saul's exact words.

But Jehosheva doesn't hesitate. "Yes, my lord; it's true. My brothers were in the king's army at Michmash, and I grew up hearing your name more than my own." She smiles softly, her tone betraying no bitterness. "When my father told me the king had asked for me, I was...pleased."

"Really?" I've been so strained lately, the pleasure warming my chest feels foreign, almost uncalled for.

Her head tilts to one side. "You don't believe me?"

"No. It's just..." I drop my shoulders. I might as well be honest. "I feel I should apologize for what happened. At the New Moon feast."

"You did nothing wrong, my lord." She barely whispers it, her eyes never leaving my face.

I sigh heavily, wishing I was a different person, that her future father-in-law was a different person, and maybe not the king. But unfortunately...

"Unfortunately, that night was a very honest expression of our relationship. He hasn't been the same since the battle with Amalek. He lost favor with Yahweh and never recovered." I don't want to cause her to disrespect the king, but if we're to be married, I want her to understand. "I don't want to fight him. I want to honor him. All my life, I've tried."

Jehosheva takes one step closer. "My father said that you are a man of honor who will teach his sons the fear of the Lord. That is enough for me."

Again, I look sharply at her, but her dark eyes glow with sincerity. I swallow hard. "I can promise you that. Yahweh is the lifeblood of our people. Anything we might gain is a loss without Him."

She nods, smiling, and I'm impressed by her focus. But there's more she should know. She hasn't mentioned my position, but that doesn't mean it hasn't crossed her mind.

"There's something else I must tell you. It won't make much sense right now, but…" I glance at the door and step in front of her, lowering my voice. "I may not be king." I can't believe I'm saying this to her, but I'm in too deep now. "I am Saul's firstborn, but Yahweh could still choose another. I do not mean that I plan to go against my father, but if I'm faced with obedience to our God or the king, you have to know what I will choose. Do you understand?"

She hasn't blinked since I started talking. Her eyes are serious, and she breathes deeply before responding. "I understand. I will not speak of this to anyone."

I nod, grateful for her quick perception.

But then she utterly shocks me, asking, "Is it David?"

"What?"

"Your brother-in-law. The commander your father raged about at the feast. Does the king think Yahweh has chosen him?"

I'm unable to respond, not only from surprise, but also deep gratitude. Only Yahweh could have set this woman apart. What other girl in Israel would discern any of this, let alone accept it? For the first time, I feel eagerness about the future.

My jaw tightens around emotion. "He's my closest friend and a man of God. We swore a covenant of peace together. David will not harm anyone in my family. But he's on the run as we speak, because my father believes he is a traitor."

Jehosheva's eyes expand. "Then, he could be planning to search for David even now. I heard that Doeg has returned to his service."

Which can only mean one thing. Saul is ready to spy on his own people in order to snare David. Alarm dances in my chest as I realize he was trying to get rid of me with this journey. I should be home right now. I need to stay one step ahead of Saul if I'm to protect my friend.

My father may resent my input, but if I keep him back from presumptuous sins, he'll thank me later. Reactionary attacks against David will only cause the king to lose the support of the people, starting with Judah, the fiercest tribe.

I turn back to Jehosheva. "I'm sorry…"

She lifts her chin, mercifully not offended. "Go to the king. When you return, I'll be waiting."

Her understanding warms my heart. She bows deeply, and I take her hands in mine, kissing them before leaving to speak to her father.

I reach Gibeah by the time dusk is falling on the next day. Sick apprehension clings closer than my garments, stretching before me with the evening shadows. Something is very wrong.

I look for Ezra first; he's easy to find. "Where's the king?" I ask him.

The disturbance I'm feeling is mirrored on my friend's face. "It's not the time, my lord," he mumbles.

"What are you talking about? Is he still holding council?"

Ezra swallows. "He's summoned the priests from Nob. Ahimelech ben Ahitub and his sons."

"All of them?" Strange. I've never known any of my father's business to require all the priests.

"Yes, all of them. And he said he wasn't to be disturbed. Just give him time."

Now I have to see for myself. Ignoring Ezra's counsel, I head straight for the throne room, only to be blocked at the door by Abner.

"Jonathan, this does not concern you."

Why does everyone keep saying that? "Everything concerns me, Abner." I push past him, and instantly a dozen pairs of eyes lock onto me.

Just as Ezra said, all seven priests of Nob are gathered before my father's throne. But he hadn't mentioned they'd be bound. Ice shoots up my spine at the sight of them huddled together like a collection of captives. Young Abiathar looks stricken, his chest rising and falling rapidly. But Ahimelech bows regally at the waist as though he's not even aware of the ropes around his wrists. "Hassar."

Saul's frustrated sigh fills the room. "Ah, yes. My son and heir. The one who makes a covenant with the son of Jesse behind my back while everyone looks the other way. Yet I am your anointed king. How am I to rule if my own priests conspire against me?" He turns an accusatory gaze on Ahimelech. The priest's gaping surprise reveals that this is the first he's heard of any trouble.

I step up next to Saul's shoulder, my voice lowered. "Abba, what is this?"

"You don't know?" He turns a triumphant sneer my way. "It has come to my attention, far too late, that David came to these men at Nob. They inquired of the Lord for him and gave him bread and the sword of Goliath, which they've been keeping in the temple." He wheels back around to face the priests. "And now the son of Jesse lies in wait for me in some cave, amassing warriors, growing stronger. Planning how to take the kingdom for himself."

Inches from Ahimelech, Saul folds his arms, staring him down. "What do you have to say to that, old man?"

My heartbeat tumbles out of control while the aged priest tries to explain.

"My lord," Ahimelech fumbles, aghast. "Truthfully, I was not aware of any treachery. Who among your servants is as faithful as David? He is the king's son-in-law and captain over your bodyguard. Your own son honored him because he was faithful to your house."

He glances at me, and I can't remember ever being so grateful to him. What a blessing to hear honest words!

The priest's expression settles. "This is not the first time I've inquired of the Lord for David, and it won't be the last. But please, my lord, banish this talk about anyone lying in wait for you, because I assure you, nothing of the sort was planned. I assumed David was being sent on some urgent business, as usual. But I knew nothing of the particulars of his mission, little or great. Nor did anyone in my household." He takes a step closer to Abiathar without removing his eyes from the king.

I am hopeful the sincere appeal is banishing Saul's suspicion—until I look at him.

I'm close enough to see the hatred eat its way through the humanity on my father's face. It's almost imperceptible, but it's chilling. And my heart shudders between beats. I have to say something. Anything to deflect his anger. But I'm utterly unprepared for the weight of it.

"You shall die, Ahimelech!" Saul shouts. "You and your whole family."

Anything I had planned to say chokes off in a barely coherent, "What?!" Aghast, I step in front of Saul, forcing eye contact. "Abba, no!"

Ignoring me, he aims the order at his guards. "You heard me, didn't you?"

"Abba, they didn't know!" I cry out. Has he gone insane? He's going to cut the priests down right here like Philistine captives? "What have they done? What is their crime?"

Unwittingly, I use the same words David did in his own defense, and of course, my father hasn't learned to listen any better since then. Mercifully, the half dozen guards shrink back, unwilling. Fumbling with their weapons, they look at the ground while Saul rails at them.

"You defy me, here and now? With my enemies standing guilty before me? Has David cast his spell on you too? Obey me, or there will be more deaths today!"

I go to my knees. "My lord and king, I beseech you!"

I reach for Saul's wrist, but he steps around me, commanding, "Abner—do it."

Abner's face drains of color so quickly, I'm amazed he doesn't collapse. He holds his hands out in front of himself, his tone dropping. "My lord, I have enough lives on my conscience. I am hardly fit to strike a priest."

I gasp in relief from the ground. *Bless you, Abner.*

But Saul won't give up that easily. My gaze follows his until it lands on the Edomite standing off to the side. Something twisted passes between them in half a second. In only three swift steps, Doeg pulls Abner's sword, pivots, and brings the blade down on the elderly priest.

"No!" I shout, too late.

The sight of Ahimelech's body cleaved in two is enough to make me feel like I took the blade instead. Abiathar wails, flinging himself down next to his father, and the other priests join him on the floor, cowering and trembling.

Their grief tears into my chest, finding the battle fury that waits at the center. A fierce growl explodes from my throat, and I lunge for Doeg, my sword aloft, ready to sever the murderer's head from his body.

But Abner grasps my fighting wrist at the last second, barely avoiding decapitation in his effort to restrain me. My father's nod sends three guards to try to wrestle me aside, and several more join in as they realize they're no match for me in the heat of anger. I am Saul's son, after all.

They can't break my hold on my sword. When I'm ready for a kill, it molds to my hand, leaving behind cramps that take days to subside. This time though, the flat of someone else's sword slamming squarely into my wrist is all it takes. Sharp pain shoots up my arm, and my weapon clatters to the floor. Cursing, I jab my free elbow backwards into someone's jaw, hoping it belongs to whoever broke my wrist.

"Enough!" Saul bellows, bending to pick up my weapon.

"Enough?!" I howl as though I've been wounded. Which I have. Bloodguilt can take generations to heal. I shout at my father over the heads of his men. "How can you do this, Abba? How can you shed innocent blood? The blood of God's priests! You have cursed us all!"

The guards press closer around me, and I throw all my strength against theirs, desperate to stop this madness.

Abner's face is pressed close to mine, his teeth clenched. "Jonathan, please! Don't make it any worse!" Sweat beads on his brow, and his eyes glisten with liquid fear.

"Abner!" Saul rotates my sword, his calmness and Doeg's smirk feeding the flames inside me. "Take the prince to his house, and keep him there under guard until I send word. Doeg, finish it."

The miserable Edomite doesn't even blink, tearing his weapon through the bodies of two more priests while Abiathar leaps through a side window, trying to escape. Screams ignite my mouth and chest, but I can't tell if I'm giving voice to them. There are too many others. The cries don't stop echoing even after every man is stretched out on the floor, blood collecting beneath them.

I feel as though I'm breathing fire, my head pounding and my throat ablaze. Doeg must die. I'll kill him, broken wrist or not—just as soon as I can break free of the horror.

My father pulls his gaze from the carnage long enough to assess me, and it's as though my thoughts leap into his mind. Without a word, he walks over, and the guards retreat, giving him room.

Before I realize what he's doing, Saul wraps his arm around my neck and tightens, sealing off air before I can get a full breath. I drop to my knees, grasping at his wrist, but even as I try, I know I can't break his hold. His arm is like the trunk of a tree.

In a matter of seconds, my breaths become painful, too much of an effort to drag in and out. Before things go dark, I force my eyes up to Saul's as the rushing in my head finally drowns out the echoes of murder. I'm almost grateful to pass out.

* * * * *

After keeping me in confinement for three days, my father sends for me. I expect to be brought to him under guard, but he only sends Ezra to attend me. I go to the king the same way I've been since the massacre—my hair unbound, my clothes dusty with ashes, my robes torn.

I've heard worse during my isolation. Saul sent men to torch the holy city of Nob, killing everyone. Men, women, and children. The city has been the home of the priesthood since the Philistines destroyed Shiloh in Samuel's youth. And now, my father is responsible for the new desecration.

The torment of Israelite lives lost at Saul's hands weighs me down, and I wonder how he can be so blind. How can he lay this guilt on our family? All the grief in the world won't wash away their blood. A thousand sacrifices wouldn't earn us mercy at this point.

Saul receives me in his private chamber. When I enter, he's seated alone at a table spread with a feast, more lavish than usual, as if we have something to celebrate.

His eyes spark with disapproval when he notices my clothes, but he has the decency not to mention them. His throat rumbles as he clears it to speak. "Hassar Israel."

I don't answer. Coals still burn in my bosom, threatening to reignite, but I'm also exhausted. The succession of sleepless nights has drained me. Forgetting my injured hand, I drop onto a cushion and grab the nearest cup of wine, only to wince at the sudden motion. I will have to get Ammiel to inspect my wrist for a break. The pain is sharp and ruling my movements. Staring at the table, I wait for the twinging to subside.

Saul sighs, unveiling a shiver of concern. "Eat something, my son."

"I'm fasting." It's the truth. I haven't touched food in three days.

Saul squints, suspicious. "What for?"

"Innocent blood." The instant the words leave my mouth, my vision spins with tears.

My father winces, clenching his fist around his cup and slamming it down. "Enough! A traitor is hardly innocent, Jonathan, and I must root their poison from our midst before it destroys us. As king, I have unpleasant duties—"

"Unpleasant?" The image of the old priest's broken body swims before my eyes. Leaning against the table, I let my pounding head drop into my good hand.

There's a heavy shove as my father gets up, shuffling several steps as he paces. Then another sigh. "I know you're grieved. I wanted to spare you. That's why I sent you away. But as usual, you ignore my commands."

"You wanted to *spare* me?" My voice breaks as my head comes up. "If you wanted to spare me, you would have spared the priests. You would have spared David."

"David still lives, imbecile! He's lies in wait now, inciting every enemy in Israel against us as we speak." He stops abruptly, his eyes cooling. "But you knew that. You were the one who let him go. You sent for him that night and helped him get away, didn't you? Don't deny it."

"I wasn't going to."

The shock filling every corner of my father's face tells me that he wasn't completely sure. He eases himself back into his chair and laces his fingers, letting a slow breath hiss from between his teeth. I can tell by the gleam in his eyes that only our shared blood is stopping him from ordering my death.

Saul lifts his chin. "You know where he went first, don't you? To Gath. The home of Goliath, our greatest enemy."

Whom he killed while we cowered in fear. Where were all Saul's suspicions then?

"So much for his noble vow of loyalty," Saul mutters. "Now he's hiding out in caves, amassing men from every corner of Israel to lie in wait for me."

I shove back from the table. I've had enough of this. "You know what else he has, my father? He has the sword of Goliath, which the priest you murdered gave to him. And why? Because it is rightly his. He fought the battle no one else would fight, therefore he carries the weapon no one else does."

I step around the table, advancing as my father stands to his feet.

"And you know what else he has? The honest loyalty of fighting men who have lived and died beside him in *your battles*. Men whose lives he has enriched with his songs and his courage while you sit here spinning lies about imaginary threats! But you know what else he has? The one thing that matters more than all this?"

I pause, inches from my father's face, and wait for the answer to flood into his eyes. It doesn't take long. He knows David carries the anointing of the Lord.

"That's right," I whisper.

Saul's eyes change, a tortured petulance slowly replacing the rage that's sure to come back. "We've done this together from the beginning. Why do you set yourself against me?"

My heart twists inside out. Hasn't a lifetime of fighting at his side and suffering at his hands been enough to make him see?

I grab his arms, steeling myself against all the pain. "I am not against you. I have stood with you my entire life. I will die by your side, fighting the enemies of the Lord. *But David is not one of them.*"

TWENTY-SIX

David

———◆——

When I open my eyes again, I'm stretched out on the other side of the fire, across from the cave's mouth. I'm still wrapped up in animal furs, supported by a folded saddlebag under my head, and my feet are pressed up against the hot stones banking the flames. My fingers fold into the coarse fur coat around me, and I wonder dully if it's from the bear I killed before leaving Bethlehem.

Joab glances over his shoulder from a few feet away. "How do you feel?"

"Thirsty." I don't even recognize my own voice, a hoarse whisper that barely goes anywhere.

Joab holds a waterskin for me to drink, then hands me a clay bottle. "This too. It'll keep you warm."

The heated liquor burns all the way down, spreading a heavy cloud through my chest, and I cough, struggling to finish it. But when Joab pulls bread and dried meat from his pack, I stop thinking. Ravenous, I devour it while Joab watches, frowning.

"How long since you've eaten?" he asks me.

I just shake my head. The last thing I remember was a woman giving me a handful of parched grain at the edge of her husband's field. But how long since I've had a full meal? No idea. When I'm finished, Joab kneels beside me, inspecting the wounds on my neck. "Where'd you get these?"

"Gath."

His eyes spark. "You know how stupid you are for going there, don't you?"

"Where was I supposed to go?" Pain bends the words.

"You know the pull I have with the resistance. You could have come to me." Joab pushes gently at my sides, checking my bruised ribs. "Nothing's broken."

He moistens a cloth, and the sharp scent of oil joins the dampness in the air. I try to keep still while he cleanses my cuts. My breathing is short and tight, like I've been stabbed. "How did you find me?"

Joab's voice tightens. "I've been looking for weeks, ever since word got out that you left Gibeah. I've never seen such unrest in Bethlehem."

I can feel the tendrils of fear starting to curl back up around my heart. "Saul didn't…"

"Saul sent word throughout all Israel that you are condemned." Joab's tone is flat, and I can hear him trying to keep the anger out of it. "If anyone sees you, they are to inform the king or face death themselves. Only a month ago, people might have hesitated to comply, but now, after what happened in Nob…"

I push up onto my elbow, suddenly alert. "What happened in Nob?"

Joab's neck muscles writhe beneath his skin. "After you disappeared, Saul called all the priests together and demanded to know why they had helped you. He slaughtered them all right there in his throne room." Eyes gleaming, Joab shudders past emotion. "Then he went to Nob and torched it. Killed everyone, even the children."

My lungs constrict, and my senses begin to burn. I have to drag my answer through the lead weight that's settled on my chest. "How did he know they helped me?"

The moment I ask, I know the answer, and we say it together. "Doeg."

At the time, I'd overlooked the Edomite lurking in Nob. Now he has the blood of an entire town of priests on his hands.

Joab shoves off the cave floor. "Everyone's afraid they'll be next. Even Jonathan is under guard. No one has any idea what you did wrong, of course. Except for us."

Us. *Oh, God.*

"Abba! Eema…" I grab Joab's arm, barely getting the words out. If Saul has touched my mother…

"They're safe, David. I got them out." It takes too long for Joab's words to make it through the flames in my mind. "I sent Asa ahead to direct them here. We took separate routes for safety. Your brothers are with them. The whole clan is coming. And the Judean resistance." The familiar fierceness bites through the shake in his tone.

I frown. "The men from the hills? They're coming here?"

"They know you're destined to be king, David. I've kept them informed, and they've been watching you, waiting for the right moment. Now Saul has forced our hand." Joab looks around us. "These caves are plenty large enough to house an army or at least the start of one."

"An army?" I hadn't pictured the tax evaders ready to fight. What has Joab been telling them?

Joab's eyes spark. "You can't just hide out until Saul hunts you down. I know you're hoping his anger will dissipate, but it won't. He's willing to kill priests and their families. He's willing to set himself against Israel and risk Yahweh's anger—all to get rid of you. The revolution has begun, David, whether you like it or not. The people will follow you now."

Grief pounds in my head. "More likely they'll hate me for what Saul does to them."

"Not if you save them." Joab's expression is calm with confidence. "Be the king Saul hasn't been. Israel will hand you the throne."

Suddenly drained, I let my head drop back against the bearskin. The last time I encountered men from the resistance, I'd ended up with a knife at my throat. Korah and his sons had tried to steal a handful of my father's sheep when I was fourteen. I'd fought them, but only Joab's arrival had stopped them from carrying out their plan.

I close my eyes as the memory drifts by. In a matter of days, I'll be surrounded by dozens of violent men like Korah. Men who want to see Saul dethroned. Men who have suffered at his hands.

"I won't kill Saul," I say firmly.

Joab's face hardens. "You're God's anointed, aren't you? You'll do what you have to do."

I push off the ground, alarm torching my trust. "Did it ever occur to you why Saul was rejected as king? Before he began oppressing Israel, before all the political moves that the resistance hates so much? Yahweh rejected him because of disobedience. His heart turned away from God, and that cursed his reign. I won't do that, Joab. I fight for Yahweh first. He loves Israel. He wants to see her thrive. And when we follow His commands, we do." I steel myself against the cough rattling in my chest. "Are you with Him, Joab?"

Finally, my nephew blinks. "Yes. But if Saul ever comes close to killing you, don't think I will show him mercy."

I lock eyes with him. "You will still wait for my direction. And if you touch Jonathan, I will kill you myself."

If Joab believes me, he doesn't show it. He turns away, his tone tight. "Only one of us saved you from freezing to death.

One of these days, you will learn the difference between a friend and an enemy."

* * * * *

Over the next several days, I struggle to regain my strength before my family arrives. Joab keeps close, making me eat, refusing to let me leave the cave. I'm amazed at the provisions he's stored away, filling several caverns nearby. As I'd guessed, he and his brothers had a plan in place long before I'd fled Gibeah.

"We'd always discussed coming here first to decide what to do. After Doeg threatened Aaron, I sent word to some of the resistance elders, warning them to be on the alert. They've known for a long time who you are."

His statement weighs a thousand pounds, but I keep my eyes on the fire. The flames still haven't warmed my bones, even after ten days crouched in front of them. I'm still coughing, shaken by shivers that reach too deep. I'm torn between incredible gratitude and the growing doubt I've felt since Joab learned of my anointing.

In spite of all I owe my nephew, I would much rather have Jonathan at a time like this. The prince's loyalty is always tempered by steadiness and honor, something Joab hasn't always exhibited.

His volatility has earned him more enemies than friends. But he's capable and fierce, and I've been forced to trust him, just like I'll have to trust the other men of war who will descend on this place in a few more sunrises.

I can't handle the confinement anymore. The broken verses I composed in Gath wander around my mind while I sling stones against the back wall of the cave, desperate to break into something that makes sense. I can hear when Joab returns from hunting, but I don't turn around, allowing him to watch me for a few minutes.

"If only that wall were your father-in-law," he mutters, dumping his kill at the mouth of the cave. "Relax. You were a child when you met Korah and his sons. They know what you've become."

So, he thinks I'm still holding a grudge for that incident? That I'm nervous to meet the men who've been known as the troublemakers of Israel my whole life? Disgusted, I don't give him the satisfaction of a reply. It isn't fear that has me wearing out the only weapon I have on hand. I just want to feel strong.

I want to erase the memory of stumbling through the countryside with icy rain pounding the fight from my body. I want to forget Gath and the weight of oppression I felt there. The way Achish's eyes transformed into something inhuman looking at me. I want to believe I'm still Yahweh's warrior, that something I'm doing is making a difference, even if I know it's not.

I keep my back to Joab, staring hard at the wall I've blistered. Waiting for my eyes to stop burning. As much as I'd dreaded leaving Gibeah, I had hoped for relief. Being removed from Saul should have given me a chance to breathe more deeply in the open air and think more clearly, waiting for Yahweh's direction. Instead, the pain has followed me here. And I'm angry. I'm so angry.

I can sling stones and shoot arrows and feel the familiar power pulsing through my hands, but what can I do about the weight in my chest? With every stone I throw, I picture the murdered ones at Nob. Michal cursing me through her tears. Jonathan under guard, possibly being accused of treason.

Years ago, I'd seen death in Abner's eyes, knowing what would happen when they found out about me. But I never dreamed it would feel like this. Knowing that I already have the blood of innocents on my head turns the earth under me until I could collapse. How will anyone follow me? I already hate myself.

The Lord be with you, as He used to be with my father.

Jonathan's words hold onto me, and I can't shrug them off. If he had the courage to say them, I can believe them. Yahweh is everything. His presence had made all the difference for Saul once, uniting Israel under him in spite of the skeptics. And I know that He's never left me.

I close my eyes, trying to force my mind back to Samuel's upper room where the *Ruach* had been thick enough to change the air. I whisper Yahweh's Name through the night, begging Him to pull me out of the fog that's keeping me from breathing truth.

But when a handful of wagons approaches, carrying my family as far up the hills as they will go, the burden lifts temporarily. I hold back for a moment, taking in the extra age in everyone's faces, letting the familiarity sink in. When I notice my mother riding in the back of a cart, something shudders deep inside me. She's ten times frailer than I'd expected, a shadow of what she used to be. I'm at her side before her feet can touch ground, sweeping her up into my arms.

"Eema..." I have to hide how terrifying it is to feel her brittle frame against me. She slides into my arms as easily as a child would, her bony fingers finding my face when I set her down.

"My David."

Beaming, she pats something in the cart, and my mouth drops open. "What's that doing here?"

My harp is supposed to be back in Gibeah, up against the wall in Saul's fortress. Where I'd left it. Yet here it is, wrapped carefully in leather against the night chill.

"Jonathan sent it to Bethlehem before we left." Eema's eyes still carry the dancing brightness of a woman half her age, and suddenly I want to laugh with her. Feeling the familiar curve of the lyre in my hands shifts everything back into place for a moment.

There's so much to say that the moment almost feels normal. Everyone's talking and embracing as though we're back in Bethlehem for some feast. My heart swells, expanding to let my family in. How did I stay away so long? Even with old Aaron and all my brothers around me, I don't think I'll be able to hold back the tears.

But when I see my father leaning on Eliab, everything tightens again. Abba's mouth slants like he's preparing to speak, but he says nothing, averting his eyes.

Just like that, the burden is back. In spite of any joy we might drag from the moment, we're still fugitives, outcasts of Israel. Because of me.

At dusk, we all crowd into the largest cave and stare at our new reality through the fire, letting our enthusiasm evaporate into the silence. I don't know how long I can sit here, feeling everything turning over in their minds.

"You know that Saul will take everything." The words are bitter on my tongue, and I hate giving voice to them. I wasn't able to feel so much anger in the initial rush to escape, the weeks of surviving in Gath, the threat of starvation in the hills. But it's all rushing in to grip me now.

The full weight of what Saul has done drops onto my shoulders as I look at my brothers. My father's house and fields will be seized or burned. People we knew in Bethlehem will be questioned and forced to choose sides. Even if things change one day, my family won't have a home to return to.

"It won't be much longer before Saul comes after us," I continue, hardening my voice. "We won't be able to stay here."

"We know." The new softness in my father's tone startles me. It's calmer than resignation. Almost humble. But I still can't look at him.

I never realized how much he mattered to me. I haven't stopped to acknowledge it for years, but he's always been in the back of my mind. With the lion, the bear, even Goliath. I had always hoped that one day he would see something in me that he could be proud of. But that's gone now. All of his fears have been realized, because of me. A stronger son would have killed Saul already, before he could do this to us.

My old insecurity crawls up close in the dark. And as usual, Eliab is ready to answer it. "Our parents can't live on the run, David. They're too old."

I look at him, ready to feel whatever contempt is in his eyes, but he's addressing everyone else. "Their only hope is Moab. We've sent word to the king in Mizpeh, reminding him of our heritage and asking if our parents might find sanctuary with him. Abinadab and I are bringing them down in a few days. Aaron will come as well."

He shifts his weight, folding his hands over his knee, closing the subject.

Whether he means it to or not, Eliab's manner is like a slap in my face, and I can feel my pride withering under his stare.

Look what you've done, Melek.

Aaron speaks up. "I'm hoping I can get word to Othniel, convince him to leave Saul's service, if he safely can. I would love to have him with me, but it would be better for him to serve beside you." The shepherd's aging voice wobbles with bravery. And it's too much for me to take.

I leave the cave and walk over to the edge where the ground drops off into a rock shelf. In the dark, you can't see it though. The ridge just cuts out into deep blackness, a gaping cavern in the valley. The air is cold and sharp, and I fill my lungs with it, hoping to bury the heat of shame. I'm still close enough to hear the crackle of the fire and the murmur of voices.

I know Moab will receive my relatives. The neighboring country has become a common refuge for Israelites during wars or famines. But at their age, my parents might not ever come back to our land. They'll die in exile. The reality cuts me open.

When footsteps shuffle up behind me, I don't turn around. I don't have to. The steps are small and labored. My eyes pinned to the darkness, I hear Eema inhale slowly, sidling closer until she's leaning against me. Her fingers slip around my arm.

It takes three full breaths before I can look at her. Before I can say it. "I'm sorry."

"Sorry?" Eema's wrinkled face wears a serenity that confuses me. How can she be so brave?

"I failed you. I've destroyed…" I can't even finish. The words burn.

Eema's grip on me tightens. "You remember what I've told you about Jesse's Moabite grandmother?"

I nod without turning my head. "Ruth."

My mother exhales the story in a few gentle breaths, like the verses of a song.

"She was younger than you when she left her homeland to accompany her mother-in-law to Bethlehem, following the God of Israel. She had no husband and very little means to make a living. She left a place where she was known and respected to come here where she would be despised as a foreigner. But she had given herself to Yahweh. She had chosen Him as her inheritance, and therefore nothing could keep her beautiful spirit hidden. She married Boaz and became a respected woman of faith in this land. Her legacy lives on today, in you."

I look sideways at Eema, a crooked smile pushing past the pain on my face. As many times as she's told me this, her voice still trembles with awe. I've heard more stories about Ruth than any other relative. But it's not likely my father sees Ruth or Boaz when he looks at me.

Eema catches her breath, and I hear the rattle of age in her voice. "Did you know your father used to play the harp?"

I frown. "I heard that Ruth taught her son Obed to play, but Abba?"

Eema nods. "He stopped. Something *in* him stopped. Despite the faith of his parents, he spent his whole life hearing from others that Yahweh no longer speaks to His people. That He had forgotten us. He felt forsaken. Unworthy. So, he settled for an ordinary life."

I feel my heart recoil. He felt unworthy because of me. He hid me away because he couldn't bear to look at the one mistake he'd made in his life.

My throat constricts, choked by a dozen memories. My father sneaking in to watch me at night while I would pretend to be sleeping. Looking the other way when Eliab called me a bastard. Saying nothing when I came home bleeding after saving his sheep from the lion.

The thoughts are so loud in my mind that Eema looks at me sharply. "He hasn't shown you the affection I have. But you have to stop hearing things he's not saying."

I scoff. "What am I supposed to hear? He made me believe I was nothing."

A tear slips off Eema's cheek onto my sleeve. "He believed he was nothing. Our own unresolved fears often harm our children. But you had a Shepherd who helped you see the truth. When your mother died, she asked me if Yahweh would accept you. I wish we had known then what I know now. You are truly beloved." She peers around in front of me, tears trailing her face. "Jonathan knows it. All of Israel will know it soon."

My heart wrenches, battling to believe. "Why are you telling me this?"

She keeps her smile steady, even as her chin shakes. "We may not return to this land. We may not see the fulfillment of what Yahweh has spoken. But you've faced bigger giants than this. Talk to him." She angles her head into the cave at my father and touches my face. "For me."

Taking her hand, I press it against my lips, then fold my arms around her, wishing I could fight a hundred Philistines rather than feel this. I love her so much. And I might not ever see her again.

* * * * *

I expect my father to doze off long before everyone else, but he's still awake even after the others have fallen asleep. I sit outside, braced against a boulder, dread pulling at me. Why am I so afraid of talking to him? It bothers me that it was so easy for me not to. I'd left Bethlehem behind and let myself forget him. I had thrown myself into serving Saul, finding enough of a father figure in the king and his son. But that's gone now.

I sigh, sensing Jesse's eyes on me. "Just say it."

But my father stays silent, too busy trying to maneuver across the rocky ground in the dark. He struggles to sit beside me, and I get up to help him. He leans on me heavily, his fingers gripping my arms while I ease him onto the ground. His breathing is shallow and labored, with a wheeze at the end of each exhale.

I wince at the stinging unfairness. At his age, he should be resting at home, with grandchildren on his knees, enjoying the fruits of a lifetime of labor. Instead, his final years have to be troubled, lived out in exile in a foreign land. All because of me.

I wait for his breathing to relax into the silence.

"I know you're disappointed." I can't believe I voiced it, but now it's in the open. Between us.

Jesse exhales softly. When he responds, his tone is lighter than I expected. "My boy, I'm not your master. I'm your father."

"What's the difference?" The words stab too harshly, but I can't take them back. Somehow, I've always wanted to know.

He doesn't answer. Instead, he sets his staff aside and edges closer to me.

When his bony hand touches my neck, I shudder, angling away from him. Something's been undone deep inside me, and I want to run from it. Starting to shake, I clamp my arms around my knees, trying to hold everything back. Abba saw me anointed. I can't fail in front of him. But that determination is already being wrestled aside by how much I need him.

His fingers tug a little, and he reaches over with his other hand, cupping my face. And my defenses tear open. I choke on a sob and bury my head in his shoulder. All I can think is how tight his grip is for an old man. He holds my shoulders until they stop shaking, and then I hear his voice from deep in his chest.

"You were strong enough for this when you were just a child watching our sheep. You are strong enough, David. And where you are not, Yahweh is."

The gratitude sweeping over me is so fierce that it frightens me. I'd never considered how much Jesse's belief would mean to me. The sincerity in his tone is something I've never heard from him before. But there's still something I have to say. I pull back and look into his eyes, relieved that he doesn't turn away.

"I'm sorry, Abba. For everything. Do you forgive me?"

Tears pool in his eyes, one trailing off into his beard, but he keeps his hand on my face. "Son, I need your forgiveness much more than you need mine."

* * * * *

My final days with my family pass too quickly. My three oldest brothers prepare to take them to Moab, along with Aaron, who's also too old to live on the run. They've brought plenty of provisions, anticipating this journey even before I did. Eliab knows the trade routes and how to avoid them, but with Saul occupied looking for me, they shouldn't be in danger. At least that's what Shammah promises.

"The king of Moab will receive us. Ruth's family was well known and respected," he tells me. But the old reassurance doesn't mean as much as it should. I don't want to let them out of my sight.

I hold my parents as long as I can, but the weight in my chest doesn't budge. Unlike my absence in battle, this really is goodbye. I feel bereft, letting them go, knowing it'll be the last time. I stare at both of them, fixing them in my mind, not as they are now, but as they were over the years. Supporting me. Keeping my secrets, and being willing to believe.

"Thank you. For everything," I say to all of them.

Aaron grips my hand, and Eema weeps silently, unable to say more than she has already. But my father, silent for too long, steps forward. He has to reach up to take my head in his hands, and when I see what he's doing, I kneel, and let him speak into my hair.

"The Lord bless and keep you. The Lord make His face shine upon you and be gracious to you. May the light of His countenance give you peace."

The ancestral blessing of our people lifts strength inside me, and I clasp my father's hands with both of mine. His affirmation means more than I can say.

When the company is ready to set off, Eliab appears at my shoulder.

"I'll take care of them," he says.

His arms are wrapped within one another, and he's squinting into the distance, but his voice sounds completely different. Without the accusation, I don't recognize it. He inhales and turns to me. "When they no longer have need of me, I will return."

I have to hide my surprise. "You will?"

"Yes." Something lifts in his face, and I wonder how long he's had to decide this. "If you weren't anointed of God, Saul wouldn't be so threatened. But Yahweh chose you. I saw it. And I'm not letting you do this without me." His eyes snap, and he shoves his shoulder against mine.

Gratitude crowds out words for a moment, turning to resolve in my chest. "I'm not sure I could."

I reach out my hand, and Eliab clasps it, finally looking at me. Finally my brother.

CPSIA information can be obtained
at www.ICGtesting.com
Printed in the USA
BVHW031158211021
619530BV00004B/42